GLOBAL CAPITALISM

SUNY Series in Radical Theory

Roger Gottlieb, Editor

GLOBAL CAPITALISM

The New Leviathan

by

Robert J. S. Ross

and

Kent C. Trachte

State University of New York Press

Published by
State University of New York Press, Albany

For information, address State University of New York
Press, State University Plaza, Albany, N.Y., 12246

Library of Congress Cataloging in Publication Data

Ross, Robert J. S., 1943–
   Global capitalism : the new leviathan / by Robert J. S. Ross and
Kent C. Trachte.
      p.   cm. — (SUNY series in radical theory)
   Includes bibliographical references.
   ISBN 0-7914-0339-4. — ISBN 0-7914-0340-8 (pbk.)
   1. Capitalism. 2. Business cycles. 3. Monopolies.
4. Competition, International. 5. Detroit (Mich.)—Economic
conditions. 6. New York (N.Y.)—Economic conditions.
7. Massachusetts—Economic conditions. 8. Social classes—United
States—Political activity. 9. Economic history—1945–
I. Trachte, Kent C., 1951–   . II. Title. III. Series.
HB501.R7456 1990
330.12′2—dc20   89–21858
                                                      CIP

10 9 8 7 6 5 4 3 2 1

Contents

CHAPTER THREE:

CHAPTER FOUR:

CHAPTER FIVE:

PART IV: POLITICS AND THE STATE

Figures

Tables

"A merchant, it has been said very properly, is not necessarily the citizen of any particular country. It is in great measure indifferent to him from what place he carries on his trade; and a very trifling disgust will make him remove his capital, and together with it all the industry which it supports, from one country to another."

—Adam Smith, *Wealth of Nations*

"The need of a constantly expanding market for its products chases the bourgeoisie over the whole surface of the globe. It must nestle everywhere, settle everywhere, establish connections everywhere.

"The bourgeoisie has through its exploitation of the world market given a cosmopolitan character to production and consumption in every country. ...[I]t has drawn from under the feet of industry the national ground on which it stood. All old-established national industries have been destroyed or are daily being destroyed....In place of the old wants, satisfied by the productions of the country, we find new wants, requiring for their satisfaction the products of distant lands and climes. In place of the old local and national seclusion and self-sufficiency we have intercourse in every direction, universal interdependence of nations."

—Karl Marx and Friedrich Engels,
Manifesto of The Communist Party

TO MARION AND SHARON: THEY KNOW WHAT IT COST

Acknowledgments

The production of this book has been marked by the small and large crises of contemporary academic life, with a bit of political drama as well. We have accomplished our work in, around, and despite Clark University. In 1979, while Robert Ross was (successfully) seeking to convince Clark University that he merited a tenure appointment, Phil O'Keefe and Don Shakow initiated a Regional Development Unit (RDU) at Clark that drew in Ross and a group of talented geography graduate students, including Julie Graham, Kathie Gibson, Cindy Katz, and Paul Susman. At various times Shakow and Graham have been Ross's collaborators and mentors. They helped a political and urban sociologist/organizer as he painfully became a serious student of political economy. Early aspects of this work were embodied in discussions, articles, and conferences organized by the RDU. When the day is done, no greater gift could be acknowledged.

Later, more crises obstructed our work. For two years we struggled together (unsuccessfully) to keep Kent Trachte at Clark; Andrea Walsh and Sidney Peck were steadfast in their personal and intellectual support for both of us even while they were both subject to similar pressures. They believed in this book. The Government Department at Clark University was a source of support and encouragement to Trachte.

We began this book in 1983, after teaching "The Seminar in Global Capitalism" together for two years. Students in that seminar have made important contributions to our research and thinking. Alan Levine found the data on infant mortality in New York City; Larry Kurzner, Mitch Ahlbaum, Jay Leader, and Bob Krinsky helped on Detroit and the automobile industry. Alex Schwartz wrote a paper for us about the economic history of Detroit. A small grant from Clark University's Faculty Development Fund allowed Ross to pay Brooks Bitterman to find time series data on Massachusetts. Anne Oberhauser taught us about the French automobile industry.

By 1986, when Trachte left Clark, our first draft was the shared product of a senior and junior author. But academic and political life pulled us in different directions. Ross worked in a political campaign, and then finished the project between 1987 and 1989, while Trachte was beginning a new career as an administrator.

In the course of this story, Chris Chase-Dunn has been a helpful and honorable critic; Roger Gottlieb and Peggy Gifford of SUNY Press refreshingly enthusiastic; Mike Miller encouraging; Dick Peet and Ruth Messinger interested; Ed Greenberg and Tom Maher as well; Dan Weiner and Mike Meyer—in different ways—personal advocates; Ben Harrison engaged; Gabe and Rachel Ross candidly bored, but willing to learn to cook while Dad was typing; Kenyon Trachte the delight of his Dad.

We did this the old-fashioned, new-fangled way: without external support, with lots of word processing. One chapter was typed (by Pat Miles). Otherwise our work is, for better and worse, the product of the politics and technology of the 1980s. No grants, no typists, no assistants (except for the noble Bitterman), one sabbatical (for Ross).

As this project ended, Irving Barrett, Ross's stepfather, died. A garment worker and high school drop-out, Irving and Ross's mother, Marsha (a schoolteacher who died in 1979), bestowed a cultural endowment that endures. James Trachte, dedicated educator, and his wife, Donna, introduced and nurtured Trachte's commitment to the life of the mind. Our wives, Marion and Sharon, to whom this book is dedicated, know the full price of these peculiar endeavors, and we acknowledge with full hearts the costs they have shared.

All of us, all together, know, with Carl Sandburg:

> "The people yes, the people,
> Until the people are taken care of one way or another,
> Until the people are solved somehow for the day and
> hour,
> Until then one hears, "Yes but the people what about the
> people?" . . .
>
> In the darkness with a great bundle of grief
>   the people march,
> In the night and overhead a shovel of stars for keeps,
>   the people march:
>   "Where to, what next?"

Part I

1
Introduction to the New Leviathan

"I authorise and give up my right of governing my selfe, to this
man, or to this Assembly of men....This is the generation of
that great LEVIATHAN...[that] hath the use of so much
power and strength...that by terror thereof he is inabled to
forme the wills of them all ... "

—Thomas Hobbes, *Leviathan, 1651*

The Irony of the New Leviathan

At the dawn of the modern era, Thomas Hobbes reasoned that the absolutist
state was erected on a foundation of implicit consent. To avoid the war of
each against all, a sovereign authority, composed by the cession of each
individual's rights to it, would impose, through the terror of coercive law,
the civil peace that he sought.

Three and one-half centuries later, after the birth of constitutional democracy and industrial capitalism, a new system of power has been erected on
a world scale, and its agents are able to obtain their will around the world.
The fiction of consent is no more real for the New Leviathan than the Old;
the social contract of the late twentieth century is just as much imposed as
that of the seventeenth century.

The New Leviathan is not the state, but a newly invigorated system of
global capitalism.

The multinational conglomerate symbolizes, crudely, the power of the
New Leviathan. Yet the irony of the New Leviathan is that its individual
agents, global firms, and financial institutions, are not sovereigns but
severely constrained competitors committed to the *economic* war of each
against all. The only Sovereign is indirect, fluid, acting upon states as well
as embodied in them. The New Leviathan is the system of global capitalism
itself, not any of its powerful parts.

Not only the terror of coercive law, but the fear of joblessness and
penury enforces the demands of the new system. The New Leviathan of
global capitalism does not defend the citizens of any given nation from
foreign invasion, as Hobbes noted of the Old Leviathan, but rather it
disciplines those who labor in every land with the weakness of others.

The Old Leviathan was jealous of all centers of competing authority; the New Leviathan welcomes all variation in social conditions, for it uses the uneven development of the regions of the global economy as a lever to bargain with each unit of government for the most profitable conditions of global production.

The characteristic "terror" of the Old Leviathan was the police power of the state. The characteristic terror of the New Leviathan is unemployment, wage cuts, the fear that a family or a community's aspiration for environmental or economic improvement may cause the agents of the New Leviathan to take their investments to some other place where working people are more vulnerable to the demands of their employers.

The Old Leviathan seemed, later—in the era of the democratic revolutions—to be permeated with irrational commitments to hierarchy, status, and the privilege of birth; the New Leviathan is the outcome of "rational" calculation.

The New Leviathan is global capitalism: an adaptive transformation of an old system to new challenges.

Discovering the New Leviathan: Global Capitalism

The global transformation of modern capitalism is part of our everyday experience. In this book, we present much data, but it is not exotic, not "unknown." As a Washington editor said recently about his journal of opinion: "The world needs to make sense of the facts that are lying there."[1]

We began our effort by trying to make sense of the distress of the older industrial regions of the advanced capitalist countries that became evident in the 1970s and early 1980s[2]. We approached the problem from the perspective of international political economy and from the analysis of metropolitan regions. Soon it became clear: separately or together, the dominant North American theories of modern capitalism, those that depicted the modern era as one in which "monopoly capitalism" described national systems, and "world system analysis" described a hierarchy of nations in the international system of exchange, did not produce satisfactory models of the way the world was working.

Our discontent, and our perception, was widely shared. Colleagues at Clark University and elsewhere were engaged in the analysis of the new era.[3] The plant closings and disinvestment of the 1970s were soon followed by the evidence of rising inequality, stagnating wages and income, and reversal in the progress made in eliminating poverty.[4] We resolved to draw together the strands of theory and empirical analysis that would demonstrate both the need for a new departure and a "middle level" formulation of new concepts for the analysis of contemporary capitalism.

We describe this book as a "middle level" of analysis because it does *not* claim new insight to the general dynamics of capitalism as a world historical phenomenon. Our goal is more modest. We *do* claim that at the centers of world capitalism there has been a shift in the alignments of power and the calculations of advantage. These shifts have changed the structure of power and politics that have not yet been synthesized as part of the "standard" analyses of capitalism. Our effort is focussed on showing that the changing structures of social relations that produced that transformation of power relations require conceptual change in the way we understand modern capitalism.

Domains of New Theory

In the vocabulary of the social science of the 1980s we have a "society-centered" view of the analysis of the state and politics, informed by Marxian social science and those who have argued within and against that tradition.[5] Because our analysis of any given "society" or social formation is highly conditioned by our understanding of its economic development, our goal of analyzing power requires that we first probe the new dimensions of global capitalist development, of the social relations that form the complex interdependence of the market-oriented societies. In order to accomplish this task we, a sociologist and a political scientist, have had to foray into territory ordinarily reserved to economists. We understand therefore, that our analytical procedures may be found wanting by those who claim professional priority in this field. But we are firm in our conviction that the structural analysis of social life, and of power among people, depends vitally on the ways men and women produce their livelihoods, and the relations into which they enter as they strive to support their families and advance their material interests.

We are forced to the conclusion that, as with war and soldiers, the social relations of "economic" life are too important to be left to economists.

Global Capitalism:
An Informal Summary

The theory of global capitalism portrays a new moment in capitalist development—a successor to monopoly capitalism and a change in the structure of the world-economy.

Levels of theory and historical perspective. Capitalism as a social system may be analyzed on three levels: its enduring logical necessity—the level that Marx ventured in *Capital*, in volumes I and II, and Smith in *The Wealth of Nations*; the level of its historical development, as in *Monopoly Capital* by Baran and Sweezy and O'Connor,[6] or Schumpeter's *Capitalism,*

Socialism and Democracy;[7] and at the level of a specific social formation in its own (often unique) development.[8]

This book about global capitalism is informed by work at the first level and uses observations from the third to develop a conceptual framework at the middle level.

The middle level of structural analysis in social science has characteristic pitfalls. The most important problem occurs in distinguishing between trends and cycles and structural change.[9]

Cyclical changes are repetitive; however painful individual or family adjustment to rising or falling unemployment may be, in the ordinary understanding of recession and expansion in the capitalist business cycle, their alternation implies no structural change, nothing new.

Trends are cumulative changes that endure: for example, the continuing concentration of capital; the movement of manufacturing facilities from central cities to suburbs and beyond.

At some point the incremental, *quantitative* accretion of trend phenomena are recognized as having produced *qualitative* differences: *structural* changes.

Cycles may execute trends (for example, when, in recessions or depressions, larger firms survive and/or acquire weaker ones, and the concentration of capital increases). And trends may cumulate to structural change (for example, when repeated waves of mergers and acquisitions transform a large number of formerly competitive industrial sectors into concentrated ones, and we observe that a basically competitive economy has become an oligopolistic economy).

Problems arise because analysis at any given moment may confuse a cycle or a trend or structural change for any one of the others. An upsurge in housing construction over a few quarters may *not* necessarily indicate a fundamental shift, lowering the proportion of income that average householders must devote to housing costs, or the onset of a housing glut more friendly to buyers than developers; an increase in employment in a given industrial sector may *not* necessarily signal a new leader in economic development. Indeed, an electoral victory by a conservative political leader may *not* indicate a fundamental change in the consciousness of the mass electorate.

This work contends that the recessions of the 1970s and the early 1980s executed a trend, and that the trend has finally amounted to structural change: capitalism is no longer well comprehended by conceiving of a system of national oligopolies (as in theories of monopoly capitalism) in which nations are in a fixed hierarchy of international exchange (as understood by world systems analysis). Rather, a new variant of capitalism is emerging on a world scale.

Global capitalism diffuses manufacturing around the world, disrupting the older model of a manufacturing intensive "core" and raw material exporting "periphery." This diffusion reflects an expanding geographic sphere of investor choice. The spatial mobility of capital, as well as its sectoral mobility, both made possible by an increasingly perfected worldwide financial market, transforms the balance of power in the older industrial regions.

Under the conditions of monopoly capitalism, labor, especially its most organized sectors in concentrated industries was able to successfully mobilize resources to win major economic and political gains.

In the new era of global capitalism, employers can counter labor's former strategic strength by the threat and reality of capital mobility toward more compliant labor and more propitious political or technological environments. A simple "labor theory of industrial location" does not capture totally the complexities of the international variations in technology, infrastructure, tariff barriers and markets.[10] Yet, it does pinpoint the global nature of the available pool of labor and the vast differences within this pool of levels of living and political potency. In all, "competitive" pressure disciplines labor and capital in ways unfamiliar to the model of monopoly capitalism.

This transformation is similar in scope and importance to that which has been generally recognized as having occurred when nineteenth-century competitive capitalism was transformed into the monopolistic form that was basically complete by the mid-twentieth century.

Perhaps. But perhaps we mistake a *cycle* of outward investment from the older industrial regions for a *structural change*; perhaps we leap too soon to claim that the world has changed when all that has occurred is a bend in the rails of a familiar line of travel.[11] Of course, time *will* yield a definitive answer.

But how much time is enough? In our examination of industries and regions (in Part III) we examine structural data since 1950, and we perceive the onset of the new era in, approximately, the late 1960s. Thus, our claim is that the new system of global capitalism is discernible over the last twenty years. In the broad history of capitalism, this is but a moment, some will contend, and we agree. But at a similar moment, around turn of the century, just such a qualitative change was observable and observed. The rise of the "trusts" and the strategic role of finance capital in modern society was broadly perceived by Marxists[12] and others such as Veblen as a central feature of a new era.[13]

In retrospect, the turn of the twentieth century was a strategic pivot in the history of capitalist development. But those who claimed that monopoly capitalism, finance capitalism, and imperial domination of the worldwide economy were the characteristics of the new era were not well honored by the canons of academic social science. Another fifty years of capitalist development were required before their insights were widely accepted, and even then, the sociological implications of that work encountered the obfuscating myths of the Cold War.[14]

We are too awed by their stature to associate ourselves with the insights of Luxemburg, Lenin, Hilferding, Veblen, Bernstein, Baran and Sweezy, Mills, or more recently, Wallerstein.[15] But we are inspired by their ability to counter the conventional wisdom (leftist or capitalist) of their times and to argue their views with vigor and confidence. Even if we have erred in claiming that there is a new moment in the development of modern capitalism, we aspire to fruitful error, to advance the understanding of power and structure at the brink of a new century.

Methods for strategic analysis. The expansion of the global capitalist economy allows investors to locate production—and "disaggregated" parts of the production itself—in states and societies in which workers are poorer, less economically powerful, and less politically potent than they are in the traditional centers of manufacturing. This, we argue, gives investors a new birth of power in the older regions themselves. The threat of capital mobility becomes a potent weapon in the old contest between labor and capital.

This view is often countered by a number of (accurate) observations: most direct foreign investment from the older industrial regions flows toward already "developed" economies; the statistical predictors of the location of investment in manufacturing (within nations, or across the regions of the world) include many more factors than labor costs, per se; the location of manufacturing investment from the rich nations, toward the Third World is highly concentrated.

There is a methodological problem involved in these apparently contradictory contentions. We do not contest the proposition that, for example, the majority of direct foreign investment by multinational corporations headquartered in the United States is destined for Europe or Canada. But the data and analysis compiled in support of the traditional view of the organization of the global economy depends too much on numerical aggregates rather than strategic analysis. For the social analysis of power, however, the problem is at least in part qualitative.

Those statistical analyses that show that the majority of U. S. direct foreign investment is *not* in poor countries do not illuminate the *strategic* impact of investments in poor countries on the United States, on collective bargaining or political contentions (about, for example, plant closing notification legislation).[16] When we learn, from a report of an interview, of a United Auto Workers (UAW) local in which potential outsourcing of parts from low wage export platforms was decisive in obtaining concessions from workers, we believe we have an indicator of a new strategic lever in relations between workers and employers.[17] The qualitative importance of this lever is not necessarily indicated by aggregate data about the magnitude of investment flows.

Quantitative analysis of international aggregates is irreplaceable to social science; but it is not, by itself, adequate to the analysis of power. Similarly, the industrial geography of capital investment is replete with the analysis of factors of location *other than* labor costs, labor discipline, and regulatory policies favorable to workers or consumers. What is qualitatively new to world capitalism, however, is that investors may find a broadening geographic field of choice in which modern methods of production and adequate human and physical infrastructure is available without the impediments of unwanted constraints. Sometimes these opportunities in the newly industrializing countries (NICs) are decisive; at others, the skill, discipline, and policy environment (e.g., West Germany's low rates of work stoppages and tariff protected membership in the European Economic Community (EEC) continue to attract investment. It is the scope and size of the *new* field of investment opportunity which has changed the strategic balance of social power in the older industrial regions.

As to the relatively few number of NICs that dominate the trade in manufacturing exports between the old industrial world and the new, we propose an additional focus to comprehend world development, that is, for the production of theory about society and capitalism in this era.

While only a limited number of NICs make quantitatively significant contributions to world export trade in manufactures, many more exhibit structural tendencies toward industrialization that were not anticipated by either the theories of monopoly capitalism nor of world systems analysis.[18] The first group looms large in the calculations of employers (and the fears of their workers) in the older regions; the second group adds reasons to seek alternatives to the standard ways we have organized our perception of the world structure of capitalism.

Power, ideology, and global capitalism.   Power, Mills wrote, summarizing Weber, is the ability to realize one's will although others resist.[19] This is the classical definition of power under conditions of adversarial conflicts, where parties to a conflict understand their interests as a zero-sum: if Party A gains, Party B loses in equal amounts.

Everyday life is usually somewhat more ambiguous. Many years ago two political scientists, Bachrach and Baratz, pointed out that one "face" of power was the ability to keep some conflicts from ever being joined, to control the *agenda* of conflict.[20] A matter not joined in explicit conflict cannot be lost: in the United States, struggle over the ownership of the means of production, that is, socialism, has hardly ever reached the public agenda. If Party A can keep a certain matter from ever reaching the stage of explicit decision, that Party, or set of interests, exerts a certain kind of power not comprehended by the classical Weberian definition. Party B may not be able to resist the will of Party A because there is no arena of explicit decision.

What then appears on the public agenda, and who controls it? Crenson showed that the "nondecisionmaking" of agenda control about air pollution was related to local dominance in a power structure.[21] By implication: if nondecisionmaking indicated power, then "unpolitics" was one of the processes of power.

Crenson's was an empirical exercise consonant with Gramsci's idea of ideological hegemony: contending parties were constrained, in the scope of the conflicts in which they engaged, and the solutions they sought, by their ability to formulate ideas, to imagine alternatives.[22] If capitalist ideas were successfully dominant in a given political culture, even challenging forces would formulate their interests within the confines of concepts that assumed the continuity and natural right of current social arrangements.

So power is not only the ability to prevail in conflict; it is also the ability to mold the ways in which actors understand any potential conflict. Sociologists typically approach this problem as one of socialization and social control in the context of stratification.[23]

The advent of global capitalism brings a new dimension to our understanding of the power to prevail via the medium of agenda control. In contemporary America, throughout the Western European economies, the "competitive" environment of global capitalism is used as the reason to restrain workers' and consumers' demands for this or that advance in their conditions. The looming presence of the "goose" of capital investment is invoked; if demands are too expansive, investors might lay the "golden egg" of jobs in some other, less demanding jurisdiction. That the probability of such a choice is relatively low, that is, it is often a bluff, merely adds to the uncertainty within which workers calculate their strategic situation.

The hegemony of capitalist culture, and the perceived realities of political choice are such that the given structure of choice appears to be rational, inevitable, "natural." There is often no "politics," that is, no large scale conflict or explicit contention about this structure of choice, because it has been accepted by potentially contending parties before public agendas are constructed. There is a "prepolitical" process which constructs the public agenda and thus predisposes "politics" to a narrowed set of choices.[24]

In our times, the erosion and stagnation of manufacturing and other wages in the United States indicates the power of capital in its direct relation to labor at the point of production.[25] But the general phenomenon proceeds far beyond the collective bargaining or wage relation. In politics, blue collar workers supported conservative political figures in larger than ordinary numbers, in the 1980s, in part because those candidates seemed to promise a more propitious environment for capital investment, that is, they plausibly promised jobs.

In short, global capitalism *does* enlist a kind of consent to its new regime, but this "consent" is not a positive political or social accord; it is more like the resignation with which humans accept the "natural" force of the weather. This resignation is based on acceptance of the parameters of capital investment in a "competitive" world in which the poor of South Korea, and tariff-protected workers of peripheral Europe and Latin America, and the middle-income workers of the industrial "core," are all part of the same global labor force, all accessible to the global firms, acutely conscious of the stakes of the game in international trade, but hardly ever conscious of their common fate.

Workers have experienced the new era in terms of regional, national, or sectoral threats. But the closely knit financial, corporate, and transport networks of world investment and production have produced new class consciousness and embracive political coalitions among employers and investors. The consequence is the political reality of the 1980s: divided workers and united employers. The power of capital in relation to state policy increases, the "relative autonomy" of the state from capital decreases.

This chapter is about the New Leviathan, global capitalism, a "variant" of capitalism, a concept similar to that of a new regime or "social structure of accumulation." This variant of an old system is based on the contradiction that arises from the near universality of global investment choices among social formations that, on a world scale, are characterized by vastly divergent political and social experience and conditions of life and labor.[26] Global capitalism is a new stage in capitalist development, a moment not anticipated by the varieties of the theory of monopoly capitalism or world systems analysis.

This is a bold claim, we realize, so we introduce it in stages. Here, an overview has described elements of our theory. We proceed cautiously, mindful of the warning implicit in the principle of scientific parsimony. As Bertrand Russell put it (in *The History of Western Philosophy*): one should not needlessly multiply entities.

The structure of our argument is inductive. There are changes in the structure of world capitalism. First, we examine what the dominant theories —monopoly capitalism and world systems—say about this. They prove to have problematic responses to these changes. Only after examining these do we venture to present our own views.

Our strategy argues that the analytical tools at our disposal have served us well, but times have changed.

Overview

In what follows, we both prosecute this contention about the reality of a change in the way capitalism is working and explain it to the best of our current knowledge. The presentation has three stages: the theoretical context (Part II), case studies (Part III), and the strategic and theoretical analysis of power and the state (Part IV).

In Part II we first introduce, chapter 2, "Tools for Analysis," the historical background for conceiving of variants or submodes of the capitalist mode of production. We define three relationships, which are central to understanding the evolution of capitalist society: capital-to-labor, capital-to-capital, and especially, capital-to-state. These three strategic relations become the themes of our analysis of change in contemporary capitalism. We show that transitions from one dominant variant of capitalism to another is accompanied by crises short of the orthodox conception of breakdown, revolution, and transition to socialism. But the evolution from competitive to monopoly to global capitalism has changed the specific matrix of these strategic relations.

In chapter 2, we also present the various analytic approaches to the theories of crisis tendencies that depress or reduce profits, thereby producing inherent obstacles to the unimpeded accumulation of capital. These theories focus on obstacles to accumulation that may arise from the success of workers' class struggle, from substituting machines for human labor, and from the inability to sell profitably that which has been produced. Here, and in chapter 5, we try to show that our work is consistent with a number of the orthodox "crisis" theories within Marxism. Readers more interested in structures than in these particular dynamics may wish to skim this material.

We then proceed to locate our contention in relation to two of the dominant theories of modern capitalism the theory of monopoly capitalism (chapter 3) and the analysis of world systems (chapter 4).

In chapter 3, we present the dominant social theory of contemporary capitalism—monopoly capitalism. From the theory of monopoly capitalism is typically derived a "model" of the strategic relations of capital-to-labor, capital-to-capital, and capital-to-state. In this model, labor in the monopoly sector has come to an accord with large-scale capital, which affords it a stable and rising material level of living, competition is dominated by American firms that do not use prices as a central instrument of competition, and the major firms acquiesce in large-scale transfers of income, through the state, to workers and the poor. In chapter 3 we show the theoretical basis of this model and suggest the ways in which we appreciate but shall later challenge it.

World systems analysis is the other major theoretical school that dominates North American analysis of capitalism. In chapter 4 we present the international hierarchy of exchange relations that are depicted by world systems analysts. In this tradition of analysis, a rich core dominates world manufacturing. To obtain these goods, a poor periphery sells its cheaper products of mines and farms, and this inequality ensures a permanent disadvantage in world trade, and thus a future of industrial stagnation.

In chapter 4 we explain both our appreciation and our analytical criticism of world systems theory, and we suggest the ways in which we shall challenge it.

Chapter 5 presents the outline of the theory of global capitalism. It closes our section on theories of modern capitalism by presenting a model of the ways in which our view of the restructuring of capitalism is different from that of the dominant models. In this chapter, we show that each of the theories of capitalist crisis are consistent with the arrangements of the global capitalist social order—that is, that the theory of global capitalism depends on no particular school of orthodoxy at the level of the mode of production in general. Again, those less interested in the classic theories of Marxian dynamics will pass over this material.

Chapter 6 begins Part III, Explorations in Global Capitalism, which illustrates the impact of global capitalism on the structure of the world system and on three areas of the United States.

We begin with a review of the diffusion of manufacturing in former colonies and poor countries. We have a dual purpose for this review. Our analyses of Detroit, New York City and Massachusetts emphasize the role of capital mobility as a lever of power and competitive necessity in this era. Chapter 6 draws together data about the industrialization of formerly nonindustrial regions to demonstrate concretely the global scope of the options now available to investors and the changes they entail. The chapter, therefore, presents evidence central to the plausibility of our argument.

Our discussion of Third World industrialization also shows how the theory of global capitalism provides a coherent explanation of this development. We integrate our understanding of the decline and restructuring of the three other regions with our analysis of the location and timing of Third World industrialization.

Chapter 6 shows that manufacturing is no longer the unique property of the rich or core nations, and that the world production process is truly global. This structural overview lays the foundation for the case studies of restructuring and its attendant crises in the 1970s and early 1980s in Detroit and the automobile industry (chapter 7), New York and its sweatshops in the garment industry (chapter 8), and Massachusetts and its transformation from mill-based industry to a service-dominated economy within which high technology electronics plays a unique political role (chapter 9).

While aggregate studies of world trade and production cannot always capture the strategic implications of structural change, case studies have inherent weaknesses. They can never be more than inferential evidence for a theoretical model. On the other hand, one test of theory is heuristic: does it make more coherent sense of a given situation than alternative theories?

The case studies were chosen to illustrate the usefulness of an approach based on the theory of global capitalism. Each city or region has a different industrial history, a different path to the current moment. These different paths present somewhat different analytical problems, and they serve to illustrate different aspects of the impact of global capitalism.

What each case has in common is that the region selected is or has been a world center of a world industry. And each industry is quite different, representing the basic types of global manufacturing: capital intensive heavy mass production; older labor intensive light industry; and new high technology. Each case focusses on the contrast between our model and one of the others (in Detroit and New York) or on the political implications of restructuring (Massachusetts).

Automobile production has been the classic exemplar of the theory of monopoly capitalism. Highly concentrated, the industry has also been the dominant force in the history of Detroit. As distinct from garment production, the automobile industry is highly unionized and, relative to wages in other manufacturing sectors, well-paid. And as distinct from New York, Detroit has not been an international center of capital, corporate services, or headquarters functions.

Thus, by turning our attention to Detroit (in chapter 7) we are able to illustrate the ways in which our approach contrasts to that of the theory of monopoly capitalism.

In our examination of New York City, in chapter 8, we ask whether the status of the City as a world center of capital and administration implies a privileged or affluent level of living for its resident workers. This examination allows us to contrast our conception of the global system to that embodied in some of the broader extensions of world system models of the global economy. We focus on the garment industry as it has been changed by global competition, and we look at some general indicators of the standards of living of working-class New Yorkers. We find, in the Global City, the decline of a competitive industry, the creation of substandard conditions in it, and conditions of life in the "core of the core," which are more typical of the "periphery."

The garment industry is among those most likely to experience internationalization. Easy entry to the market has maintained it as fiercely price competitive, and labor costs are apt to be prominent in location decisions.

As the data in chapter 6 show, this industry (along with the production of textiles) has been among the most likely to migrate to low-wage production sites in the poor countries.

While New York's garment industry remains as but a small vestige of its former centrality to the city (although a large part of its low-wage jobs in manufacturing), Detroit has not yet finished with the process of decline and restructuring in the automobile industry. By contrast to both of these, Massachusetts has seen a new manufacturing industry grow to prominence in the last fifteen years.

"High tech," and the computer industry in particular, has been claimed as the basis for the reversal of the state's economic fortunes. After decades of unemployment in excess of national averages, the Bay State now enjoys full employment. Chapter 9 examines decline and change in Massachusetts in order to illuminate the process of restructuring.

The selection of the *state* of Massachusetts as our unit should be explained. In part, our selection maintains a degree of comparability in the size of units: the population of the state of Massachusetts is about three-fourths that of New York City, and about comparable to that of the Detroit metropolitan region. Furthermore, the high tech industry, and its minicomputer fraction has a number of areas of concentration in the state, rather than a single regional concentration.

While these reasons for choosing the state of Massachusetts for our third American case study might be adequate, we have another decisive consideration. The high tech industry has impressive, perhaps unique, influence in the politics of the state. Because we are vitally interested in the question of power and public policy in the era of global capitalism, the Massachusetts experience seemed particularly relevant.

As students of class, industry, and power, we have access and insight to the politics of the commonwealth that could not be duplicated elsewhere. One of us (Ross) worked as a consultant to a member of the Massachusetts State Senate and, as we complete work on this volume, for the economic development agency for Boston. The senator was the prime sponsor of several pieces of legislation important to our story: plant closing notification legislation and legislation establishing a "right-to-know" about the presence of hazardous materials in the workplace and community. As a result, this legislator was a member of Massachusetts' Governor's Commission on the Future of Mature Industries, to which Ross acted as his liaison. Because Ross had previously acted as a location consultant for study of the high technology industry, we have been in a good position to analyze the *political* economy of the state.

Figure 1.1 is a schematic of the plan of the three regional studies.

We are aware, of course, that while our theory is global, our cases are North American. By themselves, they illustrate but cannot "prove" our

FIGURE 1.1

PLAN OF THE CASE STUDIES: RESTRUCTURING INDUSTRIES AND REGIONS

Initial Form of Manufacturing Industry Analyzed	Dominant Function of City or Region	Area
Competitive Garment industry	Headquarters Financial	New York City
Monopoly Automobiles	Heavy Industry	Detroit Region
Global High technology	Business Services/ Miscellaneous Traditional Manufacturing	Massachusetts

overall contention. Other work by ourselves and others, however, shows that the process of internationalization has had highly similar impacts on workers, industries, and areas throughout the older industrial world, and that the impact on social and political power is similar.[27] As the numbers of cases accumulate, the limits of any one or more of them are overcome.

The last section of the book focusses on the political and policy implications of the new era. The emphasis is on the basic strategic resources and orientations of classes and communities, rather than on macroeconomic policy. The analyses extend the case studies and elaborate our society-centered view of power.

Economic and social life have spatial dimensions. Any given place, a unit of governmental jurisdiction or a market area, has a history of development—social, economic, and political. Rapid economic development or change concentrated in a given area brings new people and new social (that is, ethnic, racial, or class) groups to it. Between 1880 and 1920, for example, the United States saw millions of Southern and Eastern European peoples brought to the industrializing urban concentrations of the nation. Employers used these flows of migrants as a more or less conscious means to undermine emerging working-class solidarity.

In the South Chicago Steel Works of U.S. Steel, for example, foremen were instructed to tell Italians that their English coworkers would desert them in strike action.[28]

Over time, the resident working-class may find means of overcoming its divisions, of molding itself as a class. It may (and it has in the U. S. northeast) use in its interest the liberties that legitimate the democratic state. It may and it has formed unions and other associations of class interest for class purposes. Because the state in formally democratic societies must, to some minimal degree, continue to legitimate itself as more than the instrument of capitalists, this process may result in certain accomplishments: the abolition of child labor; the achievement of workers' compensation, unemployment compensation, social security, welfare, housing subsidies, and so forth. True, some of these policies may prove to be in capital's larger interest—but not necessarily because all capitalists realize it, and not necessarily in the interests of all capitalists.

Over time, then, a place develops a particular social and political configuration, a characteristic terrain. As of the 1970s, the Massachusetts legal and social terrain (e.g., unemployment compensation and welfare payments) show the local working class to have been relatively successful as compared to others. In general, this can be said of the entire northeast-midwestern industrial belt of the United States. Rates of unionization were higher and many aspects of the social wage were also higher than, for example, in the southern United States.[29]

Thus, a nation, and, indeed, the world is a mosaic not only of technical and economic dimensions, but a differentiated juridical terrain in which capital and labor have had varying degrees of relative success. This terrain is the result of the tensions produced in part by the legitimation-accumulation dialectic.[30]

The imperatives and opportunities offered to political actors have changed in the course of capitalist development. The emergence of monopoly capitalism remade the tasks of government and the alignment of class forces.

The constellation of function and power that characterized the monopoly era is giving way under the geologic pressures of a new variant of capitalism. The terrain of the old political world is shifting in a variety of ways.

It is within this varied terrain that we observe, in chapter 10, the strategic initiatives of business and workers in the older regions of the United States.

Finally, in chapter 11, we draw together the implications of the theory of global capitalism for understanding changes in the state in recent years. The theme of our work is that a New Leviathan of global capitalism confronts the schemes of local and national actors with a stern and rigorous discipline. In this final chapter we suggest that the increase in the power of business interests in state policy, reflected in the conservative regimes of the 1980s in Western Europe and North America, is underlain by a change in the relation of the capitalist class to the state. The autonomy of state policy was partially supported by labor's political influence in the era of monopoly capitalism; it was also supported by divisions among fractions of capital. Now, with labor's power waning, and new bases of unity among fractions of capital, state policy is more responsive to the transient will of capital. The relative autonomy of the state under capitalism undergoes relative decline in the era of global capitalism. Together, the increase of capitalist class power in state policy and the global expansion of the reserve of labor have major implications for the prospects of the socialist movement in the West. Mao was wrong: the East wind does not blow red, rather it postpones the socialist project.

The study of power is never innocent of or irrelevant to value commitments. Our own biographies have surely formed the lens through which we have refracted the world of the 1980s. Sons of school teachers and garment workers, we were afforded the opportunity to be scholars in a historic moment in which working people had struggled with some success for democracy and equity, if not equality, and our parents, finally, obtained some measure of security later in their lives. The world of our maturity appears to threaten these gains.

In that sense, we have striven for a rigorous objectivity. One of us has been a local activist for almost thirty years; another has worked for more than a decade on issues of development in the Third World. Neither of us welcomes the vista which we depict.

The claim that there is a new kind of capitalism emerging in the current era is an ambitious one, it composes our maximum program. Our critics will find our errors; if in so doing we draw attention to the new strategic realities of power we will find solace in that.

Part II
Toward a New Synthesis

2
Tools for Analysis

Introduction:
Capitalist Crisis and Social Theory

Capitalism has proven to be a more adaptable system than its nineteenth century critics anticipated. Through the middle of that century, the leading capitalist economies consisted of many small firms most usually selling their products in local markets. Employers engaged labor supplied by a working class that was barely organized and included within it a large reserve army of underemployed workers. The fundamental model of capitalism shared by Adam Smith, Ricardo, Marx, and Mill was that of a competitive capitalist system whose typical (if not its only) economic unit was the small firm.

By the early twentieth century, the large firm or oligopoly had become the characteristic form of enterprise in leading industries. Fewer firms competed in these industries and workers had begun to organize themselves.

While small firms continued to be a significant and vital part of capitalist economic structure, the so-called monopoly corporation became the central institution of capitalist life.

Today another transformation is underway. Multinational or global firms control increasing percentages of production worldwide. These firms and even smaller ones employ workers and own or control facilities in many different regions and nations. Across these local communities, workers and their organizations have vastly different levels of living and contrasting opportunities to defend their interests.

In certain periods, the pace of capitalist change has been particularly rapid and acute. Economic crisis has left its mark on all those subject to capitalism's periodic waves of "creative destruction." For theorists who work in and around the Marxian tradition—and others,[1] —such moments have often been the occasion for predictions of the final collapse of capitalism and the rise of socialism.

Instead of socialism, periodic material crises in advanced capitalist nations have produced other kinds of changes. These changes include the rise of new forms of enterprise, the incorporation of new regions into an increasingly global capitalist economy, new forms of capitalist competition, and new strategic relations between the capitalist and the working class.

20

The failure of socialism to emerge in the industrial countries has demanded an explanation consistent with observable changes in the system. The intellectual history of capitalism is, consequently, marked by periods in which the prevailing understanding of the capitalist system has undergone significant revision. Marx's analysis of the fundamental logic of the capitalist mode of production has been the starting point for most radical political economists. But over time it has been extended and emended by theorists working in and around the tradition he established.

The late nineteenth century was such a period of material crisis in the centers of capitalism. Yet, what emerged was not the worldwide socialism that many Marxists anticipated but a newly expansionist form of capitalism. This result seemed to contradict the understanding of Marx held by many. The combination of secular change within capitalism and the political and economic crises churned up in its wake was the context for a period of revision and innovation in the marxist tradition.

Out of this crisis emerged the writings of Bukharin, Lenin, and Luxemburg and what has become known as the "theory of imperialism." In the same period, Bernstein argued that "evolutionary socialism" would be the developmental product of what he called "organized capitalism." While these works contain diverse ideas (and sharply contending politics), certain themes assumed particular importance in subsequent intellectual history. These themes included an emphasis upon the emergence of giant or monopoly firms and an analysis of the tendency for capitalism to expand to precapitalist or backward areas of the globe in an exploitative fashion.[2]

The material crisis of the late nineteenth century was repeated in the 1930s. But after World War II, institutional and international structural changes seemed to underlay unanticipated economic expansion in America and Europe. It was at this point that Paul Baran and Paul Sweezy articulated their theory of monopoly capitalism, while in Europe some marxists developed the theory of "state monopoly capitalism."

Baran and Sweezy focused on the growth of monopoly firms and the exploitation of nonindustrial regions that had been advanced by the earlier theorists of imperialism. Along with others, they built a theoretical framework that offered both an explicitly revised model of how the system works and an explanation of the dynamics of twentieth-century capitalism.[3] In a variety of forms, the model of "monopoly capitalism" eventually assumed a position of intellectual dominance among marxists and other radical analysts, even though Baran and Sweezy's particular theory of its dynamics remained controversial.

As the theory of monopoly capitalism gained credence among North American political economists, Third World scholars and others concerned with continuing poverty in Latin America, Africa, and Asia developed an approach known as the *dependencia* tradition. It, too, gained widespread influence, even among mainstream development theorists. Building on this tradition, as was well as the work of Baran and Luxembourg, Immanuel Wallerstein and others have advanced a perspective on the history and logic of capitalism known as world systems theory. World systems theory has now assumed a place alongside the theory of monopoly capitalism as one of the dominant intellectual influences in political economy.

Overview of Section II

The question now before us is whether these two perspectives—the theory of monopoly capitalism and world systems theory—continue to offer adequate understandings of late twentieth-century capitalism. As the previous chapter suggested, we do not think so. In the last twenty years, crisis and stagnation and new kinds of growth have signalled transformations comparable in magnitude to that of the late nineteenth and early twentieth centuries. Neither of these theories give us a firm grasp on their causes or consequences. We face another moment in which a new synthesis is required to make sense of change.

This part of the volume seeks to contribute to a new synthesis by explicitly delineating propositions from each theory's model of the way the world capitalist system is supposed to work. These propositions are then contrasted to an alternative model, derived from the theory of global capitalism. Later in Part III we apply the theory of global capitalism to change in the world structure of production and to the older industrial regions of the United States.

While the last decade has witnessed extensive analyses of the crisis of the 1970s and 1980s, there has been no widely accepted synthesis that pulls the strands of analysis together to more adequately capture the way contemporary capitalism works. We propose a new view of late twentieth century capitalism—the theory of global capitalism.

Given the recent dominance of the theory of monopoly capitalism and world systems theory we have taken some pains to summarize them and our differences with them. For some readers this may involve a journey onto unfamiliar or difficult terrain. We cling to what may be a naive faith: that social theory does make a difference in what we do in the world; that careful understanding, in the long run, repays the effort.

Ideas organize perceptions and guide actions. In the midst of struggles to defend livelihoods and communities, the stakes are high. Old ideas may not be adequate to the task.

This chapter begins the theoretical task by presenting definitions, concepts, and ideas employed in the course of this book. Chapters 3 and 4 present and critique the theory of monopoly capitalism and the world systems perspective. In chapter 5 the theory of global capitalism is elaborated.

A Definition of Capitalism as a Mode of Production

We understand capitalism as a mode of commodity production for exchange; where labor power itself is a commodity; and where a capitalist class that owns and controls the means of production extracts surplus value from a working class by purchasing its only means of survival—their labor power— through payment of wages.

At the highest level of abstraction, certain social relations have been characteristic of capitalism across time and national boundaries: competition among capitals, the extraction of value from labor by capital under a wage relationship, and (once the capitalist mode of production had reached maturity) the relative domination of the state by capital (or fractions of it).

Variants of the Capitalist Mode of Production

The concept of invariant social relationships within capitalism as a mode of production permits examination of the logic of the system at a relatively high level of abstraction. Across the history of capitalism, however, variations in the particular forms of its strategic social relations can be identified.

At a somewhat lower, intermediate, level of abstraction, the concept of variants or "submodes" of capitalism abstracts from the welter of national and historical circumstance, seeking to clarify the distinctive structure and dynamic of each submode. The Marxian tradition has tended to resist innovation in the formal concepts appropriate to the analysis of these changes. Nevertheless, these variations have, *de facto*, constituted the basis for conceiving of stages, variants or submodes of capitalism. Indeed, though not often formally acknowledged, without some concept such as variant or submode, practically all discussion of twentieth-century capitalism would be unintelligible.

The theory of monopoly capitalism articulated by Baran and Sweezy has been a major expression of the ways in which twentieth-century capitalism differed from that of the previous century. Although Baran and Sweezy have been criticized by Marxists for their specification of the dynamic problems of monopoly capitalism, broad agreement has emerged on two points.

First, many analysts concur that the history of capitalism can be fruitfully analyzed by distinguishing stages of capitalist development. Second, political economists have accepted the notion that a new structural form— monopoly capitalism—became dominant *within* the capitalist mode of production during the course of the early twentieth century.

One of the more sophisticated defenses of the utility of conceiving of stages has been offered by Olin Wright:

> A given organization of accumulation...tends to become less and less reproductive [developing "impediments to accumulation"]. This is a situation that can be described as a structural crisis of accumulation. In such situations, typically, the forms of accumulation are themselves restructured in basic ways... "Structural solutions" to those impediments...are...the ways in which the accumulation process is transformed to re-establish a compatible relations with the forces/relations of production. It is such structural solutions which define the essential character of the different stages of capitalist development.[4]

In his historical analysis, Wright agrees with Baran and Sweezy in dating the rise and consolidation of monopoly capitalism as the early twentieth century. More recent periods, he suggests, can be further specified as advanced and state-directed monopoly capitalism.[5]

As we indicated earlier, the methodological innovation of thinking in terms of change in the dominant form of capitalism is neither recent nor strictly American in origin. Already by the turn of the century, European social democracy was absorbed in discussion of "finance capital," "imperialism," and the role of trusts.

More recently, the prominent French Marxist economist, Aglietta, discussing "state monopoly capitalism," the alternative concept among French Marxists, says "It is legitimate to speak of state monopoly capitalism if the organic unity of the conditions of expanded reproduction of the wage relation modifies the expression of the laws of capitalist regulation to the point of producing historically new phenomena." He dates the emergence of this "historically new" form between 1915 and 1945.[6]

That there have been different moments in the organization of capitalist relations is also the view of Gordon, Edwards, and Reich who observe, "As the historical materialist perspective suggests, capitalist economies continually change and develop, driven constantly by the dual dynamic forces of intercapitalist competition and capital-labor conflict."[7]

Employing the concept "social structure of accumulation," these authors further assert that a new set of institutions governing capital accumulation "emerged from the class conflict and political realignment of the dozen or so years following 1935."[8]

Diverse traditions of political economy use a methodology consistent with the theory of global capitalism: they summarize historical changes within capitalism in terms of stages or variants within the mode of production. In different ways they recognize that the contradictory and dynamic nature of capitalism produces significant transformations of the conditions of working class exploitation and capitalist competition.[9]

Global Capitalism as a
Submode of Capitalism

When we speak of *global capitalism*, then, we refer to a variant or submode of capitalism that can be distinguished from two other variants extant in both present and past capitalist social formations—the competitive and monopoly variants.[10]

Capitalist social formations almost always include more than one variant of the capitalist mode of production as well as precapitalist social relations. At any given time, however, one variant can be identified as dominant in relation to others.[11] In terming the contemporary era one of global capitalism, we are suggesting that the global variant, and thus global firms, are emerging as dominant in relation to firms that continue in monopoly or competitive sectors of the social formation. Value flows from monopoly or competitive firms to global firms and from monopoly or competitive industrial sectors to sectors that are global in character.[12]

Fundamental to our conception of contemporary capitalism is that it is a system of *global production* relations. The theory of global capitalism differs from that of monopoly capitalism because it sees the dominance of global production organizations as changing the national structures and processes characteristic of the monopoly era. The theory also differs from that of world systems analysis whose starting point defines capitalism as a system of production for exchange, and which (as discussed in chapter 4) explicates the current world system as a hierarchical order of exchange rather than production relations.

Where world systems theory sees the global markets of transnational corporations as merely another form of world commodity chains that have existed since the fifteenth century, we see a system of global factories where the capitalist class has at its disposal a new bargaining power and where the balance of class forces has been fundamentally altered.

By focusing upon production, we move to the center of our analysis the strategic, that is, power and bargaining relations between capital and labor—between classes. This focus pivots on the global mobility of manufacturing capital and the capacity of giant firms to disaggregate stages of the production process across national boundaries.[13]

The Strategic Relationships
within Capitalism

Throughout this volume, the transformations of capitalism are frequently presented through an organizing device that summarizes three of the strategic social relations of capitalism. In turn, this form of presentation provides a means for contrasting the theory of global capitalism with the dominant models in political economy. These three strategic relations are those which obtain between capital and labor, between different firms (i.e., the capital-to-capital relation), and between classes, especially the dominant class—capital, and the state.

Capital-to-labor. There is no capital without labor. The conflict between workers and their employers is the central engine that drives capitalist societies through history. The most *direct* dimension of this relationship is the wage relation, which is also the easiest to quantify.

Employers engage laborers in order to make use of their ability to work—their "labor power." The problem for the employer is to make maximum use of this ability, and usually, to pay the least for it. This imperative causes employers to craft strategies for controlling and disciplining labor. Successive reorganization of the work process itself, often taking the form of "deskilling"—replacing human skill and autonomy with machine processes—is the result.[14]

Every moment of productivity of an employee that earns the employer a return larger than the worker's wage ("surplus labor," "surplus value") is a potential expansion of the employer's capital.

In any given enterprise, conflict over the wage, conditions, and pace of work is direct. However, the larger problem of a capitalist class is the aggregate accumulation of surplus value in a whole economy, for a class of capitalists. Structurally, the most critical aspect of the extraction and accumulation process is an aggregate phenomenon of sectors or economies as a whole.

The forms in which this potential for class conflict are enacted, the sites of class struggle, and the nature of class organization vary in the course of capitalist development.[15] The forms of class conflict form a crucible that tests a given submode of capitalism in comparison to others. A form of capitalist organization that proves superior in managing class struggle, in finding an advantageous niche, will obtain critical advantages in competition with other forms of enterprise. As this form becomes strategically dominant in a social formation, a new variant, or submode, of capitalism can be identified.

Different forms of capitalist organization emerge to dominance in part because each produces different strategic advantages and disadvantages as workers and employers each seek to secure their material and political interests. In each variant of capitalism, the structure of power rests on a distinctive leverage, *a lever of exploitation*, whereby capital is able to enforce its ability to extract surplus from workers.

For example, in the competitive variant, a large reserve of under-employed labor enforces discipline upon employed workers. Under monopoly capitalism, discussed in the next chapter, a segmented labor market allows monopoly capital to appropriate surplus from other capitalists and from competitive sector employees.

As global capitalism emerges, the distinctive lever of exploitation—the dominant resource for power, which becomes perfected by aggressive firms is capital mobility—the threat and reality of flight.

The relative power and bargaining position of capital and labor is central to our analysis. We refer to this changing power relation as the capital-to-labor relation.

Capital-to-capital.   The second strategic relationship is that which obtains between separate firms, proprietors, and industrial or financial blocs each of which is subject to a unitary source of control. Firms and blocs compete for inputs (e.g., raw materials, financing), in extracting value (crudely, labor costs), and for markets. These are impersonal processes that take place between aggregates of capital.

The signals that catalyze the competitive behavior of firms are profits measured in monetary terms. (More precisely, the deviation of profits from average profits among effectively available investment outlets, or the relationship of average profits to average prices of production.[16]) Whereas the relationship between labor and capital is a contest over value or surplus labor, the relationship between firms is mediated by price.

Individuals of the capitalist class, especially at its commanding heights, may have personally cordial relations facilitated by all sorts of social institutions—clubs, balls, colloquia, and associations.[17] Cartels or price-fixing conspiracies may come and go. Political coalitions may unite the interests of a variety of capitals in common cause.

Yet, these are still the cautious dances of scorpions at the alert. Whatever the form, the fundamental relation of private aggregations of capital is competitive. As against labor there may be important elements of unity; in the marketplace, more usually, an impersonal competitive necessity drives the behavior of individual firms.

We refer to these relations as capital-to-capital relations. Our focus is the ways in which the forms of competition and cooperation among capitals vary over capitalist history and within capitalist political economies. In each variant, a particular form of competition among capitalists can be identified as most typical.

For example, price competition prevailed in the era of the competitive variant. Under monopoly capitalism (discussed in the next chapter) price competition was supplanted by such strategies as product differentiation, advertising, and cost control.

As the global variant becomes dominant, prices once again become competitive even as centralization and concentration continue. What distinguishes this price competition from that of the earlier era of competitive capitalism is the extent to which a firm's success depends upon its capacity to utilize with maximal efficiency the variations in wages, skills, and so on of a *worldwide* reserve of labor.

The analysis of changing forms of capitalist competition is the second of the organizing devices through which we will explicate the theory of global capitalism.

Capital-to-[the]-state.   The capitalist state is the regulator of conditions that reproduce capitalism and the ability of the capitalist class to maintain its dominant position. As that institution with a monopoly of legitimate violence, the state is the "final" expression of power relations within its territory and within the global structure of power. Amidst the particularities of nation-states at similar levels of capitalist development are strong comparative similarities side by side with the endless variety of historical experience.

Across the history of capitalist development, the relative ability of classes and class fractions to obtain state policies that implement their interests also varies. The strategies used by class actors varies with their forms of organization and the resources available to them.

To say that the capitalist class is politically dominant in capitalist societies may be true, but it is not adequately specific. Our analysis focuses on the particular power and strategic relations which obtain between capitalists and the state. That is, "dominance" is highly relative; changes in the balance of class forces within the social formation as a whole are registered in the degree to which capital or its dominant fractions are able to obtain policies they want or need.

From the perspective of the investor, the relative balance of class forces as expressed in public policies has a spatial dimension. Within nations and between them, jurisdictions appear as a mosaic of differential conditions, some more and others less propitious for a given type of activity. Political forces, and thus differential policy profiles, are an important dimension of this national and international mosaic.

The theory of global capitalism argues that the emergence of new strategic relations between capitalists, and between capital and labor involves investor discretion in spatial location; this has produced a relative increment in the power of capital in relation to the state. In our discussion of other theories and in our case studies, we refer to this as the capital-to-state relation.

It should be noted that the label *capital-to-state*, because it always implies a relation of relative, not pure dominance, is *simultaneously* a substantive discussion of a labor-to-state relation as well. By using the phrase *capital-to-state*, rather than *class(es)-to-state*, we focus on variation in the *relative* domination of the capitalist class in the politics of capitalist societies.

Crisis Tendencies under Capitalism

Up to this point we have introduced concepts that can be used to analyse changes within capitalism, identifying the concepts of submodes, dominance, and strategic relations within a submode of capitalism.

The theory of global capitalism will use these concepts to characterize the results of a transition from one form of dominance within capitalism (monopoly capitalism) to another—global capitalism.

The idea that such a transformation has occurred requires concepts to analyse the dynamics of change within capitalism. Can one specify those dynamics of capitalism that are the source of periodic structural transformation? What, in particular, are the forces precipitating the transition to global capitalism?

Attempts to answer such questions lead to the realm of crisis theory. This is a complex and somewhat arcane area of scholarship. A comprehensive review of the various approaches, propositions, and debates is beyond the scope of this work.[18]

The objective here is more limited. We summarize the contending versions of crisis theory in order to show the way each influences an understanding of change in the forms of capitalist social relations.[19] Three different versions are explicated and contrasted. In chapter 5 we indicate the ways in these theories might each account for the transition to global capitalism.

The Tendency for the Rate of Profit to Decline

Crisis theory is built upon the proposition that capitalism generates obstacles or impediments to the expanded reproduction of the system. These obstacles or impediments are viewed as contradictions of capitalist production in so far as they emerge from the process of accumulation itself.[20] Understanding this notion requires making a distinction between the rational interest of the individual capitalist and the collective interest of the capitalist class. That which the individual capitalist is compelled to do by the forces of competition can produce at the collective level "unintended" consequences that threaten the interests of all members of the class. The cumulative effect of the accumulation strategies pursued by individual firms tend to produce crises in the larger economy.

Specifically Marxian crisis theory focuses upon dynamics that lead to a tendency for the rate of profit to decline. As Weisskopf has explained, the rate of profit is "a critical determinant of macro-economic vitality":

> Production is organised and investment is undertaken by capitalists in order to make profits; a fall in the average rate of profit—and consequently in the expected profitability of new investment—is bound soon or later to discourage such new investment. [This is] a major determinant of both the level and the rate of growth of aggregate output and employment. Thus it is quite reasonable on theoretical grounds to argue that a falling rate of profit will ultimately lead—via profit expectations and the rate of investment—to an economic crisis in which the levels and rates of growth of output and employment are depressed.[21]

Analysis of the crisis tendencies of capitalissm has thus revolved around documenting and explaining the tendency for the rate of profit to decline.

That Marx and his latter-day followers adopt the usage *tendency* is instructive—and will prove important later in our work. Assume that there *are* systemic features of the strategic relations of capitalism that create pressures (tendencies) that depress rates of profit. Such pressures will be resisted. The institutional forms of investor resistance to such tendencies may be successful in a given moment of development. The resultant institutional innovations may fall short of transformation to another mode of production, yet, over time, produce change in the way capitalism functions. Such a sequence would mask the empirical manifestation of declining rates of profit, yet simultaneously propel the system toward a new variant of capitalism.

Within Marxian crisis theory are several different explanations of the tendency for the rate of profit to decline. These may be identified as (1) interpretations that emphasize the dynamic of class struggle; (2) the thesis of the tendency of the organic composition of capital to rise; and (3) arguments that focus upon realization failure.

Each of these versions of crisis theory, as well as combinations of them, have been put forward as interpretations of the world economic crisis, which became apparent in the 1970s and repeatedly manifested itself in the 1980s.

Elements of the Labor Theory of Value

Elements of Marx's labor theory of value have played a key role in the century-long discussion of crisis theory.[22] Within the Marxian tradition, value can be created only when human beings exercise their capacity to work. Production is "measured" in terms of the total hours of human labor that go directly and indirectly into the production process. This is captured in the well-known formula:

$$P = c + v + s \text{ where:}$$

P = the total value produced

c = the value of constant capital consumed or human labor that enters indirectly into production (machines, buildings, raw materials, and so forth used in production)

v = the value of labor power used in production or variable capital (roughly, wages paid to workers)

s = the value of the surplus product produced by workers

Under capitalism, workers have available to them only one means of securing a livelihood. They must sell their capacity to work. This unique commodity was defined by Marx as *labor power*. Its cost is determined by various technical considerations (e.g., training costs) as well as "historical and moral elements" (i.e., class struggle over wages). The worker sells a commodity—labor power—in return for a wage more or less equal to the value of that commodity—an exchange that appears to many as an exchange of equivalents.

During the production process, however, it is essential, from the point of view of the employer that workers produce through their actual labor a magnitude of value greater than the exchange value of their labor power. Therefore, for one part of the day, workers labor to produce value that (through the receipt of wages) provides their means of livelihood (necessary labor). It is the value of this activity that is represented by the term v. For the remainder of the day, workers create "new" value for the capitalist (surplus labor). This "new" value is surplus value s.

Integral, then, to capital accumulation is the relationship of surplus labor to necessary labor. This is termed *the rate of exploitation* (or $e = s/v$). It indicates the success of capital in coercing labor to produce during the production process value greater than the costs of its own reproduction. Clearly, any variation in the rate of exploitation will affect directly the capitalist's rate of profit.

It is important to note that in this "classical" version of Marxism only living labor can produce surplus value, and thus profit. However, machines and raw materials also constitute a cost of production to the firm, c. Marxist value theory conceives of these as "dead" labor in the sense that machines are built and raw materials are extracted by workers. The total costs of production for a firm in a capitalist economy can then be represented by the expression $c + v$.

Finally, the value rate of profit (i.e., the rate of profit per unit of capital advanced) can be expressed by the equation:

$$r = \frac{s}{c + v}$$

where r = the value rate of profit

With these ratios and the social relations underlying them in mind, we can begin to explicate the three versions of crisis theory.

1. *Class struggle, the rising strength of labor, and the rate of profit.* One version of crisis theory proposes that the growth of working-class strength (through unionization, militance, etc.) can create impediments to capital accumulation. This version claims that class struggle explains periodic business cycles, transitions to a new stage of capitalism and long-term structural decline.[23]

Class struggle versions of crisis theory highlight the propensity for workers to organize and develop strategies for reducing the rate of exploitation. They maintain that when workers' struggles lead to a rise in the real cost of labor power (i.e., wages increase more rapidly than productivity) and/or an ability to resist increases in work intensity, the ratio s/v will decline and, other conditions being equal, with it the rate of profit. Successful struggles by workers, in this family of perspectives, trigger attempts by capitalists to restore the strategic capital-to-labor relation to one more advantageous to employers. State policies are often among the means used to achieve this.

Some renditions of the class struggle argument present the matter as a battle over the relative share of the national income going to workers and capitalists respectively. Here the success of the working class in securing wage increases in excess of productivity is seen to result in a "squeeze" on profits. In this version, the argument has been criticized by more "orthodox" Marxists as being *neo-Ricardian* or *circulationist*.[24] Class struggle theorists are said to focus only on the circulation of the money form of the commodity labor power and to ignore the production process itself.

Not all versions of class struggle arguments are susceptible to such a criticism, however. Gordon, Edwards, and Reich demonstrate how the rising strength of labor creates impediments at several moments of the accumulation process, including the work process itself. Castells has attempted to show that "the main structural barrier existing in capitalist production and circulation is the worker's resistance to exploitation."[25] Wright suggests that the perspective can be extended to include class struggles over, for example, the length and intensity of the work day or worker resistance to the introduction of new "labor-saving" technologies.[26] Wright also notes that working-class success in influencing elements of state policy and how those impact on profit rates deserve attention.

Theories that locate crisis tendencies in workers' ability to capture a greater share of the value they produce are the least determinist of crisis theories. At the highest level of abstraction in which capitalism's invariant relations are analyzed, there is no *necessary* process in which workers are able to choke capital accumulation. *If* such a result occurs, it is formed by more historically specific and conditional factors. Among these are the skills, traditions, subjective consciousness, and organizational experiences of workers. Thus, some criticize class struggle theories of capitalist crisis dynamics as being too "voluntarist"—that is, not deriving crisis from the logic of accumulation. Still others say that such theories are flawed by "economism," that is, they emphasize wage struggles in and of themselves as engines of transformation.

2. *The tendency for the organic composition of capital to rise.*   By contrast, a second tradition of crisis theory has as its central proposition the contention that capitalists are compelled to revolutionize the productive forces. This is derived from the discipline of intercapitalist competition and from

factors that limit the rate of exploitation. Firms develop and introduce new labor-saving technologies in response to these pressures. The introduction of these new technologies produces a rise in the organic composition of capital. And, as the organic composition of capital rises, there is a tendency for the rate of profit to decline unless the rate of exploitation can be increased sufficiently to offset the rise in the organic composition of capital.

An explication of this argument begins by defining the organic composition of capital. Most simply, it can be thought of as the ratio of the value of machines to human labor in the economic unit. More technically, it is the ratio of dead labor (constant capital) to living labor (variable capital plus surplus value) in production.[27] A rise in the organic composition of capital then means an increase in the ratio $c/v + s$.

The tendency for the organic composition of capital to rise can be understood as arising directly from two of the fundamental social relations discussed above. The economic vitality of a firm in a capitalist economy depends upon its success in coping simultaneously with the compulsions of intercapitalist competition and the resistance of workers to exploitation.

Intercapitalist competition forces firms to lower production costs or achieve product innovation to protect its market share, thereby forestalling bankruptcy. The firm therefore operates under a constant compulsion to lower production costs. One way to do this is to seek to drive down the cost of labor power.

The effort to lower labor costs, however, faces constraints. In the long run, wages cannot be driven below that level necessary to physically reproduce the working class.[28] Even more pertinent in the contemporary era is the capacity of workers, in contrast to machines, to resist domination. Class struggle over the conditions of production limits the capitalist's ability to lower directly the cost of labor power.

In the view of organic composition theorists, capitalists attempt to solve this dilemma through the development and introduction of labor-saving technologies.[29] Such technology increases the productivity of workers. This, in effect, reduces the portion of the working day composed of necessary labor and generates a rise in relative surplus value.[30] The firm becomes more able to compete—whether that takes the form of price competition or product innovation.

Introducing labor-saving technologies, then, is a competitive necessity for capitalist enterprises, dictated by the logic of intercapitalist competition as well as workers' resistance to exploitation. It succeeds in raising the rate of surplus extraction by increasing the productivity of workers.

Yet, contend organic composition theorists, the strategy produces its own contradictions. That contradiction lies in the fact that dead labor does not have the property of self-expansion; only living labor can create more value than is required for its reproduction. Capital, in defending its interests, replaces the ultimate source of its profits—living labor—with machines. In technical terms, the organic composition of capital ($c/v + s$) rises more rapidly than the rate of exploitation (s/v) (despite the increases in productivity), thereby causing the *rate* of profit ($s/c + v$) to decline.

The fall in the rate of profit does not typically mean an immediate crisis. Depending upon the level of demand within the economy, the mass of profits within the economy may grow. As long as this occurs, investors will continue to invest and the economy will continue to expand. Eventually, however, the continual fall in the rate of profit will discourage new investment and lead to stagnation in the mass of profit as well. No longer able to get a positive return on their investment, capitalists will cease investing. Production will be cut back, profits will fall more sharply, interest rates will rise, and unemployment will spread. At this point, the crisis has ensued.

Critics of this theory are many. They include those who reject the labor theory of value entirely. Indeed, class struggle theories do not depend on its mathematical logic at all.

In addition, one may remain agnostic as to the theoretical proposition that only living labor produces value and challenge a value theory basis for explaining capitalist behavior. Because capitalists respond to behavioral cues in *price* terms, not value categories, this argument contends, the metaphysics of value theory are irrelevant to explaining crisis tendencies. Outside of technically oriented political economists, for example, among sociological theorists of capitalism, the long expansion of the post-World War II period put *all* crisis theories in disrepute. Events of the 1970s and 1980s increased both the interest in crisis theory and its variety.

3. *Realization failure and falling profits.*   The third version of crisis theory focuses upon what Marxists call realization problems. Those who have contributed to its development include Baran and Sweezy as well as most other adherents to the theory of monopoly capitalism.

This perspective differs from the other two in that it locates profit decline in what Marxists term the sphere of circulation as opposed to the sphere of production. For both class struggle and organic composition theorists profits decline because of forces that operate during the production process.[31] For the realization failure theorist, "the threat to profitability... stems from difficulties in selling the produced commodities at profitable prices, i..e., at prices that cover the costs incurred as well as the expected profit margin."[32]

In explicating this approach, it is useful to draw a distinction between potential profits and actual profits.[33] *Potential profits* refers to the value of the surplus labor that the capitalist has managed to extract from workers during the production process. According to realization theorists, however, it is not always possible for the capitalist to sell the product at a price sufficient to realize that surplus. Actual profits can fall short of potential profits.

The failure of capitalists to realize potential profit is seen to stem from an intrinsic contradiction in capitalist social formations between the conditions under which surplus is extracted and those under which surplus is realized. As we have seen, competition among capitalists (even of the monopoly variety) drives them to minimize their wage bill. Such efforts, however, depress the effective demand for commodities on the part of workers; they drive the economy toward underconsumptionism. As capitalists succeed in increasing the rate of exploitation, they simultaneously restrict the level of demand for the commodities which they have appropriated. Unless, therefore, alternate sources of demand (state expenditures, foreign markets, etc.) can be created, some portion of the potential profits will remain unrealized.

As with other conceptions of crisis, realization theories state that the crisis is experienced by capitalist firms as a fall in the rate of profit which leads to a contraction of investment, depressed growth rates and high levels of unemployment.

Finally, most realization theorists insist either that underconsumptionist tendencies emerged with or became more acute with the advent of monopoly capitalism. For reasons explored in the next chapter, they maintain that the particular features of the monopoly stage accentuate the tendency for the surplus to rise.

Contrasts among the three crisis theories.   Marxian crisis theories agree capitalist economies are driven through history by a tendency for the rate of profit to decline. They also insist that this tendency is inherent to capitalist societies. Falling rates of profit and crisis emerge from within the strategic relations or structural logic of capitalism and not from exogenous factors.

However, the three versions of crisis theory surveyed offer contrasting interpretations of that structural logic. Class struggle theorists argue that the conflict that drives capitalism toward periodic crises emerges from the contradictory interests of capital and labor. Those emphasizing the rise in the organic composition of capital stress the contradiction between the strategies that capital must employ in order to remain competitive and the fact that living workers are the ultimate source of profit. Writers who understand crisis as realization failure suggest that the primary contradiction is that between the conditions of surplus extraction and the conditions of surplus realization.

In addition, the three approaches offer contrasting hypotheses about trends in the rate of exploitation (s/v). Realization theorists insist strongly that the rate of surplus extraction shows a tendency to rise sharply, especially under monopoly capitalism. Similarly, the organic composition approach sees the rate of exploitation rising; however, they argue that this is more than offset by the change in the composition of capital. In sharp contrast, the class struggle theory claims that a fall in the rate of exploitation is the main force driving down the profit rate.

Political economists have taken several approaches to resolving this controversy. Some have developed measures designed to test the theories and demonstrate the superior explanatory power of one or another option.[34] Mandel and Castells have argued that they are really compatible and not contradictory explanations and have sought to develop syntheses. Wright proffers the view that different tendencies can be identified as dominant during different stages of capitalist development.[35]

This work takes a very modest approach. We recognize that, optimally, a complete theory of global capitalism would specify the particular contradictions of monopoly capitalism driving the transformation to global capitalism. Absent wide acceptance of any one version of crisis theory, however, we have opted for ecumenism. Chapter 5 shows that each of the contending theses propose crisis tendencies that may contribute to the structural changes that we observe and term the emergence of global capitalism.[36]

The Concept of a Restructuring Crisis

Marxists have tended to view moments of crisis as signalling the breakdown of capitalism and the transition to socialism. While the capitalist mode of production may prove to be less than eternal, the focus here is upon a different kind of change. Along with others we assert that moments of crisis have led and can lead to a restructuring of the process of accumulation rather than its breakdown.[37]

The theory of global capitalism views the world economic crisis that began in the early 1970s as such a *restructuring crisis*. The monopoly variant or submode of capitalism, was composed of a particular constellation of the three strategic relations that facilitated, for a period of time, the accumulation of capital. For more than twenty years after World War II, the social relations of monopoly capitalism functioned to sustain expansion of the industrialized economies. Average rates of profit throughout the industrialized world were high. Investment conditions were viewed as favorable by the most dynamic firms. Investment expanded; prosperity ensued; and unemployment declined.

However, in all variants of capitalism internal contradictions begin to erode the strategic advantages of a given constellation of social relations. The monopoly era was no exception. By the late 1960s average rates of profit in most of the industrialized economies began to evidence a tendency to decline. In turn, rates of investment slowed; stagnation set in; and unemployment rose. In short, monopoly capitalism experienced a moment of crisis.[38]

In the next two chapters, we explore the two theories of contemporary capitalism most dominant in North America and highly influential elsewhere: that which asserts that the system is best understood as *monopoly capitalism* and that which depicts a *world system* of hierarchical exchange relations. In chapter 5 we present a different model of the way contemporary capitalism works—global capitalism. In the course of this presentation, we show that any one of the crisis tendencies in capitalism is consistent with the restructuring that produced the particular form of global capitalism.

3
The Birth and Death
of Monopoly Capitalism

Introduction

In their classic work, *Monopoly Capital*, Paul Baran and Paul Sweezy declared that a new era in the evolution of capitalism had come to maturity. Since early in the twentieth century the structure of mature capitalism had superceded the competitive economy of small firms which Marx had analyzed. As Lenin had done at the turn of the century, Baran and Sweezy focussed on the consequences of the ongoing process of concentration of large blocs of financial and industrial might.

Baran and Sweezy argued that the kind of competition Marx's economic theory analyzed had changed. So, too, had the dynamics of twentieth-century capitalism.[1] Their work was a culmination of a generation of Marxist and non-Marxist reflection on the meaning of the huge corporation.[2]

Subsequently, Baran and Sweezy, as well as others such as Harry Magdoff, continued the project of theoretical elaboration.[3] An especially important contribution to the later development of the tradition was made by James O'Connor, particularly in his *The Fiscal Crisis of the State*.[4]

In this chapter, we have organized the principal elements of the theory of monopoly capitalism around the three strategic social relations of capitalism: capital-to-capital, capital-to-labor, and capital-to-state. Not intended as a comprehensive review of this tradition of analysis, we derive propositions about these relationships from Baran and Sweezy and O'Connor. After examining the dynamics of the monopoly capitalism model, the chapter closes with a summary of the propositions and an indication of our evaluation of them.

The Capital-to-Capital Relation in
the Theory of Monopoly Capitalism

The capitalist class is defined by its ownership of the means of production and the extraction of surplus value from the direct producers through the wage relationship. Capitalists share an interest in the maintenance and reproduction of the juridical system that guarantees their ownership of the means of production and of those structures and laws that ensure their ability to accumulate capital. But as individual owners or firms, capitalists are in conflict or competition with one another.

This competition among capitals is more than a matter of merely personal greed or even personal choice. In a system in which decisions about allocating the means of production are made by private owners, failure to keep pace with other firms brings decline and bankruptcy. Competition remains an essential feature of the capitalist mode of production.

Baran and Sweezy have been misunderstood as arguing that monopoly capitalism is distinguished from its competitive era predecessor by the virtual elimination of competition.[5] They lend credence to this interpretation in the Introduction to *Monopoly Capital*: "We must recognize that competition, which was the predominant form of market relations in nineteenth century Britain, has ceased to occupy that position, not only in Britain but everywhere else in the capitalist world."[6] An accurate understanding of their analysis requires a closer look.

Baran and Sweezy do not argue that competition has been eliminated under monopoly capitalism. They do claim that *price* competition, which was the principal *form* of competition under competititive capitalism, has been succeeded by administered pricing. Firms in the dominant monopoly sector continue to compete with one another (and with their smaller, weaker adversaries). This competition emphasizes the techniques of cost reduction and the differentiation of products implemented by advertising. Baran and Sweezy conclude, "competition... rages on with ever increasing intensity under monopoly capitalism and the cost discipline which it imposes on its members... is no less severe than its competitive predecessor."[7] Competition does not disappear in the monopoly era; rather it takes different forms.

Baran and Sweezy's analysis of capitalist firms suggests an important moment in our understanding of capitalism. They propose that the form of capital-to-capital relations can vary within and across the history of the capitalist mode of production. Capitals may compete with one another but the form and consequences of that competition can change.

For Baran and Sweezy, therefore, *the end of price competition is a central feature of the model of monopoly capitalism*. This change in the form of competition produces other consequences that also distinguish the monopoly era from competitive capitalism. In their analyses of "price leadership," tacit "price collusion," and the planning functions of "giant corporations," Baran and Sweezy suggest that stable market shares are one of these outcomes.[8] O'Connor develops this point more fully.

According to O'Connor, what produces "stable industrial structures" under monopoly capitalism is the combination of barriers to the entry of new capital and the administered pricing techniques employed by existing firms.[9]

The second major proposition about capital-to-capital relations in the model of monopoly capitalism is the expectation of relative stability of market shares among major firms.

The absence of price competition in the monopoly era contributes to another characteristic feature of monopoly capitalism—industrial stagnation in the "backward" regions of the world economy. Baran's analysis in *The Political Economy of Growth* develops this "stagnation thesis" most completely. He argues that monopoly firms will use their economic power to structure the Third World economies as markets to absorb their productive surplus (surplus productive capacity).[10]

Baran maintains that one should *not* expect foreign investment under monopoly capitalism to bring about industrialization of backward countries because "the familiar principles of profit maximization under conditions of monopoly and oligopoly—not "spoiling the market," not engaging in cut-throat competition with powerful rivals, and the like—are as pertinent to foreign investment as they are to domestic investment."[11] While the absence of industrialization in backward regions does not distinguish monopoly capitalism from competitive capitalism, it is a logical outcome of monopoly forms of competition as these were understood by Baran.[12]

Industrial stagnation among the backward nations is the third major propostion derived from the theory of monopoly capitalism.

The major theorists of monopoly capitalism also share a view of U.S. capital as hegemonic vis-a-vis other capitals within the world economy.[13] In this view, the global economy is shaped by the interests of monopoly firms based in the United States. Baran and Sweezy, as well as Magdoff, identify these interests as ensuring access to supplies of raw materials and foreign markets.[14]

O'Connor, meanwhile, sees U. S. corporations as shaping other regions of the world to be both markets and investment outlets necessary for countering the problem of surplus productive capacity.[15]

Methodologically, this adherence to a concept of U. S. hegemony means that the theory of monopoly capitalism tends to analyze the dynamics of the U. S. economy without considering the impact of competition from foreign-based capital, whether in the form of imports or of direct investment in productive facilities. Implicitly, but centrally, the theory of monopoly capitalism (as developed in the United States) conceives of capital-to-capital relations as taking place within a hegemonic U. S. national entity.

In summary, relations between capital and capital, as described by theorists of monopoly capitalism, include the following propositions:

1. the hegemony of U. S. capital within the global economy;

2. the elimination of price competition as the characteristic form of capitalist competition; which leads to
  3. a stability of market shares among major firms; and
  4. industrial stagnation in backward regions of the world economy.

We question whether any of these propositions is accurate under current conditions.

The Capital-to-Labor Relation in the Theory of Monopoly Capitalism

The social relations of production between capital and labor compose the elemental dynamic of the capitalist mode of production. The means by which capital extracts surplus value from labor and realizes this as money capital constitute the processes by which the system is reproduced. Capitalism, as a mode of production, is distinguished from noncapitalist modes of production by the fact that the extraction of surplus value takes place in the form of a juridical wage relationship.

Within a given social formation, however, labor struggles with capital over the rate and conditions of surplus extraction. This struggle is direct, in the form of relations between employers and employees. And it is indirect, in the form of political and moral struggles over the definition of minimum decency, that is, reproduction of labor power.[16]

Although the very fact of surplus value extraction indicates the ultimate dominance of capital over labor, workers are not without some strategic assets in asserting their demands. With the advent of collective bargaining, strikes, work slow-downs, and other forms of collective action, some workers have enjoyed some success in ameliorating the degree of class exploitation. Other elements of the historic level of (decent) reproduction have been obtained through political action (e.g., the social wage).[17]

So surplus extraction—capital accumulation—is subject to constraints in the form of a struggle between classes. This focusses attention upon the means or tools that capital has available to it to control the demands of workers and ensure acceptable rates of accumulation. It raises the possibility that the primary means that capital employs on its behalf in this struggle can vary across time and space. As conditions of competition change, so do the forms of worker resistance. Capitalists may have to fashion new tools, a new strategic lever of exploitation, to ensure their individual and collective interests.

Theorists of monopoly capitalism have argued that new mechanisms of surplus extraction *did* emerge during the monopoly era. Although Baran and Sweezy have little to say about capital-to-labor relations in *Monopoly Capital*, O'Connor develops the insights of labor market segmentation researchers to argue that a bifurcation of the work force into a monopoly and competitive sector distinguishes monopoly from competitive capitalism.[18]

The economy is divided, according to O'Connor between a competitive sector, a monopoly sector, and a state sector, each roughly the same size. This produces distinct labor markets, essentially a competitive and a monopoly sector market. This bifurcation of the working class becomes the principal lever for extracting surplus. Comparing his analysis to Marx's focus upon the reserve army of the unemployed, O'Connor can be understood as arguing that the bifurcation of the working class has replaced the reserve army of labor as the principal lever of working class exploitation.

As O'Connor formulates it, workers in the monopoly sector are well-paid and relatively privileged: "...wages are relatively high,...the demand for labor is relatively stable,...and average wages tend to rise somewhat faster than productivity."[19]

Supporting this outcome is a tacit agreement between monopoly capital and organized labor in that sector. In return for allowing wages to keep pace with both improvements in productivity and the rate of inflation, monopoly firms enjoy the cooperation of labor leaders in their quest for a disciplined work force.[20]

While monopoly capital made some gains from such an agreement, this compact limited control or reduction of direct labor costs as a strategy for capital accumulation. The practice of monopoly pricing and the reduction of input costs from suppliers and subcontractors located in the competitive sector emerged as the alternative accumulation strategies available to monopoly firms. Under both these options the ultimate source of surplus is the competitive sector labor force.

When monopoly firms utilize their market power to impose price increases, the resulting inflation has less effect on monopoly sector workers than on others. In the unionized monopoly sector, collective bargaining agreements typically included cost-of-living adjustments. In contrast, workers in the competitive sector, lacking such contractual protection from the vagaries of inflation, experienced decline in their real wages.[21] In effect, monopoly pricing power allowed monopoly capital to extract indirectly from competitive sector workers an additional increment of the value they produced.

Certain of the products utilized by monopoly firms in the production process are subcontracted from small, less capital-intensive firms located in the competitive sector. Harrison and others have called this the *industrial periphery*.[22] Given the bargaining relationship that obtains between these competitive sector firms and the giant firms—many small firms supplying the same product to one or several large firms—monopoly capital is able to impose unfavorable prices or terms of trade on competitive sector capital.

As a consequence of monopoly firms' market power, competitive sector firms must offer lower wages to their workers. Again monopoly capital receives indirectly some portion of the surplus generated by competitive sector workers.

In *The Fiscal Crisis of the State*, O'Connor proposed that monopoly sector workers had become relatively immune to the strategies employed by monopoly capital to maintain and augment rates of capital accumulation. Instead, the burden of exploitation had been shifted to the competitive sector worker. In O'Connor's words, "The result of the bifurcation of the work force...is that both unemployed and underemployed and fully employed workers in this [competitive] sector are increasingly impoverished..."[23] The bifurcation of the working class had become the principal lever of exploitation available to monopoly capital. Therefore, *the theory of monopoly capitalism proposes a model in which the monopoly sector working class is well-paid and relatively secure.* We will subject this contention to criticaly scrutiny in Part 3.

The Capital-to-State Relation in the Theory of Monopoly Capitalism

In the Marxian tradition, the state is understood as performing functions that maintain and reproduce the dominance of the capitalist class. This process may be neither simple nor mechanical nor direct.[24]

The capitalist class is not a monolithic entity that is unified in its views about what constitutes appropriate state policy in every instance. An even more diverse working class, meanwhile, conducts its struggle to ameliorate the conditions of its exploitation in the political arena of state policy formation, and, on occasion, it achieves some relative successes.

Variations in the nature of state activity exist among capitalist social formations. This variation is both systemic or developmental, and it is spatial or geographic in its manifestation.

Should a newly dominant fraction of the capitalist class emerge on the basis of changed markets and enterprise structures, one would expect such change to be registered in both the political climate and public policies of the state apparatus.

Similarly, if the relative balance between capital and labor is altered or a new lever of class exploitation emerges, this change should produce new patterns of state activity. If the sensitivity of investors to variations in policy among states or regions is effectively heightened, then one would expect the spatial deployment of capital to reflect this.

The major theorists of monopoly capitalism observe patterns of state activity that are typical of the monopoly era and that differ from those evident under competitive capitalism. Baran and Sweezy and O'Connor emphasize rising government expenditures as a response to the tendency of the surplus to rise under monopoly capitalism (see "Crisis Theory" above).

Although writing prior to the period of most accelerated growth, Baran and Sweezy argued that the transition from competitive to monopoly capitalism entailed a dramatic growth in state expenditures. As they view it, the problem for the state is the absorption of the rising surplus. They show that growth in government spending does not result in lower corporate profits, but rather that the effective demand thus created supports capital accumulation."[25]

Baran and Sweezy also relate this expansion of state expenditure to the emergence of a newly dominant fraction of the capitalist class when they state that "...the function of the state under monopoly capitalism is to serve the interests of monopoly capital."[26]

Given the central dynamic in their work—the tendency of the surplus to rise—Baran and Sweezy devote less attention to any impact that change in the capital-to-labor relation has on state policy. They note that transfer payments increased during the period ending in the late 1950s. They also acknowledge in passing that low income and working-class citizens benefitted from aspects of the expansion of state activity. However, they place more emphasis on the limits to government spending on social needs. These limits are established by what they call the "private interests of the moneyed oligarchy."

It is in this context that Baran and Sweezy point out the strategic role of military spending within monopoly capitalism: the way in which the "rising surplus" can be absorbed by the state, consistent with the interests of monopoly capital, is through the growth of a giant military establishment that nourishes a wasteful branch of industry. For the theory of monopoly capitalism, military spending is "wasteful Keynesianism."

Whatever the limits on the *type* of state spending, Baran and Sweezy propose that the expansion of government spending in the United States is a manifestation of the specific logic of monopoly capitalism.[27]

O'Connor extends the analysis of Baran and Sweezy. In what has become a classis formulation, he contends that the state acts under two often mutually contradictory imperatives: accumulation and legitimation.[28] The accumulation function entails facilitating the conditions of capital acumulation. The legitimation function entails ensuring the conditions of orderly social processes—social peace.

According to O'Connor, the monopoly capitalist state facilitates private accumulation by engaging in social capital expenditures.[29] In particular, the state allocates resources to social investments such as physical capital (highways, airports, railways, industrial development projects, etc.) and human capital (teaching, administrative, and other services in education, R&D, and science). Other outlays are directed toward social consumption programs (suburban development and urban renewal projects, child care and medical facilities, as well as social insurance programs), which assist the accumulation process by lowering the reproduction costs of labor that must be borne by the private sector.[30] Expanding state expenditures in these categories are an important base for monopoly sector growth; they are necessitated by the irrationalities of the monopoly sector, especially the growth of a surplus productive capacity.

Performing the legitimation function involves the state, in O'Connor's view, in social expenses. These allocations of state funds are not productive (of surplus value, of capital), but have the purpose of producing "social harmony."[31] The welfare system, "which is designed to keep peace among unemployed workers," is his obvious example.

O'Connor's language is more "structuralist" than Baran and Sweezy's; these patterns are the result of imperatives experienced by state managers. Legitimation costs function as responses to the tendency of monopoly capitalism to produce surplus population. They are driven by a grudging need to preserve the social peace. Therefore,

1. The principal theorists of monopoly capitalism share the view that monopoly capitalism brings about new forms of state activity.

2. In their work, working-class people are seen as receiving some portion of these rising outlays while monopoly capital is viewed as adopting a positive or tolerant attitude toward the expanding role of government in the economy.

We will examine, in Parts 3 and 4, changes in state activity over the last twenty years in order to show how the emergence of global capitalism changes the nature of state activity.

Dynamics in the Theory of Monopoly Capitalism

The theorists of monopoly capitalism share with the Marxian tradition the view that capitalism as a mode of production, by its very logic, produces contradictions and exhibits tendencies toward crisis. There is a long and sometimes highly technical tradition of controversy about the precise nature of these "tendencies."

Marx's own analysis of the contradictions inherent in capitalism culminated in his formulation of "the law of the tendency of profit to decline." Put succinctly, this law posits that "...all firms operating under the 'anarchy of capitalist production' are obliged simultaneously to increase their portion of dead labor relative to living labor and, despite the rising rate of surplus brought about by productivity increases, to suffer a falling rate of profit."[32] From these falling rates of profit emerge crises, and presumably an ultimate breakdown.

Convinced that Marx's analysis applied only to competitive capitalism, the theorists of monopoly capitalism rejected "the law of the tendency of profit to decline" and replaced it with "the tendency of the surplus to rise, both absolutely and as a share of total output."[33] On this point, Baran and Sweezy are quite clear:

> The law immediately invites comparison, as it should, with the classical-Marxian law of the falling tendency of the rate of profit. Without entering into an analysis of the different versions of the latter, we can say that they all presuppose a competitive system. By substituting the law of the rising surplus for the law of falling profit, we are not rejecting or revising a time-honored theorem of political economy: we are simply taking account of the undoubted fact that the structure of the capitalist economy has undergone a fundamental change since that theorem was formulated. What is most essential about the structural change from competitive to monopoly capitalism finds its theoretical expression in this substitution.[34]

In Baran and Sweezy's view, monopoly capitalism produces its own contradiction—the tendency of the surplus to rise. By *surplus*, Baran and Sweezy (in the Introduction to *Monopoly Capital*) mean "the difference between what a society produces and the costs of producing it."[35] Later the surplus is referred to as "the difference between total output and the socially necessary costs of producing total output."[36] In Marxian terms, Baran and Sweezy are suggesting that under monopoly capitalism the amount of value that is appropriated by monopoly capital as a class increases both in absolute terms and as a proportion of the total value produced in the society. In more conventional terms, Baran and Sweezy's argument is similar to saying that the aggregate profits of monopoly capital increase both absolutely and as a proportion of the value of total national output.[37]

What causes the surplus to rise? As Baran and Sweezy understand it, the combination of the monopoly pricing powers of the giant firms and a tendency for their costs of production to fall is responsible.

Baran and Sweezy first argue that as a result of the structure and price behavior of oligopolistic firms, price competition passes away.[38] In this situation, firms in a given market share a common interest in seeing that the prices established maximize the interests of the group as a whole. Monopoly firms become "price makers" obtaining extra large or monopoly profits through the exercise of their price-setting power.

Despite the alleged elimination of price competition, Baran and Sweezy insist that the monopoly firm remains under a compulsion to lower cost. For the firm with the lowest costs "...can afford the advertising, research, development of new product varieties, extra services, and so on, which are the usual means of fighting for market shares and which tend to yield results in proportion to the amount spent on them...," while "any company which falls behind in the race to cut costs is soon in trouble."[39] As a consequence of "nonprice" forms of competition, production costs under monopoly capitalism exhibit a downward trend (while the costs of the "sales effort" grows).

Under competitive capitalism, such cost reduction might have led to a lowering of prices and stable or lower profit margins for firms. However, under monopoly capitalism, this will not happen. As Baran and Sweezy explain: "...the monopolistic structure of markets enables the corporations to appropriate the lion's share of the fruits of increasing productivity directly in the form of high profits. ...[U]nder monopoly capitalism, declining costs imply continuously widening profit margins. [These] imply aggregate profits which rise not only absolutely but as a share of national product."[40]

Having established the tendency of the surplus to rise, Baran and Sweezy then complete their argument by suggesting that the central problem or crisis tendency facing monopoly capitalism is the absorption or utilization of the surplus.[41]

In their view, consumption, including that of workers and capitalists, rises more slowly than the rate of increase in the surplus. Total surplus, *and* the proportion of the surplus available for investment, rises. Productive capacity tends to rise faster than consumption.

In order to support this expanding stock of capital available for investment, it would be necesary for consumption to expand at an equal rate. Yet, the very logic of monopoly capitalism prevents consumption from expanding at such a rate. Absent some positive action, a situation of underconsumption would ensue. Firms would cease making new investments, employment would contract, and consumption and profitable investment outlets would decline even more. These declines would continue until the system reached "a point low enough on its profitability schedule not to generate more surplus than can be absorbed."[42] Of its own logic then, monopoly capitalism has a tendency toward stagnation or depression.

In his work, O'Connor has accepted the proposition that monopoly capitalism exhibits a tendency for the surplus to rise. His specific formulation differs somewhat from that of Baran and Sweezy: "Monopoly sector growth tends to generate surplus capital in the form of surplus goods [or surplus productive capacity] and surplus population [or technological unemployment]."[43] Similar to Baran and Sweezy though, O'Connor concludes that productive capacity tends to grow faster than the demand for goods and services.[44]

O'Connor attributes this tendency for production to rise more rapidly than demand to two principal causes.[45] First, he notes that wages among what he calls *competitive-sector workers* rise more slowly than the ability of monopoly firms to increase productivity. Second, he argues that the monopoly sector receives a "smaller than proportional share of total demand" while the competitive and state sector absorb a disproportionate amount in the form of taxes, services, trade, and so on.

Unique to O'Connor's analysis is the view that this crisis tendency ultimately takes the form of a "fiscal crisis of the state." As do Baran and Sweezy, O'Connor notes that state expenditures expand to correct or offset the surpluses generated by monopoly sector growth. O'Connor specifically notes two general areas of the state sector that expand markedly.[46]

First, as surplus population is created, the social expenditures of the state expand in the form of programs such as welfare benefits, public housing, supplementary education programs, and other increments to the incomes of the unemployed and working poor. These are legitimation expenses.

Second, as surplus productive capacity expands, the social capital expenditures of the state, in military and related programs, for example, also grow thereby absorbing some of the surplus. Where Baran and Sweezy emphasized military expenditure as the chief mechanism of surplus absorption, O'Connor says "the growth of state expenditures in the form of welfare expenses and warfare expenses is also a single process."[47]

The major theorists of monopoly capitalism see a contrast in the dynamics of that era and the competitive period. While falling rates of profit plagued competitive capitalism, the crisis tendency of monopoly capitalism finds expression in an overproduction/underconsumption formulation. Baran and Sweezy see the logic of monopoly capitalism as tending toward a state of stagnation or depression induced by a tendency for the surplus to rise more rapidly than available consumption and investment outlets. The rise of the military-industrial complex is the destructive way in which monopoly capitalism attempted to avoid this looming crisis.

O'Connor understands the manifest form of the crisis to be a fiscal crisis of the state as the state expands its expenditures in response to the tendency of monopoly sector growth to generate both surplus population and surplus productive capacity.

The Theory of Monopoly Capitalism:
An Assessment

The theory of monopoly capitalism expanded our understanding of the capitalist mode of production. Particularly noteworthy was the contention that changes that matter can occur *within* capitalism.

That the characteristics of early twentieth-century capitalism differed dramatically from those prevailing during the nineteeth century was demonstrated rather conclusively. Baran and Sweezy, O'Connor, and others have shown that the forms of capitalist competition, the structure of the labor market, the mechanisms of surplus extraction, and the nature of state activity all changed in important ways during the first half of the twentieth century.

The theory of monopoly capitalism accurately depicted the structure of social relations prevailing in the United States and world capitalist economies for a substantial period of time. Indeed, in chapter 7, we find that the model derived from the theory of monopoly capitalism offers a coherent understanding of the world motor vehicle industry between 1930 and 1970.

The past two decades, however, have witnessed yet another change. In each of the major areas we have examined, the theory of monopoly capitalism produces propositions about the way the world should appear that are no longer accurate.

Each of the following propositions contrasts with those which might be derived from the theory of monopoly capitalism. In the case studies and policy studies of this volume we demonstrate the basis for our judgement.

Capital-to-capital relations. Capitalist competition includes a vigorous price dimension, especially evident among global firms of different national origins. Market shares have changed markedly, and in some instances are volatile. U. S. firms are not nearly so dominant as they once were; the United States is losing global economic hegemony in a more competitive global environment.

Capital-to-labor relations. Monopoly sector manufacturing workers have been unable to protect their purchasing power or their jobs. Their unions are not stable, but weakened. A new bargaining tool, the threat of capital mobility, provides employers of both monopoly and competitive sector labor a new lever of exploitation.

Capital-to-state relations. State expenditures that benefit the working class—the social wage—are under effective attack. Capitalist class interests are more directly effective in molding state policies. The automony the state had to pursue "legitimation" policies is declining. The threat of capital mobility across local jurisdiction or national boundaries is a political resource of major proportions.

Such strongly contrasting propositions about strategic relations may stem from one or both of two sources: the system may have changed once again, therefore requiring new concepts. It may also be the case that the dynamics of the theory of monopoly capitalism were not correctly understood. We are more or less certain about the first; we are interested in pursuing the possibility of the second.[48]

Whatever our skepticism about crisis tendencies in the theory of monopoly capitalism, they receive little empirical attention in this work. Rather our method is to concentrate on analyzing concrete change in the three social relations of production: capital-to-capital, capital-to-labor and capital-to-state.

This analysis becomes the basis for our central contention that contemporary capitalism is undergoing a transition from a monopoly to global variant comparable to the transition from competitive to monopoly capitalism detailed by the theorists of monopoly capitalism.

A central factor in the differences between the conception of global capitalism and that of monopoly capitalism is the role of international capital mobility and the migration of capital toward low wage, vulnerable labor. This is also an important factor in distinguishing the theory of global capitalism from that of the other major perspective in political economy—world system theory. It is to this theory we now turn.

4

The Present as the Past:
World Systems Theory

Introduction

- The modern world comprises a single capitalist world-economy which has emerged since the sixteenth century.
- Nation-states do not have separate and parallel histories; rather their fates are determined by their positions within the world-economy.
- A permanent and necessary feature of capitalism is a world system comprised of a hierarchy of rich ("core") and poor ("periphery") regions.
- This hierarchy takes the form of an international division of labor which operates to the advantage of the rich, or core, states.

In the mid-1970s, Immanuel Wallerstein introduced these propositions as the premises of an approach to political economy he termed "*world systems theory*."[1] In subsequent years, the intellectual influence of world systems theory has grown.[2] An impressive body of scholarship concerned with the origins, history, and contemporary features of world capitalism now exists.[3]

The intellectual heritage of the world systems approach can be traced to the critique of "developmentalism" found in the work of Paul Baran.[4] The approach has also been influenced by the *dependencia* tradition of political economy that developed in Latin America.[5] Andre Gunder Frank's work, in particular, shaped Wallerstein's sense of the determinants of poverty in the underdeveloped countries: poverty and underdevelopment were the *result* of capitalist development, not its absence.

Despite its shared roots in Baran's work, world systems theory differs in important ways from the theory of monopoly capitalism. It constitutes an alternative understanding of the structure and tendencies of modern capitalism.

This chapter presents an overview of the world systems perspective. We begin with an exposition of the methodology, concepts, and propositions that anchor the approach. An examination of the role of cycles and long-term secular trends in the theory follows. These concepts are then applied to develop a world systems understanding of current changes in the world-economy. Finally, a brief assessment of the perspective is offered.

World Systems Theory: Methodology, Concepts, and Propositions

World systems theory begins with the proposition that there has been a capitalist world system since the sixteenth century. The histories of individual states are understood to be conditioned by their place and function within that world system.

Wallerstein credits Andre Gundar Frank as the source for these ideas. As Wallerstein put it, Frank's crucial insights were that:

> ...the modern world comprises a single capitalist world-economy, which has emerged since the sixteenth century and which still exists today. It follows...that national states are *not* societies that have separate, parallel histories, but parts of a whole....To the extent that stages exist, they exist for the system as a whole. ...[T]o understand the internal class contradictions and political struggles of a particular state, we must first situate it in the world-economy."[6]

World systems theory, then, follows a holistic logic. Specific events within the world system are explained in terms of the laws of the system as a whole.

The logic of the world system compels action according to the structural positions of its various actors. Class struggle, international war, and transnational economic conflict are all explained as "efforts to alter or preserve a position within the world-economy which is to the advantage or disadvantage of particular groups located within a particular state."[7]

The division of the capitalist world economy into rich core and poor periphery regions is another premise of world systems theorists. They consider it one of the "institutional constants of capitalism as a system."[8] In their view a *capitalist* world-economy *necessarily* produces unequal development: a rich core and a poor periphery.

In Wallerstein's view capitalism is to be defined as a system of "...production for sale in a market in which the object is to realize the maximum profit."[9]

In such an economic system producers in a given region will choose to specialize in the production of those commodities that yield higher profits. This privileged, *core*, position was attained by Western Europe, which became capitalist and entered (read, created) the world market earliest. Achieving and maintaining core status depended in part upon the strength of the state. Other regions, meanwhile, had imposed upon them productive tasks that were necessary and complementary to those of the core, but that yielded lower profits.[10] These regions constitute the *periphery* of the world system.

Since its origins, the capitalist world system has been divided into core and periphery regions. Unequal development has prevailed as the core has specialized in relatively more mechanized, higher profit, higher wage, and more skilled activities.[11]

Some world systems writers, notably Wallerstein, have also posited a third region—the semiperiphery.[12] It is defined as a region "containing a relatively equal mix of core, peripheral and intermediate types of production."[13]

In Wallerstein's view, semiperiphery regions are integral to the proper functioning of the world system.[14] He sees the existence of this "middle stratum" of states as contributing to the political stability of the system. Because they are both "exploiter and exploited," the interests of the semiperiphery do not coincide with those of the periphery. As a result, the core is not faced with the unified opposition of all the other states.

From their analysis of the world division of labor, world systems theorists adduce another "permanent and necessary feature" of capitalism as a system. Integral to capitalism since its inception has been "primitive accumulation" or the transfer of value from the periphery to the core.[15] World systems theorists have described the principal mechanism which facilitates this transfer as "unequal exchange."[16]

What most economists view as mutually beneficial trade between developed and developing countries, world systems theorists see as unequal exchange. In world systems theory, when goods are traded between core and periphery regions, value is transferred from the periphery to the core.

Unequal exchange results from the fact that the price differences of the goods exchanged are greater than the respective amounts of human labor embedded therein. As a result of wage differences between core and peripheral workers, some measure of the surplus value extracted from workers in the periphery is transferred, under the guise of "international trade," to capitalists in the core. Such exchanges have always been in favor of the core, although the intensity of the inequality may be increasing or decreasing during different phases of the world economy.

In summary, in the world systems theory tradition, capitalism, from its birth, is understood to have as its principal constant feature a definite core-periphery division of labor. This division of labor, in turn, facilitates the transfer of value (i.e., capital) from the periphery to the core and is central to the processes of capitalist accumulation. Capitalism produces and sustains unequal development.

World-Systems Theory:
Changes and Cycles

The theory of monopoly capitalism observed that fundamental, structural change had taken place within the history of capitalism. By contrast, world systems theory sees no fundamental change in the structure of the world-economy since its origins in the sixteenth century.[17]

Cycles of expansion and contraction, even upward or downward movement in the hierarchy: these patterns persist. But the characteristics of world capitalism do not change, however much they may vary. Cycles repeat themselves within the history of capitalism.

Employing the concept of cycles enables world systems theory to emphasize the similarities, rather than the differences, of periods of the capitalist world system.[18]

Two types of cycles figure prominently in recent world system literature. The first is the alternation of dominance in the capitalist core. Periods of hegemony by a single state are followed by periods of competition, or multicentricity, in the core. State power and competitive advantage govern the arrangement of core structure.

The second type of cycle is the Kondratief cycle. These are alternating periods of growth and stagnation constituting (the seventy-year) "long waves" on charts of capitalist history.

Cycles of hegemony are seen as instrinsic to the capitalist world-economy. According to Wallerstein, one can observe a pattern whereby the producers from one state within the core attain, as a result of technical innovation, the ability to produce goods relatively more efficiently than producers from other core states.[19] This comparative productive efficiency then becomes the foundation for achieving hegemonic status. Mature hegemony includes the relative domination of world production, trade, and finance.

Moments of hegemony are transitory, however; other states catch up and the competitive advantage disappears.[20] Alternating periods of hegemony and core competition can therefore be observed throughout the history of the capitalist world-economy. In hegemonic periods, one state dominates world production and imposes a system of relatively free international trade. In periods of core competition, the former hegemonic state experiences a relative decline in its competitive advantage and its domination of world markets and that state and others turn toward political constraints on world trade.

Kondratief cycles or long waves are also understood by world system theorists as repeating themselves throughout the history of the capitalist world economy.

According to Wallerstein and Hopkins, periodic downturns in the world economy derive from a tendency for production under a capitalist world economy to outstrip world demand.[21] They root this claim in the fact that production is undertaken by units whose goal is to optimize/maximize profits while demand is a function of income distribution which is socially and politically determined.

For a variety of reasons, they contend, the share of the surplus accruing to capital tends to increase during periods of expansion. In turn, much of this is reinvested in new production facilities, thus further increasing the supply of consumer goods. Supply expands rapidly while demand tends to stagnate. Ultimately, a crisis of overproduction results and the global rate of profit declines. At this point of decline, (the "B-phase" in the Kondratief cycle) the world system enters a period of acute political struggle.

In the short run, this struggle leads to expenditures on immediate consumption which alleviate partially the crisis of demand; in the middle run, it results in increases in the real income of fully proletarianized workers, which activates the next phase of expansion.[22] Accompanied by some transfer of production to lower-wage, semiperipheral sites (and in some eras a geographic expansion of the size of the world-economy), this succeeds in restoring world demand. The next cycle of expansion then ensues.

Cycles of hegemony and alternating periods of growth and stagnation are thus an essential element of the world system understanding of the capitalist world-economy.

World Systems Theory and Secular Trends

World systems theorists note several secular trends observable over the whole history of the capitalist world system.[23] These trends represent characteristics of the world system that have increased or intensified throughout its history. It is understood that their rate of increase or intensification can be more rapid at certain times than others. The secular trends that have received the most attention include the following.

1. Geographic expansion.   Since its inception, the world system has incorporated new populations and territories into the capitalist system of production for exchange. Territories are considered incorporated to the capitalist system even if the wage-labor relationship is not dominant as long as production is for the purpose of exchange in the world market. Historically, such expansion has been a principal means of overcoming periods of stagnation, but it has now reached its limits.[24]

2. Commodification.   This takes two principles forms: the proletarianization of labor and the commercialization of land. In other words, more and more labor and land come to be bought and sold. In the core, most spheres of life have been commodified (witness fast food restaurants and laundromats replacing the household performance of these functions). In the periphery, commodification has increased but is less developed than it is in the core.

3. Mechanization. More and more of the value created within the capitalist world-economy comes from machines. In Marxian terminology, the organic composition of capital rises. Again, this process has occurred more rapidly in the core than in the periphery, but it shows a tendency over time to intensify in the periphery as well.

4. Polarization. The capitalist world-economy is seen to produce an increasing "uneveness" in its development. In more conventional terms, the system over time exhibits increasing degrees of inequality.

5. Concentration. The world system exhibits a tendency for the average size of economic enterprises to increase over time. This trend has gone through periods in which it has slowed or even reversed temporarily, but in every epoch, there is a definite trend toward concentration.[25]

6. Internationalization of capital. Capital is seen as having been international since the sixteenth century when direct investments were made in plantations and mining. Increasing internationalization is a long-term tendency of the system. Transnational corporations are thus understood as but the most recent institutional manifestation of a continuing long-term trend. Global capital mobility, from the world system perspective, has not changed the essentially continuous dynamics of world capitalism.

The World System since 1945

Such developments as the transnational firm, the growth of manufacturing production and an industrial working class in the periphery, and an increase in the average size of firms are seen by many analysts as unique characteristics of the twentieth century. In contrast, world system theory sees them as tendencies evident since the inception of the capitalist world-economy. These events do not, in this perspective, justify the use of the phrase a *new stage* to characterize recent developments in capitalism.[26]

In this section, we review the way world system theorists have explained recent developments in the world economy. To facilitate comparison with the theories of monopoly and global capitalism, the discussion is again organized around the capital-to-capital, capital-to-labor and capital-to-state relations.

Capital-to-capital relations. According to world system theory, one dominant characteristic of capitalist class relations in the contemporary period of the world-economy is the hegemonic decline of the United States. Wallerstein recognizes that, "By the 1960s the United States could no longer outsell Western European and Japanese producers in their own markets, and by the

1970s it could no longer easily do so in the U.S. market."[27] From this perspective the intensified competition of the recent period is understood simply as the United States experiencing a moment of hegemonic decline similar in its essentials to that which struck the United Provinces in the mid-seventeenth century and Great Britain at the end of the nineteenth century.[28]

A second important feature of the present phase of the world economy from a world system perspective is that the system has entered a crisis of overproduction. As a result, we witness producers from different core states beginning to "scramble for markets." In Wallerstein's view, the world economy entered such a Kondratief B-phase of stagnation in 1967; and much of the accelerated competition of the past twenty years can be explained as adjustments in market shares that always accompany such periods of stagnation.[29]

World system theorists have also paid attention to what a variety of other commentators have termed the emergence of a "new international division of labor."[30] The issue concerns the comparatively rapid growth of manufacturing production outside the core since 1960.

In world system analysis, this development has been treated as a cyclical, rather than a structural phenomenon. Wallerstein argues that one way for entrepreneurs to restore profit levels during the "transition" periods that come at the end of a cycle of contraction is the relocation of production to lower-wage, usually periphery or semiperiphery, zones.[31] About the most recent phase of stagnation, he notes,"...many of the largest firms sought to solve their immediate problems by reducing costs through the most classic of operations in a B-phase—the runaway shop—and in the late 1960s and 1970s a significant proportion of mechanized production shifted out of the core countries to 'free-trade zones' in the periphery, to the so-called newly industrializing countries, and even to the socialist bloc....in all of which the work force receives less remuneration."[32]

Similarly, Chase-Dunn and Wallerstein have both characterized recent industrial growth in certain Latin American and East Asian states as instances of the upward mobility of states into the semiperiphery—an event said to be typical of periods of economic stagnation.[33] They emphasize that because the periphery as a whole is the most strategic source of value—of capital—flowing into the core, most of the periphery is structurally inhibited from development which might bring it to equal terms with the core.

World system theory rejects the notion that the recent growth of manufacturing in the periphery and semiperiphery is indicative of a new stage of core/periphery relations; it is but a moment of cyclical repetition.

In summary, from the perspective of world system theory, hegemonic decline, intensified competition among capitalists of different core states and the growth of manufacturing production in the periphery are not evidence that there is anything new or unique about the recent history of the world economy.

We dispute neither the contention that the history of capitalism evidences the rise and fall of hegemonic states nor the argument that the capitalist mode of production has an internal logic which leads to cycles of growth and contraction.

We do question the proposition that there has been no significant change in the world-economy and the theoretical understanding of capitalism that leads to that conclusion.

From a certain vantage point—one distant from everyday life—the rise and fall of nation-states within a hierarchy of privilege has taken place in the past, is evidently occurring in the present and will continue in the future. The object of analysis determines, in part, the patterns one observes.

By contrast, we contend that the primary units of analysis for political economy are the concrete experiences of classes and parts of classes. From our perspective, changes in the structure of their relations—in this case, in the forms and strategies of capitalist organization that offer competitive advantage—are significant and not merely repetitive. Similarly, the shift of manufacturing activity to formerly underdeveloped regions is not a marginal note about a basically constant structure. A vast body of social science, and political and revolutionary controversy has centered on the proposition that *no* development in the backward regions could proceed in the context of imperialism.[34] Rather than an episodic matter, therefore, the view here is that the industrialization of the backward regions is symptomatic of a new era of global capitalism.

Capital-to-labor relations. In the realm of capital-to-labor relations, perhaps the most notable trend of recent decades has been the changing structure and material condition of the working class in the core. Recent work by world system writers has paid some attention to this development. In contrast to some of the earlier dogmatic propositions of Emmanuel and Amin about the homogeneous well-being of workers in the core, Hopkins, Wallerstein, and Chase-Dunn have noted current trends toward greater working-class differentiation and regional variation.[35]

In typical fashion, however, these world system writers conceive of change involving the working class in the core as cyclical in nature. Hopkins and Wallerstein have argued that job loss among full-time workers and growth in the number of low-paid workers in the core always occurs during periods of contraction.[36] Similarly, Chase-Dunn has linked the expansion of lower-paying service and nonmanual jobs in the United States to hegemonic decline and likened it to the historical experience of the United Provinces and Great Britain.[37]

Wallerstein has also stated that periods of contraction evidence shifts in the location of wage employment. He contends that this explains rising employment in the core as well as increases of real employment in the semiperiphery.[38]

Despite this contention, Hopkins and Wallerstein have hypothesized that one can observe throughout the history of the world economy a growing material well being of the fully proletarianized workers of the few core countries.[39] Elsewhere Wallerstein has argued that, even in phases of contraction in the world economy, the acute class struggle that ensues in the core produces, not a decline, but an increase in the real income of the regularly employed sector of the full-time proletariat.[40] Indeed, such increases are understood as essential to restoring demand and initiating the next phase of expansion.

In summary, world system writers have explained the recent trend toward the loss of well-paid jobs and the creation of lower-income jobs among the core working class as cyclical in nature. They anticipate, however, that those workers who remain employed will experience improvements in their real income. Overall, they see no movement toward a fundamental restructuring of the working class in the core.

By contrast, the theory of global capitalism analyzes the recent era of world capitalism as one of accelerated global mobility of capital. This mobility becomes the new central lever in capital's strategic relation to labor—its new lever of exploitation. This changing means by which capital extracts value from labor is central to the contention that there is a new variant of capitalism.

Consequently, our empirical expectations are also somewhat different. We view the loss of well-paid manufacturing jobs and the creation of less well-paid service and manufacturing employment as part of lasting restructuring of the working class in the older regions. We expect that through the use of its new lever of exploitation, capital has succeeded recently in driving down the real wages of even the most organized workers in the core.

Capital-to-state relations.   Some analysts have argued that the growth of the global firm has reduced the effective regulatory powers of single nation-states.[41] World system theorists have rejected this sovereignty-at-bay thesis.

We, too, observe that important areas of state regulation have been evaded and weakened by the global firms. While observing such a change in capital-to-state relations, we do not, however, adopt the sovereignty-at-bay thesis. We agree with Chase-Dunn and other writers from the world system perspective that state power, including military power, remains a prominent element in ordering the global system. We also accept and second Chase-Dunn's criticism of those who have suggested that the present era is characterized by an integrated world bourgeoisie.[42]

Our point is a different one. The sovereignty-at-bay thesis views the state as a neutral, classless entity. We understand the state as an arena of class conflict, as a set of institutions that both reflect and mediate disputes both among capitalists, and more importantly, between capital and labor.

In contrast to both world system analysis and those who claim states are less potent in the current world system, we present the proposition that the essential change is in the nature of the power relation between investors and states.

Summary. In its depiction of cycles and secular trends, world system analysis has adopted an eagle's eye view of capitalist history. Just as it does not note the transition from a competitive form of the capitalist mode of production to a monopoly form as a significant "moment" in the evolution of the system, neither does it consider recent changes in the world economy to be evidence of capitalist transformation. This stands in contrast both to the theory of monopoly capitalism and the theory of global capitalism.

World System Theory: A Conclusion

The tremendous contribution made by world systems theory to the analysis of the capitalist world-economy is widely and appropriately appreciated. The central thrust of this analysis, that capitalism must be understood as a global system, is the proper starting point for intellectual work.

But world systems analysis—perhaps because of its immense scope and historical perspective—does not incorporate easily the substantial changes in relations between capitalists, capital and labor, and the state that accompany changes in the dominant form of capitalist organization.

Just as world systems theory does not acknowledge the transition from competitive to monopoly capitalism as central to the story of the world system, neither do they accept easily the idea that there is a successor to monopoly capitalism.

For the world systems theorists, the many changes that have occurred in the world capitalist system since 1960 are not evidence of anything new. They see the global economy as in the midst of cycles of contraction and competition not unlike those of earlier centuries in the history of capitalism.

The theory of global capitalism challenges that interpretation of the present moment in the history of capitalism. Fundamental change can occur within the capitalist mode of production. That change can be apprehended by focussing upon the social relations that constitute the system.

In the course of this work, we make the case that important change has taken place, and continues to transpire, at the level of social relations. While we accept that a structural hierarchy and unequal development may be a constant throughout the history of capitalism, we also maintain change that matters has occured during the capitalist era. That this change is qualitative, and not merely cyclical as world system theory would have it, is one emphasis of our analysis.

This debate has implications for matters of practice as well as theory. The fate of the working class in the older regions depends upon whether their class strategies incorporate an accurate understanding of the system. The fate of revolutionary movements and regimes in the Third World is also involved.

If the system has not changed, then class practice and revolutionary tactics proven successful in earlier eras should offer the best guidance. But, if change has occurred, then following the past may invite disaster in the future, which is a prospect we fear.

We begin our search for the character of the new era in hopes that the long tradition of egalitarian, democratic, and socialist struggles can be informed, made more practical, more effective—somehow and sometime—with aid of a more adequate understanding of the changing social system of capitalism.

In the next chapter, we present an outline of the theory of global capitalism. In the course of explicating our alternative to the two theoretical perspectives we have reviewed, we indicate the ways in which we think the theory of global capitalism more accurately depicts the structure and the dynamics of contemporary political economy.

5
Global Capitalism

Introduction:
The Theme is Power

Power—the ability to realize one's will—is a constituent element of the direct confrontation of labor and capital at the workplace. Labor and capital also contest with one another in a variety of mediated relations—the most important of which is their contest over state policy.

The theory of global capitalism is particularly concerned with relations of power between the main classes of capitalist society. It is a theory about the changing structure within which politics are acted out. Power relations have both political and economic dimensions and expressions. The particular perspective of this theory is its comprehension of the political (i.e., the power) dimension of relations that are usually analyzed in a mechanically economic framework.

Political power relations do not simply reduce themselves to economic ones, they are not *simple* reflections of relations of production. But the global form of capitalism is changing the balance of political power that held through the post-World War II period, and into the late 1960s. This changing balance at the level of political relations is—*in this case*—appropriately understood as derived from a changing balance of the direct relations between employers and employees.

That there is a changing balance of class forces in contemporary capitalism, and that there is something "new" about the global dimension of the structural forces driving this change, has been noted by many observers of the signs and sources of labor's retreat in the older industrial nations.

This changing balance of power is a central feature of the global variant of capitalism. Just as many observers both within Marxist orthodoxy and outside of that tradition share the view that capitalism was transformed with the emergence of its monopoly form, so, too, do many observers share our view of the multifaceted nature of recent change in structures of power.

Tabb, for example, notes that "...the cross-national practice of multi-sourcing...[increases] the bargaining power of capital," and says that

"What is unique about the present crisis (unlike the 1930s and earlier important crises) is the internationalization of production...."[1]

In similar fashion, Castells notes the "economic restructuring of the world capitalist system," which, although still capitalist, is as different from the period between 1945 and 1973 as the latter was from the pre-Depression era.[2] He, too, observes "capital gaining the initiative again over the wages and regulations conquered by the labor movement after decades of class struggle."[3] Castells, too, links these developments to a "new international and interregional division of labor," and to a change in the political balance of class forces "not so much reducing government intervention...but shifting from legitimation to domination."

And, James O'Connor, who made a major contribution to the theory of monopoly capitalism, later acknowledged that "...a full analysis of crisis trends in the USA requires study of the new internationalization...of production and labor migration and changes in the composition of capital in favor of high technology industries and sevices, among other developments."[4]

The emergence of global capitalism is facilitated by a series of technological "revolutions." Among these are the postwar changes in ocean transport (containerization, more efficient engines) and airfreight. Transportation technology has reduced shipping costs in relation to both bulk and value-added.

Information technology (e.g., electronic telecommunications and data processing) has made world financial markets a reality, and worldwide command and control immeasurably faster and easier than ever before. Vast magnitudes of capital move across the globe at the speed of light, and are appropriately discounted, and accounted for, instantaneously.[5] The physical separation of stages in the production process is less costly under these conditions.

Enabled by these technologies, and impelled by the imperatives of the accumulation process capital can now locate, for example, research and development, skilled machining and fabrication, semiskilled assembly, administration, and services in various regions throughout the globe.

Storper and Walker see these developments as highlighting the comparative cost of labor "as the key to locational competitive advantage" on a world scale.[6]

In each of many separate regions, a firm may employ workers who are objectively linked in a single production process but whose organizational and political linkages across regions are minimal.

The observation of structural changes giving rise to a new balance of power is, as the above sampling suggests, relatively widespread. The strategic relations of global capitalism (i.e., power relations) express the overall transformation.

The Capital-to-Labor Relation
under Global Capitalism

As new variants of capitalism emerge and become dominant, the mechanisms of extraction available to capital in its struggles with workers change. In the competitive era, the presence of a reserve army of labor provided the leverage that capital needed to discipline labor. Under monopoly capitalism, the principal lever of exploitation resided in the bifurcation of the working class into two relatively distinct segments: the monopoly and competitive sectors. In turn, for the dominant monopoly firms this translated into two primary strategies for maximizing rates of capital accumulation: unequal exchange with competitive sector firms and monopoly pricing.

The social regime of monopoly capital included the unionization of labor in basic industries. Monopoly pricing power, given stable technologies, allowed employers to accept unions and accommodate their wage and benefit demands by passing on their costs to consumers and suppliers. A new stratum of consumers was created, "middle-income" workers, whose wage allowed them to purchase the output of mass-production industry. This has been termed the regime of *intensive accumulation* or Fordism.[7]

The relative gains of labor, particularly in the well-organized monopoly sector firms became problematic in two distinct ways. There is some evidence that compensation outdistanced productivity in the late 1960s. This depressed average rates of profit in manufacturing and was particularly evident in some sectors, such as steel and automobile production. The stagflation of the 1970s was part of the result. Another result was the pursuit of locations for production that cut labor costs or pursued local policy advantages.

The successes of workers in the industrial nations, and within them, in their older industrial regions, had the additional effect of making their employers vulnerable to challengers who could bring the same (or more up-to-date) products to the market with less costly labor embodied in them.

Both these forces—internal stagnation and external challenge—brought forth a new axis of competition: labor costs, to be sure, but this axis had, by the 1970s, taken on a spatial character: labor from some areas was cheaper than that from others. The result is global competition that erodes monopoly pricing power. Under global capitalism the most dynamic firms seek alternative strategies of capital accumulation. More specifically, enterprises in globally competitive markets exercise intense efforts to control cost factors with particular attention devoted to direct labor costs.

However, the organization of production relations characteristic of monopoly sectors is not usually propitious for the control of direct labor costs. A new lever for reducing the bargaining power of organized monopoly sector labor is required. The use or threatened use of capital mobility provides this capacity and becomes the primary lever of exploitation in sectors where the global variant emerges as dominant.

More concretely, monopoly sector and other firms become global by locating parts or phases of their production processes in regions where low-wage and/or politically-repressed working classes are located.[8] In a direct manner, this lowers labor costs, and indirectly the *threat* of further relocations provides the leverage needed to extract concessions from the work force still employed at older production sites.

The increased bargaining power of employers reinforces existing tendencies to replace living labor with machines. Now the employer can make explicit that "survival" of the firm, of some jobs, requires the sacrifice of many others to new techniques. Labor is forced to relinquish many of its prerogatives (e.g., work rules) and to accede to technological change.

By altering the relative balance of power between capital and organized labor, capital mobility undermines the ability of monopoly-sector workers to defend the relative material well-being gained during the era of monopoly capitalism. At the workplace, this takes such forms as job loss, decline of real wages, and a loss of control over work rules.[9] In the sphere of reproduction, deteriorating housing and health conditions are among the losses suffered by those workers most vulnerable to offshore competition.

The Capital-to-Capital Relation under Global Capitalism

In comparison to the competitive era of capitalism, monopoly capitalism was marked by the emergence of giant firms, the end of price competition in many industrial sectors, and the stabilization of market shares. Yet the production processes of firms, and especially of given commodities, were relatively concentrated with the space of national economies.

Under global capitalism, giant firms of different national origins compete aggressively for shares of a global market that encompasses many different national markets. Price competition frequently returns and erodes the monopoly pricing power of the dominant enterprises. Market shares of older firms become vulnerable, some firms fail to survive, mergers become numerous, and new strategies for accumulation are designed and implemented.

A variety of factors account for the intensified competition of the contemporary global era. Some of these are conjunctural and others can be derived from the basic dynamics of the capitalist mode of production.

The conjunctural factors include the reconstruction of European and Japanese economies in the aftermath of World War II, the development of new technologies for gathering, storing, and communicating information, the maturation of specific products and markets (making their production more routinized, thus exportable to formerly nonindustrial sites), and the emergence of more nationalist regimes in the Third World.[10] The more systemic processes are discussed below.

The characteristic (but not the only) organizational form of global capitalism is the multinational corporation (MNC) or the global firm. Often such firms are not only global in that they produce and sell in many nations, they are also conglomerates—they unite under a singular authority divisions and subsidiaries in a potentially vast variety of disparate products or services.

The global firm and conglomerate is a design for survival under the competitive conditions of the new era. Its ability to "scan" the globe for investment possibilities makes possible a rational assignment of resources and ruthless pursuit of the exact combination of local policies, labor conditions, transport considerations, and so forth for any commodity or part.

Both the multinational producer and the conglomerate are extremely well-adapted to conditions of class struggle on a world scale. Multisourcing, for example, allows a firm to avoid the consequences of labor difficulties at any one site. Conglomeration, for another example, prevents labor organized in a given industrial sector from jeopardizing the profit flow of a highly diversified corporate structure. Both insulate the employer from labor's power and organization and increase the employer's bargaining power.

The Capital-to-State Relation under Global Capitalism

During the monopoly era the state expanded its role as a regulator of the conditions of capital accumulation. Elements of this role implied devoting increasing shares of the state budget to the assumption of the social (i.e., legitimation) costs of accumulation. Included among these costs were additions to the social wage. The expansion of these forms of state expenditures depended politically upon an uneasy accord between monopoly capital and monopoly labor.

To some extent, although monopoly capital exercised relative domination over the state, the expansion of such government expenditures also reflected a relative increment in the capacity of organized monopoly-sector labor to influence state policy. In short, under monopoly capitalism, the state was relatively autonomous from the interests and political power of capital—even its dominant fraction, monopoly capital.

Under global capitalism, we witness the relative decline of this relative autonomy of the state. Capital, particularly its global fraction, finds state regulation less acceptable and social expenditures designed to maintain the social peace less necessary. With an enhanced ability to move production to other regions where state policies may be more favorable to capital, global capital is in a position to demand changes in state policy. The relative decline of the relative autonomy of the state under global capitalism is linked in fundamental ways to the internationalization of production that is characteristic of this era.

In any current era of capitalism, it is in capital's interest that labor be disciplined and that the potential for labor militance be controlled. Given the particular configuration of high degrees of labor organization, oligopolistic market structures, and the geographic concentration of production found under monopoly capitalism, the expansion of social expenditures by the state played an important role in ensuring labor's acquiescence. With the global firm becoming dominant, however, the threat of capital mobility (i.e., job loss) provides capital with a means of disciplining labor directly. In this sense, from the point of view of capital, state social expenditures become less necessary.

At the same time that global capital finds itself more able to discipline labor, such firms find the behavior of their competitors less disciplined. Faced with competition from global firms of different national origins, national fractions of capital prevail upon their home states to reduce regulations, cut taxes, and allocate more public funds toward subsidizing their production costs. Once again the threat to relocate production and/or to shift assets to alternative investments is utilized as a lever to convince state officials to enact (or repeal) appropriate legislation.[11]

The emergence of global capitalism restructures the relationship of relative autonomy that characterized the monopoly capitalist era. This autonomy had material and ideological sources. One source was based in the need for capitalists to compose their differences (at least enough to face the political efforts of labor successfully) and to guide state activity toward acceptable ends. This produced state activity that was, in a general sense pro-business, but that was justified in terms of its "consensual," "public interest" nature. Technical considerations often appear dominant in this realm. Quantitative evaluations of alternative public policies are the ideological fig leaves on successful conflict resolution.

In the era of global capitalism, this source of state autonomy continues. Technical calculation continues to be the language that mediates disputes between fractions of capital, and which, further, molds the claims of other strata into acceptable forms. What is changed under global capitalism are goals and mechanisms: equality drops away and markets are elevated as preferred agencies. Metaphors of "competition" expand the profitmaking realm into human services, and some firms face the new rigors of "deregulation."

Another source of relative independence of state policy under monopoly capitalism was the ability of labor and consumers and other democratic forces to win legislative benefits and small bridgeheads of bureaucratic influence. This declines as capital's bargaining power increases. Any given advance for workers, or consumers, may be subverted by allusion to a bad "investment climate."

Yet another source of state autonomy has been the need to cloak the actions of state policy in terms that reflect its alleged democratic nature. The democratic form of the political process does, indeed, make possible the benefits that labor and other noncapitalist forces are able to obtain. In the monopoly era, however, state expenditures on the poor and regulations and programs for the working class served to justify those aspects of state policy that made capital accumulation possible. With more choice, this motive has declined: *the fear of want pacifies discontent where the charade of compassion once sufficed.*

In summary, global capitalism is characterized by a relative decline in the relative autonomy of the state.

Summary: Global Capitalism

Global capitalism entails the domination of that variant of the capitalist mode of production characterized by the disaggregation of stages of production across national boundaries under the organizational structure of individual firms or enterprises. An accelerated or qualitatively different mobility within a global context offers capital a new lever of exploitation. These features qualitatively distinguish the current era of the world economy from that which preceded it.

Until very recently the production process "was primarily organized within the national economies or parts of them. International trade ... developed primarily as an exchange of raw materials and foodstuffs ... [with] ... products manufactured and finished in single economies ... In terms of production, plant, firm and industry were essentially national phenomena."[12]

The consequences of the global shift in economic structure and political power noted here and elsewhere are, in summary, the following:

1. stagnation in working-class purchasing power, pushing real income to levels achieved ten and fifteen years and more ago;
2. steady decline in rates of unionization of the work force;
3. at the state and local level of politics, the dominance of the rhetoric of the business climate argument (Working-class political demands are

resisted by claims that the resultant investment climate will discourage business activity and thus lose jobs for the local working class.); and

4. at the national level, the parallel dominance of the argument that the rigors of international competition require a shift of public expenditure toward investors' interests and reduction in the social wage. Illustrations of the application of this argument are: reduction in regulation and enforcement of occupational health and safety matters; reduction in expenditures for income and social service support; and tax relief for affluent households and the corporations.

While these observations are broadly shared, they have not been carried through to the logical conclusion: the more well-articulated models of contemporary capitalism are not fully consistent with the changes in structure which compose most commentary on the current realities of the system. While they certainly capture important aspects of the recent past and some aspects of current reality, neither world system analysis nor the theory of monopoly capitalism would predict one of the items listed above.

In the late 1970s, projections based on the theory and model of monopoly capitalism proved to be misleading in their expectations about structural and political trends in America and the leading capitalist countries.

The theory of global capitalism accounts for the shift in the relative balance of power between labor and capital—toward capital—by proposing that a new variant (or submode) of capitalism is emerging as the dominant form of capital and capital accumulation. Most simply, the vast expansion of investor choice as to the physical location of business activity gives capital an immense increment of bargaining power, directly in its relations with employees and indirectly in matters of state policy.

A Crisis of Restructuring: The Transition from Monopoly to Global Capitalism

As noted in chapter 2, Marxists have proclaimed and conservatives have warned that the particular contradictions of capitalism will produce its ultimate breakdown. We described the three general types of crisis tendencies emphasized in political economy: class struggle, rising organic composition, and realization crisis.

Evidently, however, the obstacles to capitalist accumulation, the manifestation of its crisis tendencies, may result in changed relations *within* capitalism rather than its extinction (i.e., restructuring). This volume does not endeavor to "choose" which among these proposed tendencies is "fundamental" or "decisive" in the current restructuring process. Rather, we find that *any* one (or combination) of the proposed obstacles to accumulation could plausibly produce a "global" solution in the medium run.

Graham and Gibson *et al.*, for example, provide evidence that a restructuring model for the U. S. crisis can be disaggregated to allow for analysis on a sector-by-sector or region-by-region basis.[13] Their work also makes plausible the first of the dynamics of capitalism that may be driving this transition. Employing an innovative technique for transforming National Income Accounts data into data organized appropriately for use in a marxian analysis, Graham and Gibson *et al.* rejuvenate a branch of crisis theory that had fallen into some disrepute—the contention that the rate of profit (in value terms) tends to fall with an increasing organic composition of capital.

In particular, they observe that, for the United States since 1958, one can discern (1) at an aggregate level both an increasing organic composition of capital and a measurable decline in rates of profit as measured in value terms;[14] and (2) at a sectoral level that the leading firms in those sectors that exhibit more marked declines in the value rate of profit are more likely to have globalized their production processes than firms in those sectors where the declines in the rate of profit are less severe. This work provides considerable evidence for concluding that the global restructuring of capitalism in the older regions can be linked to a tendency for the rate of profit to decline and that this decline is driven by the tendency of the organic composition of capital to increase in the mature industries in the mature capitalist regions. The link from this finding to the transition to global capitalism is as follows:

1. $s/c + v$ (the rate of profit) tends to decline because c (constant capital) increases relative to v.

2. Increases in s/v (the rate of surplus value, or the rate of exploitation) can compensate for this decline through the mechanism of depressing v (wages).

3. This mechanism has but limited use in the older regions where labor retains some bargaining resources, some political influence, and where the historical level of reproduction is high.

4. By performing substantial fractions of the production process in low- or "lower-" wage sites of production, where the rate of exploitation is higher, the rate of surplus value is buffered. Thus, the flow of production capital from the older core to the NICs and to the "semiperiphery" of the core itself (Ireland, Greece, Spain).

Class struggle theories (i.e., those analyses which emphasize the ability of workers to raise their share of national income under monopoly capitalism) would similarly produce a flow of capital away from political economic jurisdictions where labor is strong, toward those in which it was weak, or in which the combination of discipline and state policy kept its costs low (e.g., those socialist bloc countries courting foreign investment for export production). This dynamic depends on the uneven development over space of working-class organization and of class struggle. While the two views are often depicted as mutually exclusive, elements of the "class-struggle" analysis are behaviorally and conceptually compatible with organic composition theories, as follows:

Capitalists in the older industrial regions are replacing living labor with dead labor. This occurs because living labor has become more costly or less disciplined, from the perspective of the firm, than the alternative machines. The economic bargaining power of monopoly-sector workers in some of the older industrial regions is relatively high. Their political influence in some states and regions supplements this bargaining power through increases in the social wage and other regulations that favor working-class interests.

Faced with this *relative* shift in the balance of class power, monopoly-sector firms seek out means for employing alternative, lower cost, less powerful reserves of labor. The relative shift in the balance of class forces characteristic of monopoly capitalism in the older regions then creates a dynamic that also propels the restructuring of capitalist *production* on a *global* basis.

The last of the crisis tendencies that could plausibly lead to global transition is that of realization failure—insufficient demand in the mature economies, leading to a dearth of acceptably profitable investment opportunities. This is linked to the historic tendency for capital to become more concentrated. Firms within industrial sectors of a given national economy in the older regions become fewer in number and larger in size. Their immense capital plants afford them economies of scale; but that same size requires very large production runs to reach a break-even point. Thus, concentration of capital *permits*, and surplus productive capacities *compel*, firms to penetrate one another's markets. And they embark upon a course of fierce competition for markets located in newer regions. This competition impels each capital to search for, among other things, cost advantages over their rivals. Labor costs are obvious candidates.

The immense reserve of low-wage workers in less industrialized places offers itself as an attractive source of competitive advantage. At the same time, it offers new investment opportunities for capital goods. When one firm brings to the world market a commodity produced with contemporary technology and with a substantial fraction of low wage labor in it, the others are forced to follow. The concentration of capital, a dynamic inherent to the capitalist mode of production, thus produces global diffusion of manufacturing facilities.

Consequently, the transition to global capitalism is the plausible result of each of the proposed crisis tendencies of capitalism.

Restructuring Crisis or
Cycle of Contraction?

The theory of global capitalism, then, contends that the era of monopoly capitalism has passed. The dynamic tendencies of capitalism (systemic properties that create impediments to continuous expansion) are driving the restructuring process past the point at which the monopoly capitalism model works well in describing the system.

The theory of global capitalism analyzes this transition in ways which are also distinct from the world systems view of the logic of cycles of contraction.

As noted in chapter 4, world systems theory understands phases of stagnation in the world economy as being initiated by crises of overproduction. These crises of overproduction are then seen as causing a decline in the global rate of profit. The world system then enters a moment of acute class struggle during which the real income of workers in the core is said to increase.

According to world systems analysts, such periods witness an increase in the number of wage workers and middle strata bureaucrats in the semi-periphery. This results from a limited transfer of production to these regions. In combination with increase in workers' real incomes, these developments succeed in restoring world demand. With world demand restored, another phase of expansion begins.

In later chapters, we show that this scenario is not an accurate account of this era. The tendency of world systems theory to emphasize trade, and therefore demand, factors leads to an analysis of cyclical crises that views overproduction as the triggering mechanism. By contrast, we are inclined to focus on concrete power as between employers and employees, and in political affairs.

Graham and Gibson *et al*, as well as data presented later about the world automobile industry, indicate that a decline in the rate of profit initiated the most recent episode of contraction and crisis. In part, this was accounted for in their work by a rising organic composition of capital. But we also note that the 1960s saw an increase in the bargaining power of monopoly labor, which lead to increases, *not* decline, or stagnation, in their real income levels (see chapter 7).

To this capital reacted by expanding production in low-wage, overseas sites, thereby seeking to restore the rate of surplus extraction. In the short run, overproduction ensued, but in the middle run this provided an ability to close down production facilities in older sites. With the ability to move globally thus established, capital then presented production workers in those older sites in the core with the demand for wage constraint/ concessions and enforced its demands with the lever of global mobility.

For workers in the core, what resulted was stagnating or declining, not increasing real wages.

Both our use of the concept of a restructuring crisis and our understanding of its dynamics distinguish the theory of global capitalism from world systems theory. This difference in conceptual foundation also lies at the root of the dispute about whether the present era is marked more by change or by continuity. Where we see restructuring crises, world systems theorists see cycles of competition and contraction.

Implications for the Older Industrial Regions and Cities

Examining alternative conceptions of the nature of contemporary capitalism on the ground of our older regions and metropolitan areas is particularly appropriate. If one proceeded from the model derived from the theory of monopoly capitalism, one would expect such areas as the Detroit region and its working class to enjoy a rising standard of living, protected by the market power of the region's dominant firms and the bargaining power of its relatively strong unions. In such a local setting, relatively immobile capital would be apt to come to accommodation with broader working-class forces in the policies of the local state.

Baran and Sweezy do not directly comment on the role played by industrial structure or class relations in the differential urban or regional deployment of resources. O'Connor, however, does.[15]

In O'Connor's work, the suburbs are the location of monopoly sector production and corporate executive residence. The inner city houses increasingly poor people dependent on state transfer payments or employment in competitive-sector, secondary labor markets. The shift of production to suburbs is a function of a search for lower taxes and less expensive land. This understanding was, and continues to be, accurate in important respects.

However, the model of urban space derived from the theory of monopoly capitalism does not anticipate the rapid desertion of the older industrial suburbs. By contrast, the theory of global capitalism anticipates that the venerable deployment of capital will be restructured as a result of the changing structure of capitalist relations. While regional flows of capital within national boundaries are included within domain of the theory of global capitalism, its distinctive perspective is the analysis of local change in the context of the global theater of capitalist choice. The restructuring crises we examine are more profound than city to suburb shifts in the location of manufacturing.

Examining concrete regions is appropriate for another reason. New theory must establish something more than its logical plausibility. If we are correct, if there really is a new moment in the history of capitalism, this understanding should be helpful. It should be more helpful than other theories are in the analysis of concrete change in describable environments. We intend to show that there is an advantage in our mode of analysis.

Implications for the Periphery

The theory of monopoly capitalism was associated with a stagnation thesis for the backward nations. World systems theory was extended to acknowledge that some manufacturing capital migrates to Third World sites for production during cycles of contraction. But this has not been seen as a qualitative change of the past two decades.

The debate over the "Monthly Review" model of the world division of labor has centered on the role of "peripheral" nations in the dynamics of modern capitalism.

A New International Division of Labor?: The State of the Debate

During the 1960s, the Monthly Review model of the international division of labor achieved widespread acceptance among radical political economists. Even mainstream international political economists and development theorists came to treat the Baran/Frank model and related notions of *dependencia* as serious challenges to their understanding of the status of the Third World within the world economy.[16]

The model assumed material prosperity in the older regions. Radical scholarship concentrated on specifying the way the appropriation of value from the Third World countries by those of the First World accounted for the latter's high rates of growth and working-class affluence. Among the mechanisms identified as explaining these phenomena was the idea of unequal exchange advanced by Emmanuel and Amin.[17]

Baran's stagnation thesis and the "development of underdevelopment" formulation of A. G. Frank became the starting points for understanding the logic and consequences of capitalist development in the Third World.[18]

As signs of change in the world economy became evident during the 1970s, however, the Monthly Review model of the world economy was challenged. One part of that challenge was composed of attempts to explain the end of prosperity in the older regions. These have already been reviewed. Other challenges provided an alternative conception of the international division of labor as depicted by Baran and Frank.

Warren was among the first challengers to the Monthly Review model. He attempted to revive the "orthodox" Marxist thesis that imperialism is a "progressive force" that accelerates the development of precapitalist areas of the world.[19] In so doing, Warren rejected emphatically the industrial stagnation thesis of Baran and Frank. He showed that Third World rates of industrialization had exceeded those of the developed world from 1960 through the mid-1970s.

Just as Warren was formulating his view of orthodoxy in the Marxist theory of imperialism, Fernando Cardoso formulated a revision of Frank's "underdevelopment" argument from within the *dependencia* tradition.[20] Cardoso argued that capitalism in the center countries had moved into a new phase of "monopolistic expansion" that produced in some Third World countries a foreign investment-driven phase of industrialization. In contrast to Baran and Frank, Cardoso saw foreign investment in the periphery as flowing toward industrial sectors rather than traditional sectors. Cardoso contended that these new flows of foreign investment were producing "associated dependent development" rather than underdevelopment.

As the debate intensified during the late 1970s, the world systems theory of Wallerstein and others began receiving increasing attention. With their intellectual roots in the work of both Baran and Frank, world systems writers tended to oppose both the resurrectionism of Warren and the revisionism of Cardoso. Emphasizing the continuous and unchanging structures of the capitalist world-economy, they adopted as the foundation of their model the notion that there are distinct differences between core and peripheral production processes. They maintained further that these differences always operate to the advantage of the core.

As the prominence of the world systems perspective increased, a conceptual critique was unleashed by Marxian scholars who considered that the world systems approach had lost sight of the primacy of the relations of production. The most influential was Brenner's careful and lengthy attempt to refute what he termed *Neo-Smithian Marxism*.[21] Focussing principally upon Frank and Wallerstein, Brenner sought to show that by failing to take into account the dynamic nature of class structures, these authors had locked themselves too quickly into the proposition that underdevelopment in the periphery is inherent in capitalist expansion.

Other scholars turned their attention to conceptual modification and empirical assessment of the theses put forward by Warren and Cardoso.

Szymanski gathered extensive data in support of his contention that "during the late phase of monopoly capitalist imperialism that began around 1960...the predominant tendencies have become the evening out of the general level of industrialization as well as a homogenization of the class structures of the core and the periphery of the world capitalist system."[22] Szymanski maintained that the flow of industrial capital from the core to the periphery in search of cheaper labor was a central aspect of this new phase of imperialism.

Landsberg presented updated evidence challenging the industrial stagnation thesis and formulated the concept of "manufacturing imperialism."[23] Cypher argued that the 1960s and 1970s had "revealed a host of incongruities," including the export of manufacturing capital and peripheral industrialization. He linked their emergence to "the internationalization of capital."[24]

Building upon Cardoso's concept of "associated dependent development," Evans conducted a detailed study of Brazilian industrialization.[25] Evans showed how the model of class relations underlying Baran's stagnation thesis had evolved and created the political conditions in Brazil permitting industrialization.

Frobel, Heinrichs, and Kreye finally came forward with the thesis that the classical manufactured goods/raw material international division of labor that informs the work of Baran, Frank and the *dependistas* was being replaced by a new international division of labor.[26] They argued that, "For the first time in the history of the 500-year-old world economy, the profitable production of manufactures for the world market has become possible to a significant and increasing extent, not only in the industrialized countries, but also in the developing countries."[27] This historic development was attributed to the coming together of three preconditions: (1) a worldwide reserve of labor; (2) technological advances which allow for the decomposition of production processes; and (3) technological progress that renders the management of production largely independent of geographical distance.

Focussing more upon relations of production, Lipietz articulated an "accumulationist" equivalent of the new international division of labor.[28] He termed the new system "global fordism." As Lipietz saw it, sometime in the late 1960s, capital's strategy of substituting machinery for workers as a means of increasing the rate of exploitation (fordism) reached its limit. Capital responded by shifting unskilled manufacturing to the cheaper wage zones of the periphery. Fordism was applied globally. Lipietz concluded that one result of global fordism was a circumscribed, but definite, industrialization of the periphery.

Despite their emphases upon the revolutionary nature of peripheral industrialization, most of the Marxist and dependency writers evaluated negatively the overall impact of the process upon Third World countries.[29] Among others, the superexploitation of workers, the stifling of local capital, increased economic inequality, a deepening of dependency, and the introduction of inappropriate technologies were all cited as costs associated with this phase of Third World industrialization.

The debate has also involved more conventional international political economists and economic geographers. Caparoso attempted an eclectic interpretation that drew from Marxist, dependency, and neoclassical perspectives and categorized their various ideas in terms of "push, pull, facilitative and conversion factors."[30] Grunwald and Flamm accepted the basic thesis of Frobel et al. in their analysis of the "global factory."[31] Dicken coined the phrase "global shift" to denote the internationalization of production capital and the relatively high growth rates of manufacturing in the developing market economies.[32] In contrast to most of the Marxist and dependency writers, however, the mainstream scholars offered generally favorable judgments of the impact upon peripheral countries.

Scholarship in recent years has mounted a substantial conceptual and empirical critique of the Monthly Review model of the international division of labor. The validity of the industrial stagnation thesis has been severely weakened. The proposition that foreign investment would not create the growth of industry in the Third World has been revised. Broad agreement seems to be forming that in recent decades a new international division of labor has emerged.

Monopoly Capital and World Systems Views of the New International Division of Labor

Influential currents of dissention to the new view do remain. Writers wed to the monopoly capitalist tradition have been uncertain in their embrace and have resisted any serious reformulation or departure from the theory of monopoly capitalism. Some have chosen to question the magnitude of the recent trends as well as their conceptual significance.[33] Others have acknowledged the tendency toward industrialization in the Third World, but have argued that it can be explained according to the essential elements of the theory of monopoly capitalism.[34]

The response of world systems theorists has been more unyielding. Wallerstein, as mentioned in chapter 4, without any specific mention of his critics, has contended that both the current slowdown in the core as well as the transfer of production toward the periphery is nothing more than a cyclical phenomenon that has occurred during every Kondratief B-phase throughout the history of the capitalist world-economy.[35]

Chase-Dunn has minimized the magnitude of peripheral industrialization and rejected the concept of a new international division of labor. He also maintains that any change that has transpired can be explained by cycles and trends present since the inception of the capitalist world-economy.[36]

Global Capitalism and the New International Division of Labor

The debate has yet to be resolved. The next chapter gives a detailed presentation of evidence in support of the proposition that the transition to global capitalism has brought about a new international division of labor. The slowdown of industrial growth in the older regions and the rapid industrialization of areas of the periphery are a consequence of the transition from monopoly to global capitalism.

The contributions to the debate thus far fail to offer an adequate explanation of the forces driving the restructuring of the international division of labor.

Cardoso and Evans, who focussed on dependent development in Latin America, do not consider the relationship among contradictions of capital accumulation and the dynamics of class conflict in the core and the development process which they observed. Similarly, the three factors cited by Frobel et al., while of undoubted conjunctural importance, are not linked, by them, to changes in power and industrial structure in the core; their discussion of surplus value is not linked to tendencies toward crisis under capitalism and the role of class struggle in bringing about change.

Warren's contention that imperialism has always been a progressive force is not convincing for the era of monopoly capitalism. Szymanski's schema of late monopoly capitalist imperialism and Landsberg's analysis of manufacturing imperialism leave one wondering how a form of capitalism, which in its early life produced peripheral stagnation, can now drive a process of peripheral industrialization while retaining its essential characteristics.

Cypher's emphasis upon the internationalization of capital leads in a useful direction, but he fails to link it to capital-labor relations—the elemental social relation of capitalism. Lipietz's exposition of global fordism, while insightful, stops short of linking global fordism to change in the capitalist mode of production. He does not consider whether this is the occasion for a revision of the theory of monopoly capitalism. Alternatively, *global fordism* really should be understood as an underspecified version of the proposition that monopoly capitalism has been transformed to something new—global capitalism.

Conclusion

The next section illustrates the impact of global capitalism in a series of concrete cases. While "cases" cannot "prove" theory, each case demonstrates that dependence on one or the other of the older models of capitalism would lead to different expectations about the course of capitalist and working-class development.

We examine New York City, testing whether its role as the location of major global command and control functions makes it a particularly "privileged" environment for workers. We analyze the crisis of Detroit, asking whether the theory of monopoly capitalism leads to correct understandings of the working-class situation in the city and in the automobile industry. We also examine the restructuring process in Massachusetts, showing the role that capital flight and internationalization have played in that state. We begin by looking at industrialization and the growth of manufacturing in formerly backward countries, asking whether the older theories have correctly anticipated those developments. Together, these case studies illustrate the dynamics of global capitalism, suggesting that it is the appropriate starting point for analysis of the current era.

Part III
Explorations in Global Capitalism

6
The Restructuring of the World Economy under Global Capitalism

Introduction

That the world economy is in transition to a new era dominated by the global variant of capitalism is a proposition that builds upon the work of those who have sought to identify and document the recent upheavals of contemporary capitalism. Much of this body of work concludes that for more than two decades monopoly capitalism has been in crisis in most of the older industrial economies. Mandel, Castells, and Bowles; Gordon and Weisskopf; and Armstrong, Glyn, and Harrison, for example, find that this crisis has been manifest as a decline in the rate of profit.[1]

The consequences and outcomes of this recent crisis are the focus of the remainder of this volume. The leading firms in many sectors have been compelled to form new strategies of capital accumulation. Those strategies amount to a restructuring of capitalism from a monopoly to a global variant.

In previous chapters we introduced the idea that transitions from one variant of capitalism to another can be grasped by observing changes in three strategic social relations, identified as the capital-to-capital, capital-to-labor and capital-to-state relations.

In this section empirical evidence and case studies are introduced to substantiate and illustrate the changes in these three strategic relationships.

The plan is as follows:

- Because the strategic lever of capital mobility, especially toward cheaper labor, is central to the idea of global capitalism, this chapter documents extensively the "new international division of labor" and places our understanding of it in the context of other interpretations.
- In succeeding chapters we use case studies of world centers of three industries—automobile, apparel, and electronics—to illuminate separate aspects of the global perspective.
- In the chapter on Detroit, center of the automobile industry, the contrast between a global analysis and that of monopoly capitalism is the central focus, in particular the erosion of labor's position in relation to capital.

- In the chapter on New York City, a center of apparel production until recently, the focus is on a contrast to world systems analysis, and in particular on spatial aspects of capitalist competition.
- Concluding the case studies, the chapter on Massachusetts focusses on the electronics industry and political implications of its internationalization.

The perspective of global capitalism contrasts with the theoretical models of capitalism most prominent in North America: the theory of monopoly capitalism and the world systems approach. The following chapters illustrate the impact of the globalization of capital on the older regions of the United States. While case studies cannot, by themselves, "test" a theory, we believe that these case studies show that neither of these models adequately anticipates important aspects of structural change.

Under global capitalism, the economic geography of the world is reorganized. The international division of labor associated with the era of monopoly capitalism becomes altered. The concentration of manufacturing production in the older regions of Western Europe and North America has broken down. Industrialization is occurring rapidly in the Third World.

During any given era of capitalism, a definite spatial arrangement of production tasks can be discerned. Leading enterprises make investments across space in a manner designed to maximize their rates of capital accumulation. Regions come to perform certain functions within the capitalist economy and their economic fates are a direct consequence of that function. The particular dynamics of any given variant of capitalism generate a corresponding international division of labor.

As different variants of capitalism emerge to dominance, changes in the international division of labor can be expected. As change occurs within the capitalist mode of production and the logic of the system is modified, the fate and function of different regions within the capitalist world economy also become transformed.

During the monopoly capitalist era, an international division of labor that reflected the interests of monopoly capital in the older regions was established. Manufacturing production was concentrated in the more mature capitalist economies while the primary role of the lesser developed countries of the periphery was the production of raw materials for consumption in the core.

Following Szymanski, we call this the Monthly Review model of the international division of labor.[2]

In the First World, especially after World War II, this international division of labor produced *relative* prosperity. High rates of industrial growth prevailed, real wages of certain workers rose, total manufacturing employment expanded, and unemployment declined. The welfare state was created and, in part, alleviated the suffering of those excluded from the fruits of this "golden era."

As Baran and Frank have shown, industrial stagnation was the typical fate of Third World economies. First World capital concentrated its Third World investment in raw material extraction and tropical agriculture. In those regions, imports of manufactured goods from the older industrial regions stifled the initiative of local capital.

This chapter presents the view that the transition to global capitalism results in a new international division of labor. In particular, industrial growth in core regions has levelled off or declined while industrialization has been launched in the periphery. This occurs as a consequence of the new conditions of capital accumulation that prevail under global capitalism.

Since the mid-1960s, firms in many manufacturing industries traditionally located in the core have faced declining profits. The prevailing conditions have compelled a search for new strategies of capital accumulation. New forms of competition among firms have become evident. These include price competition, conglomeration, and spatial mobility in search of the lowest cost production sites with adequate infrastructure.

This chapter focuses on the way these new modes of capitalist competition have altered the structures of the world production economy, including the structures of national economies and the corresponding international division of labor. Particular attention is devoted to the strategy of spatial mobility—the *relative* withdrawal of manufacturing capital from the older industrial regions and its relocation to sites in the Third World. That firms in such industries as clothing, automobiles, and electronics have pursued this new strategy of competition is demonstrated by examining data on foreign investments in manufacturing in the Third World in recent decades.

Many Third World sites of production offer a lower cost labor force, which also has a history of being less militant. By lowering labor costs through production in low-wage sites firms have been able to circumvent or defeat high-wage labor of the traditionally powerful sectors of the First World. In the era of global capitalism, these new forms of competition—price and spatial mobility—emerge as necessary in the struggle for market shares.

At the same time, the movement of capital to Third World sites serves to restructure the capital-to-labor relationship characteristic of the monopoly era. Spatial mobility across the globe gives capital a new lever of exploitation, a new strategic resource. By substituting workers in the periphery for workers in the core, manufacturing firms have been able to increase their rates of surplus extraction. Even when this substitution is a *relatively* small fraction of a global firm's *total* employment, it looms large in the strategic relation between employers and employees, lending firms important leverage with remaining employees in the core. Spatial mobility has been the critical instrument used to restore the rate of profit.

A world market in sites for manufacturing production emerges in the era of global capitalism. New investment capital flows toward those locations possessing the requisite infrastructure and where the balance of class forces is more favorable to capital. The Third World becomes an attractive site for the location of manufacturing production, and the spatial organization of production tasks within the world economy is transformed.

This chapter is divided into four parts. The first part examines evidence that supports the contention that spatial mobility to low-cost production sites has become a characteristic form of capitalist competition in the current era. The massive flow of foreign manufacturing investment to the Third World from 1960 to 1980 is documented. In addition, the logic of foreign investment under global capitalism is developed in order to explain the sectoral and national patterns of this investment.

The second part documents the sustained and rapid growth of manufacturing production in the Third World after 1960. We show that Third World industrialization has been fueled by the relative relocation of manufacturing capital from the core to the periphery. We also explain the concentration of Third World industrialization among a few countries.

The third part presents evidence in support of the proposition that a new international division of labor exists. The rapid growth of manufactured exports from the Third World in recent decades is examined. The new role of the periphery within the world economy is outlined. These developments, too, are linked to the emergence of global capitalism.

The last part offers some observations about the costs and constraints of Third World industrialization.

A NEW FORM OF CAPITALIST COMPETITION: THE STRATEGY OF GLOBAL SPATIAL MOBILITY

The discussion of the capital-to-capital relation in chapter 5 presented the view that the forms of competition among capitalists characteristic of the monopoly era were being replaced. Specifically, we argued that under global capitalism, price competition, conglomeration, and spatial mobility (which includes lower-cost Third World production sites) had become the principal strategies employed by the most successful firms in their struggles to retain, or acquire new, market shares. The following evidence substantiates the importance of global spatial mobility as a new form of capitalist competition.

The Growth of Foreign Investment
in Manufacturing in the Third World

During the era of monopoly capitalism, investment in manufacturing sites in the Third World was not a typical form of capitalist competition. Foreign investment in the Third World was concentrated overwhelmingly in raw material extraction. Monopoly capital from the older regions structured Third World economies to be sources of raw materials and consumers of surplus manufactured goods.

Data on U. S. direct investment support these propositions. In 1950, U. S. direct investment in manufacturing accounted for only 12 percent of total U. S. direct investment in the periphery. In contrast, U. S. direct investment in mining and petroleum constituted 51 percent of total investment. In the period between 1952 and 1959, new U. S. direct investment in manufacturing facilities in the periphery averaged only $70 million annually.[3]

Since the early 1960s, manufacturing capital has made increasing use of spatial mobility as a new strategy of competition. Concretely, there has been a relative and absolute increase in foreign investment in manufacturing production facilities in the Third World.

The available data on U. S. direct investment support this proposition. By 1966, U. S. direct investment in manufacturing rose to 25 percent of total U. S. direct investment in the Third World while mining and petroleum fell to 48 percent.[4] In the following years, this trend intensified. By 1979, U. S. direct investment in manufacturing reached 33 percent of total direct investment in the Third World and mining and petroleum declined to 18 percent.[5] The flow of U. S. direct investment in manufacturing averaged $498 million annually, from 1970 to 1972, but between 1979 and 1981, the flow of U. S. manufacturing investment grew to an average of $1.7 billion each year.[6]

U. S. foreign investment in manufacturing in the Third World has grown both absolutely and relatively to investment in traditional sectors. This supports the proposition that spatial mobility has emerged as a new and critical form of competition for U. S. manufacturing capital.

The available data show recent increases in the flow of manufacturing investment to the periphery for the other major core industrial powers. As of 1971, 42 percent of the stock of British direct investment in the periphery was in manufacturing industries; by 1979, that figure had increased to 57 percent.[7] In 1980, 68 percent of the outflow of German direct investment to the periphery was in manufacturing.[8] The surge of Japanese foreign investment to the periphery during the 1970's was also concentrated in such manufacturing industries as textiles, iron and steel and electronics.[9]

Overall, according to the United Nations Centre on Transnational Corporations, in the 1970s, particularly the latter years, foreign investment in manufacturing accounted for an increasing share of direct investment from developed to developing countries.[10]

In contrast to the era of monopoly capitalism, manufacturing capital from the older regions is now flowing to the Third World in substantial amounts. In fact, investment in manufacturing in the periphery now exceeds investment in raw material extraction.

Other Means of Relocating Manufacturing Production to the Periphery

While the data on foreign direct investment in manufacturing are impressive, they do not capture comprehensively the relocation of manufacturing production to the periphery by core capital. Subcontracting is one means of capital relocation not included in direct investment data.[11] For example, in the apparel industry, firms frequently subcontract the sewing of garments to independent "jobbers" located in a low-wage country. The "jobbers" are not formal subsidiaries of the apparel firm, and the firms may make no direct equity investment in plant and equipment in the low-wage site. Yet, in a very real sense the payment to a "jobber" is the functional equivalent of a direct foreign investment. For it is the foreign apparel firm that provides the capital to finance the sewing machines needed to sew the garment.

Joint ventures are another means of redeploying production whose impact is not fully reflected in direct foreign investment data. General Motors's joint venture with a Korean automobile manufacturer illustrates the point. By acquiring a share of the Korean firm and agreeing upon a joint project to produce a new subcompact car for the U. S. market, GM began the process of shifting production from plants in the United States that currently make subcompacts to plants in Korea. Yet, because the Korean firm has existing plants, the amount of capital flow recorded is less than would have occurred if GM had to build new plants in Korea.

Global finance capital has also played a role in the movement of manufacturing production to the periphery that is not reflected in direct investment data.[12] The available research suggests that a significant portion of the enormous loans that have been extended to Third World countries in the past fifteen years have financed private and state-owned manufacturing facilities in the periphery.

The means global capital has available for shifting manufacturing production to sites in peripheral countries are many and varied. Direct investment is the most visible but it understates the magnitude of the redeployment that has transpired in recent decades.

Capital Relocation to the Periphery and the Balance of Class Forces

In relocating some production to the Third World manufacturing capital is attracted by the more favorable balance of class forces present in those countries.

While the working class has attained, in the First World, a measure of ability to achieve material, cultural, and political goals, in the periphery working-class accomplishments have often been meager. There exists as between the core and the periphery considerable variation in the balance of class forces.

Many indicators of the balance of class forces at any given location in the global mosaic can be conceptualized. Wages and industrial disputes are among those for which comparative data can be assembled.

Table 6.1 presents data on wages and industrial disputes for 1974 and 1980 for several core countries that were the major sources of foreign manufacturing investment and for a number of the peripheral countries that were the leading recipients of such investment. The extraordinary variation in wages as between core and periphery makes evident the way moving production to the periphery can assist in restoring the rate of surplus extraction. The low number of disputes in the periphery means that costly disruptions of production are unlikely to occur.

The Sectoral Pattern of the Relocation of Manufacturing Production to the Periphery

Analysis of the conditions and the sectoral pattern of recent investment reveals that manufacturing investment in the former periphery is leading to a significant restructuring of both the core and periphery.[13] We begin this discussion with an analytic distinction between *import substitution* and *export oriented* foreign investment. *Import substitution* manufacturing investment occurs among a small number of Third World recipients whose domestic markets are large enough to attract foreign investment to service those domestic markets. Brazil is a prime example.

Under monopoly capitalism core manufacturing capital—primarily U. S. capital—tapped these markets by exporting goods produced in plants located in the core. This marketing strategy is rendered increasingly obsolete by the intensified competition for world markets shares that is characteristic of global capitalism. It has also been made difficult by national content policies that have prevailed in some of these countries.

TABLE 6.1

WAGES AND INDUSTRIAL DISPUTES: SELECTED COUNTRIES

| Country/Region | Wages 1980 | | Industrial Disputes 1974 | |
	Average Wage Manufacturing ($ U.S.)	Period	Disputes Per 1,000 Worker	Working Days Lost Per 1,000 Worker
Periphery				
Malaysia	N/A	N/A	0.31	0.38
South Africa	475.58	month	N/A	N/A
Argentina	1.11	hour	N/A	N/A
Chile	279.23	month	9.36	N/A
Colombia	1.00	hour	N/A	N/A
Mexico	1.70	hour	1.84	N/A
Venezuela	610.53	month	0.18	0.20
Hong Kong	9.07	day	0.03	0.02
India	67.49	month	0.57	7.86
Korea	241.48	month	0.04	0.01
Singapore	0.99	hour	0.05	0.03
European semiperiphery				
Spain	3.97	hour	0.68	0.59
Greece	2.40	hour	N/A	N/A
Ireland	4.76	hour	1.04	2.63
Portugal	1.63	hour	N/A	N/A
Yugoslavia	280.04	month	—	—
Selected core				
United States	7.27	hour	0.30	2.39
Japan	1078.64	month	0.43	0.80
France	5.38	hour	0.60	0.60
West Germany	7.25	hour	N/A	0.11
United Kingdom	6.20	hour	0.37	1.87

N/A: Not available.

Source: International Labor Organization, *Yearbook of Labour Statistics 1983* (Geneva: International Labour Office, 1983).

Therefore, much of the manufacturing investment made in the large market peripheral countries protects or expands the world market shares of the global firms that have invested in these countries.

Export oriented manufacturing investment has as its purpose the production of goods in a peripheral site for export, primarily to core countries. In some instances these goods are finished products that directly enter the market; in others, they are intermediate products shipped to plants in the core for further transformation. For most Third World recipients of manufacturing investment, export oriented investment is more typical. Singapore is a prime example.

Two principal sets of conditions determine industries where export oriented manufacturing investment will occur. First, certain technological characteristics must be present. For both finished and intermediate products transportation costs must not exceed wage and other savings that may be realized by moving to the periphery. In the case of intermediate products, the production process in the industry must be such that labor intensive phases of production can be physically removed from others.[14]

Second, those industries where competition is most acute and where rates of profit evidence decline can be judged most likely to relocate to manufacturing sites in the periphery. These factors vary across industries as well as within an industry over time. State policies that affect competition, mechanisms of capital accumulation and possibilities for relocation also vary across industries.

A wide variety of industries that have traditionally been located in the core face conditions of accumulation that compel the relocation of production to the periphery. Peripheral countries have received substantial investment in *heavy* industries such as machinery, metals, and transportation and *advanced* industries, such as chemicals and electronics, as well as light industries, such as textiles and food. Foreign investment in manufacturing in the periphery cannot be dismissed as composed of obsolete technology or limited to light industry.[15]

Investment in some of these industry groups is overwhelmingly for import substitution. Food, chemicals, and machinery fall into this category. The same is true of transportation equipment; although (as we will see in chapter 7), the value of exports of motor vehicle parts from the periphery has grown rapidly in recent years. These investments tend to be concentrated in the large market countries.

In contrast, much of the investment in electrical machinery (especially electronic components and accessories) and textiles are of the export oriented type. In these industries, a greater percentage of the investment flows to export platforms such as Hong Kong and Singapore. Although direct foreign investment is low, the clothing and garment industry should also be included among the export oriented group. Subcontracting often serves as a substitute for direct investment.[16]

Electronics, textiles, clothing and garments, and motor vehicle parts, then, are the most important industries where the relocation of production is export oriented.

Each of these industries meet the technological criteria for relocation to the periphery outlined above. A high value-to-weight ratio reduces transportation costs as a barrier to relocation. The production process can be disaggregated into discrete phases separable over geographic space.[17] Available evidence also suggests that international competition and profit rates have influenced relocation to the periphery in each of these industries.

Frobel et al., as well as our study of New York City, document that international competiton and profit considerations have been the crucial factors determining the use of production sites in the periphery in textiles and clothing.[18] Investment in the production of electronic goods in the periphery for export increased dramatically during the 1970s. Flamm's study of the semiconductor industry establishes this as a period of intense global competition.[19] Graham's analysis of rates of profit shows that the electronic components and accessories sector were among those experiencing the most severe rates of decline in profits between 1958 and 1972.[20] Finally, chapter 7 demonstrates that increased foreign investment by U. S. automobile firms could be explained by the intensification of global competition as well as declining rates of profit.

The National Pattern of Manufacturing Investment in the Periphery

While the logic of global capitalism anticipates a substantial flow of manufacturing investment to the periphery, the specific location rationale for manufacturing investment in the periphery can be understood primarily as the intersection of assessments of market size, the balance of class forces and the adequacy of the local infrastructure.

In cases where import substitution investment is being considered, all three conditions must be present. The local market must be large enough to absorb goods. Wage levels must be low enough, the working class must not have a history of militance, and state policy must not be heavily influenced by workers' interests. (International businessmen use the term *stability* as a composite for these considerations.) The local infrastructure of energy production, transportation facilities and the like must be adequate to meet the needs of the projected plant.

Very few countries meet all of these criteria. Those peripheral countries with the largest stocks of foreign direct investment in manufacturing (as of the late 1970s and early 1980s) included Brazil, Indonesia, Mexico, Singapore, India, Nigeria, South Korea, the Philippines, Colombia, and Hong Kong. Malaysia was beginning to replace its Southeast Asia competitors as a location for export platform activity as was Thailand.[21] Among those that could be considered recipients of import substitution investment are several of the South American countries—Brazil, Mexico, and Colombia. Others include Nigeria, India, Indonesia, and South Korea.

Locations for export oriented investment are influenced by the balance of class forces and the adequacy of infrastructure. Competition among possible sites is acute. Only those with very low wages, tightly controlled labor forces, few restrictions upon capital, and modern infrastructure can expect to be recipients of such investment.

As of the late 1970s, Singapore, the Philippines, Hong Kong, Malaysia, and Morocco were clear examples of peripheral countries attractive as export platforms. Some of the import substitution sites, such as Brazil and Mexico, also receive important amounts of export oriented investment.

The competition among sites yields conditions quite favorable to capital. The example of Singapore makes the point. In 1981, the average wage of all manufacturing workers in Singapore was $1.21 (U. S. dollars) per hour, while that in electrical equipment (the sector of the greatest investment in Singapore) was $1.05 (U. S. dollars) per hour.[22] Meanwhile, Singapore's Chamber of Commerce advertised that in 1981 *no* working days were lost to strikes.[23] Finally, the Singapore government offered ten tax-free years to foreign investors.[24]

As a result of the competition for export oriented investment and the fact that few countries are of interest as import substitution sites, manufacturing investment in the periphery is heavily concentrated in a few countries. As of 1979, for example, 62 percent of U. S. direct investment in manufacturing in the Third World was located in three countries—Argentina, Brazil, and Mexico. The five-country concentration was 71 percent, and the ten-country concentration was 82 percent.[25] Among the leading recipients of manufacturing investments, the amounts received by Brazil, Indonesia, Mexico, and Singapore dwarf those of Ecuador, Morocco, and Venezuela.

A Note on the Semiperiphery

We introduced the concept of the semiperiphery in chapter 4. It was defined as a region with a balance of core and peripheral forms of production. As we understand the new global system of production, the semiperiphery, especially its relative low-wage and/or authoritarian areas, should have received major shares of footloose manufacturing capital from the core. Semiperipheral sites, such as the European semiperiphery countries of Spain, Ireland, Portugal, and Greece, offer conditions of capital accumulation relatively more favorable to capital than core sites while being geographically proximate to core markets. In addition, several of these European semiperipheral countries joined or were preparing to join the European Common Market.

As a consequence, direct investment in manufaturing in the European semiperiphery increased dramatically in the 1970s. In 1966, the stock of U. S. direct investment in manufacturing in Ireland was only $61 million; in Spain, the figure was $199 million. By 1979, the stock of U. S. manufacturing foreign investment in Ireland has grown to $1.3 billion; in Spain it had reached $1.6 billion. Overall, the European semiperiphery's share of total U. S. direct investment in manufacturing in Europe increased from less than 5 percent in 1966 to more than 8 percent in 1979.[26]

Summary

In contrast to the era of monopoly capitalism, the transition to global capitalism brings about a flow of manufacturing capital from the core to the periphery. We understand this relocation of manufaturing production to be a response to intensified global competition and falling rates of profit. Manufacturing capital moves to the periphery in part because production sites there offer a balance of class forces that is more favorable to capital.

The sectoral pattern of foreign manufacturing investment shows that investment has occurred in heavy and advanced industries as well as traditional light industry. Distinguishing between *import substitution* and *export oriented* strategies of investment facilitated further explanation of the sectoral pattern. Investment of the export oriented type was shown to have been compelled by conditions of capital accumulation and enabled by certain technological features of production in the industry.

The national pattern of foreign manufacturing investment revealed a high degree of concentration among a few countries. Only a small number of countries combine the market size, class situation, and infrastructure that attract import substitution investment. Similarly, the absence of an adequate infrastructure in many countries combined with acute competition restricts export oriented investment to only a few favored sites.

Finally, the European semiperiphery has also been the recipient of substantial flows of foreign manufacturing investment in recent years.

THE RESTRUCTURING OF THE GLOBAL PRODUCTION ECONOMY

As a consequence of the new strategic importance of global spatial mobility, historically different patterns of growth and decline can be observed in the geographic regions that compose the world economy. Specifically, industrial decline or deindustrialization in the older regions of North America and Europe have accompanied the rapid growth of manufacturing industry in parts of Latin America and Asia.

During the era of monopoly capitalism, the dynamics of capital accumulation dictated a world production economy where manufacturing remained and became increasingly concentrated in the First World while the Third World suffered from industrial stagnation. The current epoch of global capitalism generates a changing geography of world manufacturing.

Earlier in this chapter data was presented in support of the contention that global spatial mobility has become a principal form of capitalist competition during the past two decades. We turn now to an overview of the historically different geographic patterns of growth and decline that result from this strategy. The emergent geography of world manufacturing is outlined. We devote specific attention to the phenomenon of Third World industrialization.

Regional Patterns of Growth

The traditional theory of monopoly capitalism maintains that countries in the older regions will experience manufacturing growth while the Third World suffers from industrial stagnation. While the term *stagnation* may be an exaggeration, the available data do indicate that during the monopoly era the rate of manufacturing growth in the First World exceeded that of the Third World. From 1938 to 1950, for example, the annual rate of manufacturing growth in the older regions was 4.5 percent annually compared to 3.8 percent in the Third World.[27] Table 6.2 confirms that, on an aggregate basis, this trend continued from 1950 to 1960. Manufacturing growth in the industrial market economies averaged 6.1 percent annually while in the developing countries it averaged 5.0 percent.

In spatial terms, these comparative growth rates mean that during the era of monopoly capitalism, world manufacturing production was being concentrated increasingly in the core. Data on annual average rates of growth in manufacturing portrayed in Table 6.2 suggest that, since 1960, a historically new spatial pattern of growth has emerged. The evident changes correspond with the proposition that there has been a transition from monopoly to global capitalism.

The aggregate rates of manufacturing growth shown in Table 6.2 for the Third World exceeded those of the First World for the periods 1960–1965, 1965–1970, and 1970–1981. From 1970 to 1981, the manufacturing growth rate in the Third World was 6.9 percent, nearly two and one-half times more rapid than the 2.7 percent rate registered by the older regions.

Comparison of the growth rates for individual countries listed in Table 6.2 offers further confirmation of the emergence of a new world manufacturing order. The twenty Third World countries listed in the table represent, with the exception of Taiwan, the largest Third World producers of manufactures. During both the 1965–1970 and 1970–1981 periods, the

TABLE 6.2
RATES OF GROWTH IN MANUFACTURING: 1950–1981

| Country/Region | *Average Annual Real Growth Rates* | | | |
	1950–60	*1960–65*	*1965–70*	*1970–81*
Industrial Market	6.1	5.7	5.7	2.7
Developing	5.0	6.7	6.5	6.9
Middle Income	6.6	6.3	7.0	7.4
Low Income	N/A	8.7	4.1	4.2
Periphery				
East Asia				
Singapore	N/A	7.8	15.8	10.6
Hong Kong	N/A	12.5	14.0	10.4
Republic of Korea	16.8	13.8	25.7	20.9
Malaysia	N/A	N/A	11.5	11.0
Thailand	6.4	10.8	11.4	10.4
Indonesia	N/A	1.0	7.9	13.9
Philippines	10.2	6.2	5.0	4.2
Latin America				
Brazil	9.1	3.8	10.0	7.4
Mexico	6.0	9.0	8.7	6.0
Colombia	6.5	5.7	6.2	5.7
Peru	7.3	9.7	6.7	3.2
Venezuela	13.0	9.5	3.6	5.2
Argentina	0.4	3.9	6.1	0.3
Chile	N/A	6.7	1.6	−0.4
South Asia				
India	3.2	9.0	3.3	4.3
Mid-East/Africa				
Algeria	8.8	1.5	13.3	11.6
Egypt	8.8	20.0	3.8	9.3
Morocco	5.2	3.3	5.8	5.8
Nigeria	N/A	11.1	10.4	9.5
Turkey	8.6	12.7	11.6	6.3
European semiperiphery				
Spain	8.8	12.6	10.1	4.8
Portugal	6.7	8.7	8.9	3.2
Greece	7.9	7.9	8.7	6.1
Ireland	3.0	6.6	7.1	4.9
Yugoslavia	10.4	11.7	6.1	7.4
Selected core				
United States	3.4	6.3	3.8	3.3
West Germany	9.8	5.7	6.5	1.7
France	6.8	5.5	9.6	2.2
United Kingdom	3.5	3.4	3.0	−0.6
Japan	18.3	11.5	16.3	4.2

N/A: Not available.

Source: The World Bank, *World Tables*, 3rd edition, vol. 1 (Baltimore, Md.: Johns Hopkins University, 1983).

growth rate of the manufacturing sectors of seventeen of these countries equalled or exceeded that of the United States. Comparisons to the United Kingdom, France, and West Germany are also favorable through most of this period.

Notable in Table 6.2 is the extremely rapid industrialization of Japan between 1950 and 1970. In world systems terminology, Japan was a *rising core power*. At the same time that world manufacturing production was being shifted from the core to the periphery, there took place a within the core shift from North America and Europe to Japan.

Yet by the period between 1970 and 1981, even Japan's rate of growth slowed. In fact, in sixteen of the Third World countries the rate of growth of the manufacturing sector was more rapid than that of Japan. That industrialization in these Third World countries was even more rapid than that of the rising core power, Japan, offers dramatic testimony to its historic importance. Finally, rates of manufacturing growth among those countries that compose the European fringe must be mentioned.

Historically, Spain, Portugal, Greece, Ireland, and Yugoslavia had been industrially underdeveloped regions within the European continent. Yet, during most of the recent period, manufacturing growth in the five countries of the European fringe outstripped significantly the pace of growth in West Germany, France, and the United Kingdom. Manufacturing growth in these previously underdeveloped parts of Europe that is more rapid than the rate in the historic economic powers of Europe is another feature of the new pattern of regional growth.

The regional patterns of growth characteristic of the era of monopoly capitalism have been altered. Not only has the Third World experienced manufacturing growth, but it has grown more rapidly than the mature industrial economies. The same is true of the recent pattern of growth within the European continent.

These new patterns of growth produce a changing geography of world manufacturing production.[28] Manufacturing production on the globe has been shifting away from its traditional locations toward previously underdeveloped regions. While the precise magnitude of this shift is difficult to gauge, it has been estimated that during the 1970s alone, the developing countries as a whole increased their share of the manufacturing output of the world market economies from 11 percent to 15 percent.[29]

Regional Patterns
of Structural Change

Samir Amin has captured well the contrasting structural changes that theorists of monopoly capitalism anticipate for developed and underdeveloped regions: "...in the central model (in the older regions) industry, as it develops, provides work for a larger number of workers than the number of craftsmen that it ruins. Industry recruits from declining agriculture and from the natural increase in the population. In the periphery, industry employs workers in fewer numbers than those of the craftsmen that it ruins and the peasants who are 'released from agriculture' "[30]

The theory of monopoly capitalism suggests that the industrial/manufacturing sectors of countries in the older regions will increase significantly in relative importance while the share of these same sectors in the Third World declines or stagnates. Available data tend to confirm the accuracy of this view for the older regions for the first one-half of the twentieth century. In the United Kingdom, industry moved from 48.9 percent of Gross Domestic Product (GDP) in 1907 to 56.8 percent by 1955. In France, the relative share of industry rose from 46.2 percent in 1896 to 51 percent by 1963. In the United States, the share of GDP accounted for by industry expanded from 37.7 percent in 1889–99 to 45.3 percent by 1953.[31]

Data for the more specific manufacturing sector exhibit the same tendency toward relative growth. The share of British GDP accounted for by manufacturing increased from 27.1 percent in 1907 to 36.8 percent in 1955. West German manufacturing rose from 34.6 percent of GDP in 1911–13 to 40.4 by 1936–38. In the United States, manufacturing went from 21.1 percent of national income in 1879 to 30.7 percent by 1965.[32]

Finally, data on the share of the labor force employed in manufacturing show the same tendency toward relative expansion. The United Kingdom went from 35.9 percent in 1921 to 37.3 percent in 1961; West Germany showed a shift from 32.9 percent in 1907 to 39.6 percent by 1961; and the United States evidenced a gain from 17.8 percent in 1869–79 to 25.9 percent by 1965.[33]

Data for the Third World during the same period are limited, unreliable, and incomplete, and some of the data exhibits developments contrary to the expectations of the theory of monopoly capitalism.[34] Kuznets's data show a healthy relative expansion of the industrial work force in Argentina, Columbia, and Mexico throughout the early twentieth century.[35] Yet the data that Kuznets reports for Chile, the Philippines, and India could be interpreted as evidence of stagnation.[36] Amin, meanwhile, argues that the proportion of the work force in the Third World engaged in the industrial sector during this period declined, and he reports that in Egypt between 1914 and 1958 the percentage of the population employed in industry, building, and construction work fell from 34 percent to 25 percent of the nonagricultural employed population.[37]

Available data generally support the proposition that from about 1890 to 1960 the patterns of structural change in the different regions of the world economy are consistent with the theory of monopoly capitalism. The older regions of North America and Western Europe were characterized by an expansion of the share of economic activity accounted for by manufacturing. Trends in the Third World are less certain, but they do not clearly contradict the views of Baran, Frank, Amin, and others.

As stated above, the theory of global capitalism leads to the expectation that different regions of the world economy have been restructured since the mid-1960s. We anticipate a relative decline in the importance of the manufacturing sector in the older regions and a rising importance of the same sector in previously underdeveloped regions. In contrast, the theory of monopoly capitalism would anticipate a continuation of the patterns of structural change characteristic of the early twentieth century.

The data in Tables 6.3 and 6.4 provide quite striking support for the proposition that the structures of national economies no longer resemble that of the theories of either monopoly capitalism nor of world systems.

Table 6.3 shows over time the proportion of GDP accounted for by manufacturing for selected countries in different regions of the world economy. The Third World countries listed therein represent most of the leading exporters of manufactured goods from these regions. The four countries from the older regions are the same as those for which data were reported above. Data are also reported for five countries from the underdeveloped fringe of Europe.

For each of the four countries of Europe and North America, Table 6.3 shows that manufacturing production declined as a percentage of GDP. This development represents a reversal of the tendency for the share of manufacturing to increase in these countries that was evident during the era of monopoly capitalism. It is consistent with the pattern of deindustrialization anticipated for these regions by the theory of global capitalism.

For most of the Third World countries listed in Table 6.3 the data show that the importance of manufacturing to the national economy rose fairly significantly. Only three countries—Argentina, Mexico, and Chile—deviate from this pattern; and these seem explicable by unusual circumstances that characterized each of these countries during the 1970s.[38] This pattern of structural change also varies from that experienced by the Third World early in the twentieth century.

Overall, the data in Table 6.3 support the proposition that regional patterns of structural change during the last two decades have been inconsistent with the theory of monopoly capitalism. They evidence a pattern of diminishing shares of manufacturing in the older regions and rising shares of the same sector in the Third World that is consistent with the theory of global capitalism.

Examining changes in the levels of employment in manufacturing in various countries offers further evidence in support of this interpretation of historically new regional patterns of growth and decline.

TABLE 6.3
CHANGES IN NATIONAL ECONOMIC STRUCTURES

| | Manufacturing as Percent GDP | | | |
| | Ave | Ave | Ave | |
Country/Region	1950–60	1960–70	1970–81	1982
Periphery				
Korea	13.1	19.0	27.0	28.0
Peru	23.2	21.8	27.5	24.0
Hong Kong	15.5	30.9	27.4	N/A
Argentina	29.4	31.1	26.9	N/A
Brazil	25.5	26.1	26.6	N/A
Egypt	20.1	21.5	24.9	27.0
Singapore	11.6	16.3	23.3	26.0
Philippines	20.3	20.8	24.6	24.0
Mexico	24.2	21.4	23.1	21.0
South Africa	20.5	22.5	22.5	N/A
Turkey	12.0	15.9	20.5	22.0
Colombia	16.6	17.6	21.0	21.0
Chile	20.9	24.7	21.7	20.0
Thailand	12.6	14.7	18.9	19.0
Malaysia	8.7	10.8	19.2	18.0
Morocco	14.6	16.1	16.9	16.0
Venezuela			16.2	16.0
India	15.5	14.4	16.3	16.0
Indonesia	N/A	8.9	10.6	13.0
Algeria	8.3	11.9	11.3	10.0
Nigeria	3.5	6.5	5.2	6.0
European semiperiphery				
Greece	16.0	16.8	19.5	18.0
Portugal	28.0	32.2	35.4	35.0
Spain	N/A	24.9	25.4	22.0
Ireland	N/A	18.5	19.5	N/A
Yugoslavia	35.9	28.2	30.3	32.0
Selected core				
United States	28.6	27.9	24.1	22.0
West Germany	40.5	40.4	38.1	35.0
France	29.1	28.7	27.4	25.0
United Kingdom	32.1	29.2	24.0	19.0

N/A: Not available.

Source: For 1982, The World Bank, *World Development Report 1984* (New York: Oxford University Press, 1984); other years, from The World Bank, *World Tables* (Baltimore, Md.: Johns Hopkins University, 1983).

As Table 6.4 shows, employment in manufacturing has grown in recent years in most of the fourteen Third World countries for which data are available. Overall, as many as 8 million more jobs in manufacturing were created than destroyed in these fourteen countries between 1967 and 1980. In contrast, more than 1.5 million more jobs were destroyed than created in France, West Germany, and the United Kingdom from 1970 to 1980. Among these countries, only the United States continued to show any growth of manufacturing jobs, and this trend has been reversed during the 1980s.

Further evidence suggests that global firms have played a major role in the restructuring of world manufacturing employment. Employment in manufacturing in developing countries by multinational enterprises was estimated to have increased by 560 percent from 1960 to 1977.[39] Other studies have shown that multinational firms have been responsible for the loss of millions of jobs in industrialized economies.[40]

Under global capitalism the objective conditions for a global working class become realized. Discrete phases of the production process may be performed as readily by Korean, Brazilian, or Filipino workers as by French, American, West German, or British workers. Finding peripheral workers to be less organized, poorly paid, and politically repressed, manufacturing capital has elected increasingly to shift production toward those workers.

Summary

In the past two decades historically new regional patterns of growth and structural change have emerged in the world economy. These patterns do not correspond with the stagnation expectations of the theory of monopoly capitalism. They are consistent with the theory of global capitalism.

Foreign Investment and Peripheral Industrialization

Our theory of global capitalism maintains that the relocation of production by core capital to the periphery is the crucial factor that has brought about industrialization in the periphery since 1960. The available evidence supports this contention, although some countries stand as exceptions.

That the same countries accounting for the bulk of the growth of manufacturing production in the Third World have also been the principal recipients of foreign direct investment in manufacturing suggests strongly that the upsurge in manufacturing investment has been instrumental to the accelerated growth of manufacturing in these peripheral countries.[41] The twenty-one peripheral countries that are the leading recipients of foreign investment

TABLE 6.4

CHANGES IN WORLD MANUFACTURING EMPLOYMENT BY REGION
SINCE 1967

Country/Region	Number of Employees in Manufacturing (In Thousands)			Jobs Lost (−) or Created in Manufacturing (In Thousands)	
	1967	1970	Latest	Since 1967	Since 1970
Periphery					
Brazil	1,537	2,635	3,951	2,414	1,316
Mexico	243	1,321	587	344	−734
Republic of Korea	644	861	2,015	1,371	1154
Turkey	416	501	745	330	244
Venezuela	210	219	447	236	227
Philippines	378	389	1,561	1,183	1,172
Indonesia	209	887	963	755	76
Hong Kong	405	549	871	466	322
Egypt	548	596	754	206	158
Nigeria	70	127	305	235	178
Colombia	278	339	508	230	169
Chile	261	244	218	−42	−25
Singapore	59	123	285	226	162
Malaysia	90	153	415	324	261
Total 14 Periphery	5,347	8,944	13,626	8,278	4,681
European semiperiphery					
Greece	230	253	357	128	104
Ireland	176	198	206	30	8
Spain	1,907	2,013	2,175	268	162
Portugal	298	308	668	370	360
Yugoslavia	1,190	1,292	2,106	916	814
Total 5 SP	3,801	4,063	5,512	1,711	1,449
Selected core					
United States	18,422	18,213	19,210	788	997
France	5,250	5,114	5,002	−248	−112
West Germany	7,365	8,203	7,141	−224	−1,062
United Kingdom	7,751	7,951	6,462	−1,289	−1,489
Total 4 Core	38,788	39,481	37,815	−973	−1,666

Source: The World Bank, *World Tables* (Baltimore, Md.: Johns Hopkins University, 1983).
Note: The data reported under the column labelled "Latest" vary from 1976 to 1980. Data for the majority of countries are for 1979 or 1980. The numbers reported under jobs lost/created should therefore be treated as approximations of trends rather than precise measures.

are, with two exceptions, the leading industrial producers in the Third World.[42] Together, they account for more than 75 percent of all manufacturing production in the periphery.[43] By and large, they are also among the leading recipients of foreign manufacturing investment.

Foreign-owned or -affiliated enterprises accounted for major shares of manufacturing employment, production and exports of Korea, Argentina, Brazil, Colombia, Mexico and Singapore during the 1970s.[44]

The role of foreign investment in Third World industrialization does need some qualification. First, considerable variation exists among countries for which data is available. In Singapore, the dominance of foreign capital cannot be questioned; in Argentina, Brazil, and Mexico, it is important but not clearly dominant. Second, two of the leading peripheral industrial powers have achieved their growth with little participation of foreign capital. Korea and India are examples. Third, even where foreign capital is important, local capital has been extensively involved as well.[45]

Despite these qualifications, the evidence overall does support the view that foreign investment has been the driving factor in peripheral industrialization.

A World System Cycle or a Transition to Global Capitalism?

The recent shift of manufacturing capital toward what world systems analysts would call the periphery and semiperiphery is not entirely consistent with their theory.[46] In their view, the transfer of some manufacturing production to the periphery occurs during the B-phase of a Kondratief cycle (a contraction in the long cycles of worldwide capitalist accumulation). Because such a cycle was, retrospectively, said to have begun *circa* 1967, world systems theorists were able to incorporate the expansion of manufacturing that occurred in the periphery during the 1970s into their long-term view.

For a world systems theorist, however, these developments did not signal a new moment or stage of capitalism. They represent a pattern that has been repeated throughout the history of the capitalist world-economy. This distinguishes the world systems interpretation of the new international division of labor from ours, as well as from that of many of the other writers cited herein.

These contrasting views cannot be resolved solely by appeal to empirical evidence. They depend upon two strategic issues: first, when does quantitative structural change become qualitative; and second, these matters depend in large part upon the definitions of capitalism employed by world systems writers compared to ourselves and others. In world systems lexicon capitalism is a system of production for exchange in which the object is the maximization of profit. To the extent that stages exist in this conception, they are determined by whether agriculture, merchant activity, or industry is the principal productive activity of the core. For world systems writers, the manner in which surplus is extracted from labor and the ways in which capitalists compete to maximize profit are *not* essential features of the system.

In contrast, we understand capitalism in terms of the social relations through which surplus is extracted by capital from labor and then realized in competition with other capitals. What is important about the new international division of labor to us is that it can be linked to transformations of social relations. In particular, this chapter shows that it can be linked to a new form of capitalist competition: the search for comparatively low-waged industrial labor.

World systems writers have asserted that global production has been present in the capitalist world-economy for centuries. Colonial trading monopolies are cited in support of this proposition; and the world role of metropoli such as Amsterdam in the 1600s are said to be parallel to the role of London in the nineteenth century, or New York City in the twentieth century. This response misses the point.

Eighteenth-century colonial trading monopolies were not the typical nor dominant form of capitalist production in their era. Their fundamental source of value was *coerced* labor, that is, the articulation of precapitalist forms of production with dominant capitalist (i.e., merchant) forms of marketing. But global firms with their multinational assembly lines operated by wage laborers have become the typical or dominant form of capitalist production only in the past thirty years. More importantly, these global firms employ a new lever of exploitation—the relative conditions of *wage* labor—and engage in new forms of competition based upon the widespread diffusion of this "proletarianization."

As indicated in chapter 4, on some issues our differences with world systems theory turn on conflicting views as to what is essential in defining capitalism as an economic system. Whether recent developments in the world manufacturing order and the international division of labor mark a new stage of capitalism is an issue that falls into that category. Other differences are empirical disputes and some of these are taken up in subsequent chapters.

A NEW INTERNATIONAL DIVISION OF LABOR

The Growth of Manufacturing Exports from the Periphery and Semiperiphery

The industrialization of the Third World has transformed the international division of labor. The classical model of the international division of labor associated with Baran and Frank is no longer an accurate depiction of the world system of trade. Describing the periphery as the producer of raw materials for export to the core fails to note significant change that has occurred in recent decades.

Table 6.5 shows that manufactured exports from peripheral countries expanded sharply between 1962 and 1981. Included in Table 6.5 under the category *Periphery* are sixteen of the most important exporters of manufactured goods in the Third World. Whether measured in gross value (Table 6.5) or per capita terms,[47] exports of manufactured goods for each of these countries grew. Countries such as Hong Kong, Korea, South Africa, and Singapore now export billions of dollars worth of manufactured goods. Comparable growth can also be noted for five of the countries of the European fringe.

Foreign capital is a major force behind the growth of manufactured exports from these peripheral countries. The countries lisited in Table 6.5, with few exceptions, also rank among the leading recipients of foreign manufacturing investment. These sixteen countries account for more than 90 percent of all manufactured exports emanating from the periphery.

A Comparison of the Growth of Manufactured Exports from the Periphery with the Growth of Core Exports

As is evident from Table 6.5, exports of manufactured goods from the core countries increased at a rapid rate, until 1980; yet the rate of growth of Third World manufactured exports exceeded that of the leading industrial powers.

Using the data of Table 6.5, Figure 6.1 shows that manufactured exports from the sixteen countries of the so-called periphery have grown more rapidly than those of the United States. In 1962, the combined manufactured exports of the sixteen leading peripheral countries equalled 17 percent of U. S. exports. By 1981, their total exports were more than 60 percent of those of the United States. Individually, fifteen of the sixteen peripheral countries and the five countries of the European fringe improved relative to the United States.

This gain relative to the United States may not be that surprising to some observers. The U. S. was after all a hegemonic power in decline for much of this period. However, Figure 6.1 also indicates that the manufactured exports from the leading sixteen developing countries also fared well relative to two rising core powers, West Germany and Japan.

Among the core countries, Japan is considered by many to be the "economic miracle" of the post-war period. Many analysts hold Japan up as a model of industrial efficiency and export-led growth. Yet the periphery and semi-periphery as a whole have fared well relative to Japan.

TABLE 6.5
GROWTH OF MANUFACTURED EXPORTS BY COUNTRY

Country/Region	Manufactured Exports (Millions of Dollars)			
	1962	1977	1980	1981
Periphery				
16 Countries	2,370	36,457	78,971	96,075
Hong Kong	642	7,267	18,208	20,076
Republic of Korea	10	8,480	15,722	19,188
South Africa	317	2,576	5,166	15,317
Singapore	328	3,626	10,452	11,712
Brazil	39	3,141	7,770	9,465
India	630	3,356	4,117	4,424
Mexico	122	1,182	3,389	N/A
Philippines	26	764	2,141	2,552
Kuwait	11	1,059	2,123	2,453
Malaysia	58	1,121	2,464	2,359
Thailand	21	647	1,886	1,869
Argentina	39	1,349	1,861	1,800
Turkey	4	431	782	1,748
Pakistan	97	681	1,285	1,439
Colombia	16	466	804	838
Tunisia	10	311	801	835
European semiperiphery				
Spain	205	7,214	14,967	14,320
Yugoslavia	344	3,415	6,570	8,574
Ireland	134	2,420	4,909	4,820
Portugal	205	1,420	3,322	2,961
Greece	27	1,373	2,441	2,266
Selected core				
United States	13,957	82,521	147,336	157,217
West Germany	11,623	104,361	165,447	151,043
France	5,317	48,585	81,654	73,675
United Kingdom	8,947	46,884	84,287	70,115
Japan	4,340	77,514	124,027	146,635

Source: The World Bank, *World Development Report* (1980, 1983, 1984). Oxford University Press: New York.

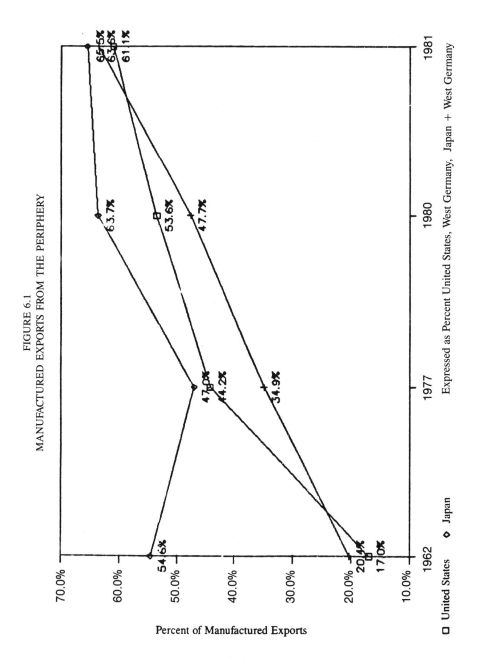

FIGURE 6.1
MANUFACTURED EXPORTS FROM THE PERIPHERY

Expressed as Percent United States, West Germany, Japan + West Germany

□ United States   ◇ Japan

The New Role of the Third World
in the World System of Trade

The traditional view of the periphery as producer and exporter of raw materials within the international division of labor needs to be revised. Table 6.6 portrays the role of the periphery in the international division of labor in 1960, 1970, and 1980. It gives the percentage of exports from the periphery for each of these years that fell into the categories of non-oil primary commodities or manufactures.[48] A transformation of the role of the periphery within the international division of labor can be observed.

As of 1960, the function of the periphery within the world trade system corresponded roughly to the classical monopoly capitalist/dependency theory description of the international division of labor. Nearly two-thirds of the exports of the periphery consisted of non-oil primary commodities, and the value of these commodities was almost six times that of manufactured exports. In the American periphery, the value of primary commodities exceed that of manufactured exports by more than a factor of twenty. Among the Asian periphery (which includes the oil exporters of the Middle East), exports of non-oil raw materials had a value three times that of manufactures.

By 1970, the relative importance of these two categories of goods had changed notably. By 1980, the classical description of the international division of labor no longer bore much resemblance to reality.

In 1980, exports of non-oil primary commodities and manufactured goods were nearly equal in value for the periphery as a whole. For the American peripheries, the ratio of non-oil primary commodities to manufactured goods had declined dramatically from more than 20-to-1 to approximately 2.5-to-1. In the Asian periphery, the value of manufactured exports had nearly doubled that of non-oil primary goods.[49]

This analysis of the transformed function of the periphery within the world trade system is supported by data for individual countries. In 1960, manufactured goods accounted for more than 50 percent of the value of exports in only one (Hong Kong) of the important peripheral exporters of manufactures. For seven of these countries manufactures were less than 10 percent of their exports. These countries as a group displayed an export profile consistent with the classical international division of labor.

From 1960 to 1981, the share of exports accounted for by manufactures rose markedly in each of the sixteen countries. By 1981, manufactured goods totalled more than 50 percent of exports in six countries. In every country, except oil-exporting Kuwait, manufactured goods had reached at least 20 percent of total exports. Once again, similar trends are evident for the five European semiperipheral countries. The provision of manufactured

TABLE 6.6
CHANGING INTERNATIONAL DIVISION OF LABOR

Percentage of Exports by Commodity Class

Region	1960		1970		1980	
	Non-Oil Primary Commodity	Manufacture	Non-Oil Primary Commodity	Manufacture	Non-Oil Primary Commodity	Manufacture
Periphery	62.3	11.7	46.7	22.2	25.1	22.5
American periphery	63.2	3.1	64.4	12.5	39.3	15.6
African periphery	84.4	10.9	58.6	11.0	39.3	7.8
Asian periphery	49.6	16.0	30.0	26.5	11.6	22.9
Core	29.0	65.7	22.2	72.8	19.6	71.9

Source: The World Bank, Commodities and Export Projection Division, *Commodity Trade and Price Trends*, 1982–83 ed. (Baltimore, Md.: Johns Hopkins University, 1982), p. 2.

goods has become an increasingly important aspect of these countries' participation in the world trade system.

So far, the data discussed have shown that manufactured exports come to play a much larger role in the world trade activity of countries previously understood as peripheral. From their perspective, manufacturing production is now a major aspect of their "insertion" in world trade. It is also true, and of historic importance, that their share of the world market in manufactures is expanding. This is not just important to the so-called peripheral or semi-peripheral countries; it is a structural feature of the new world market in manufactured goods.

While the share of the developed market economies in world exports of manufactured goods remains much larger than that of the developing market economies, a shift toward the periphery has been seen since 1960. Within each of the major industrial categories for manufactures, the share of the core declined and that of the periphery increased between 1960 and 1983.

Overall, the peripheral share of world manufactured exports rose from 5.5 percent in 1960, to 12 percent in 1983.[50] The growing presence of Third World manufactures in world trade is *not* simply a phenomenon of traditional labor intensive products such as apparel. For example, in the category "Machinery," exports from developing market economies zoomed from from less than 1 percent (0.7 percent) of total world exports in 1960, to 7.7 percent in 1983. The logic of global capitalism indicates that the surge of manufactured exports from the periphery should have the old industrial "core" as a primary destination. Indeed, the selective migration of manufacturing capital from the core to the periphery is and was largely aimed at reducing the cost of manufactured products destined for the markets of the core—a strategy of market share retention in a competitive world economy.

As of 1979, nine of the sixteen peripheral countries and three of the five European semiperipheral countries listed in Table 6.6 sent more than 60 percent of their manufactured exports to "industrial market" or core countries. More than 70 percent of the manufactured exports of Hong Kong, South Korea, South Africa, Mexico, Philippines, Turkey, and Tunisia are consumed in the industrial market economies.[51]

Many of these Third World manufactured exports are one component of a production process that has been disaggregated to distant locations around the globe. A recent study published by the Brookings Institution finds that "about a quarter of imports of manufactures from developing countries" to the United States are "U. S. products and components that come back to the United States."[52] The same study found that European and Japanese firms, as well as U. S. firms, utilize Third World assembly locations extensively for reexport to third country core markets.[53] Such behavior is precisely consistent with the return of price competition and falling profit rates in the older industrial regions characteristic of the transition to global capitalism.

Under global capitalism then, a transformation occurs in the international division of labor. Peripheral and semiperipheral economies increasingly perform the function of providing manufactured goods for consumption in core markets.

A Sectoral View of Peripheral Industrialization and the New International Division of Labor

Szymanski studied in statistical detail the nature of Third World industrialization. He concluded that

> ...the economic growth of the less-developed capitalist countries is centered in the manufaturing sector; within the manufacturing sector it is centered in heavy industry; heavy industry represents a considerable share of the total manufacturing sector; and the sectoral distribution within the manufacturing sector between the developed and the less-developed capitalist countries is being undermined along with the overall traditional agrarian-industrial specialization between them.[54]

The wide variety of industries where developing country exports now constitute an important share of world trade is striking. In heavy industry, such as the production of pig iron (19 percent) and in high-tech electronic industries (30 to 35 percent) as well as more traditional light industries such as clothing and leather (38 percent, 22 percent), developing countries have taken their place in world trade.[55] A Brookings Institution study of "production sharing" found that the most significant groups of products imported under U. S. tariff items 806/07 were motor vehicles and parts and semiconductors and parts.[56]

The sectors where the periphery has become important as an exporter of manufactures correspond closely to those where production has been relocated from the core. This also supports the contention that the changing function of the periphery within the world trade system results from the mobility of capital *from* the core, a critical aspect of the transition to global capitalism. The periphery has assumed a new role in world trade largely due to decisions taken by global firms to relocate production to sites offering more favorable conditions of capital accumulation.

A Qualifying Note

Despite the historical significance of the new international division of labor, its implications must not be overgeneralized. More than 90 percent of the manufactured exports from the periphery originated in only sixteen countries. The five leading peripheral exporters of manufactures account for approximately three-fourths of all manufactured exports originating in the periphery.

For the vast majority of peripheral countries, mineral and agricultural raw materials remain their principal export. More than sixty peripheral countries remain primarily dependent upon raw material exports for their export earnings. A sizable number of Third World economies continue to be highly dependent upon one or two such commmodities. Subsaharan Africa, with the exception of the Republic of South Africa, has been virtually excluded from the new international division of labor.[57]

Although the conditions of capital accumulation in the core drive global firms to relocate production to low-wage sites, not all Third World sites meet the required conditions of social, political, and physical infrastructure favorable to capital. And among those states that do, there is a fierce competition to attract investment.

Many volunteer for inclusion in the new international division of labor of global capitalism, but under the logic of the system, few are chosen.

Summary

The transition to global capitalism brings about a new international division of labor. The periphery assumes a new role as an exporter of manufactured goods. Despite its historical significance, the new system excludes many peripheral countries.

THE COSTS AND CONSTRAINTS OF GLOBAL CAPITALISM IN THE THIRD WORLD

While global capitalism produces industrialization in the periphery, it may not, and often does not lead to improvements in human welfare in the newly industrializing countries.

Szymanski showed that rapid industrialization in the Third World has been associated with a general reduction in the quality of the diet of the majority of people and a tendency for income inequality among classes to grow.[58] Other studies have supported the relationship between manufacturing growth or penetration by multinational corporations (MNCs) and income inequality.[59] Frobel et al. document the low wages, long hours and high intensity of work, physical and mental exhaustion that prevails among workers, typically women aged sixteen to twenty-four, who labor in the free trade zones so attractive to global firms.[60] A burgeoning literature has established the particularly exploitative conditions under which Third World women labor in the new global industries.[61] Kentor has linked "overurbanization" in the periphery with its consequent squatter settlements, high levels of unem-

ployment, and teeming mass of peddlers, to dependence upon foreign investment by transnational corporations.[62]

These and other findings about the costs of industrialization in the
Third World are consistent with our model of global capitalism. The logic
of global capital mobility dictates that the conditions of workers, both
employed and unemployed, in the periphery remain marked by poverty,
malnutrition, and vulnerability.

Manufacturing capital has been attracted to the Third World precisely
because the work force receives low wages, has few rights, and offers little
threat to the interests of capital. While such investment may provide some
additional jobs at wages that are attractive by the standards of the local labor
market, any consequential change in the local wage rate or the degree of
militancy among the working class can send global capital in search of new
more attractive sites for production.

"Development" programs that are premised upon entry to the capitalist
global economy are policies whose success depends upon maintaining a
work force that is "attractive" to investors who scan the globe looking for
the most lucrative opportunities. Global firms have many choices when
locating production in the periphery. Competition among sites is keen.
Remaining competitive usually means that the state enforce discipline and
austerity on the working class.

Global capitalism also promotes political authoritarianism in the
periphery.[63] The choices open to Third World states are severely
constrained.

Global investors frequently cite stability as a principal factor affecting
their locational decisions. Given that low wages, growing income inequality,
and high levels of unemployment are typical outcomes of industrialization in
the periphery, the possibilities for political instability are high. Democratic
regimes, which in the Third World typically come to power through a
populist alliance of workers, peasants, and small local capital, are ill-suited
to the maintenance of favorable investment conditions. Democratic populist
or progressive regimes such as that of Manley in Jamaica or Alfonsin in
Argentina have little chance for long-term survival. Domestically, their
political life depends upon their capacity to deliver better economic conditions to their constituency of workers, peasants, and small local capital.
Attempts to achieve these goals, however, are met typically by the
withdrawal or withholding of investment by global firms, credit denial by
the International Monetary Fund (IMF) and global banks, and economic and
political pressures by core states.

In the global mosaic, the Third World economy governed by a populist
government becomes an unattractive investment site. Alternatives are
available. Either the populists must agree to alter policies and impose

austerity and discipline or investment and credit will be withheld. And even if assent is not given, the economic conditions that obtain upon the withdrawal and denial of capital and credit by the global firms and banks generally lead to the forced adoption of an austerity program. Under these contradictions, the populist regime tends to disintegrate and replacement by military-backed authoritarian government is a high probability.

Even conservative improvements in wage and working conditions can decrease the attractiveness of an investment site. The same is true of modest moves toward greater economic nationalism. In recent years, for example, wage increases in Singapore and Hong Kong have led investors to look increasingly to Thailand, Malaysia, the Philippines, and other Asian countries as sites for investment.[64]

Ensuring social stability, restricting the rights of workers, facilitating a lid on wages, and repressing leftist movements are tasks that the state must perform in those periphery economies that are included in the new international division of labor. Authoritarian states in which the military directly exercises state power, or supports actively those in power, are best able to impose this combination of economic austerity and political stability.

As industrial capitalism in the periphery matures, its contradictions become more acute.

As we noted above, the industrial working class in the Third World and the semiperiphery has grown substantially in the past two decades. As this tendency continues, one can expect that industrial working-class politics will become more central than peasant politics to the forces of opposition in these countries. Given the exclusionary nature of Third World industrialization, the absence of participatory means of legitimizing state power, and the failure of populist governments, it seems likely that political support for socialist alternatives will grow.

In the meantime, the New Leviathan will continue to restructure peripheral economies bringing industrialization and a new role in the global economy but leaving in its wake poverty, increasing inequality, malnutrition, and political oppression.

Reprise and Prospect

This chapter has shown that the structure of world manufacturing production and trade was transformed between 1960 and 1980 in ways that the theories of monopoly capitalism and world systems analysis did not anticipate. Together as the Monthly Review school of thought, they had in common a view of the world division of labor which projected an industrial "stagnation thesis" for the Third World. Yet, the material reviewed here shows that First World production capital uses major fractions of the Third World as part of its competitive strategy. Rapid industrialization has been part of the Third World experience of the last quarter century; industrial decline has appeared in the First World.

This lengthy analysis has now brought us back to our early and continuing theme: power in modern capitalism. That investors based in the older industrial regions can and do make use of investment sites where labor is poorly compensated and politically feeble has direct relevance to industrial and political relations in those older regions. The next chapters analyze Detroit, New York City, and Massachusetts: in each region and for the industries centered there, the internationalization of capital has proven to be of central importance.

7

The Monopoly Sector in the Core: The Crisis of Detroit

DETROIT AND THE ERA OF MONOPOLY CAPITALISM

Introduction: Detroit and the American Way of Life

For most of the twentieth century, the industrial heartland of the United States lay in a region defined by the great cities of Buffalo, Pittsburgh, St. Louis, Minneapolis, Milwaukee, Cleveland, and Detroit. Most of the country's and much of the world's steel, machines, rubber, electrical machinery, and automobiles were made by the men and women working in the factories of this region. Although the region experienced hard times during the periodic recessions that plagued the U. S. economy during the century, the period from the end of the World War II through the late 1960s was one of unprecedented prosperity and the future seemed to promise even greater accomplishments and wealth for the residents of the industrial heartland.

The automobile industry was the engine driving this growth. By the 1950s, total passenger car production in the automobile industry had reached 5 or 6 million units annually.[1] In the postwar period, the industry has been estimated to have been responsible for one-fourth of the value of all retail sales, the economic health of one in six businesses, and the jobs of one in six American workers.[2] When Charles Wilson, a former president of General Motors serving President Eisenhower as Secretary of Defense, claimed that what was good for GM was good for the country, he offended the protocols of American ideology, but not the conventional data.

In the midst of the auto-industrial heartland, Detroit was the home of the automobile industry. From 1949 to 1952, the Detroit metropolitan region accounted for more than 40 percent of automobile employment in the United States. Even as late 1958, Detroit's auto workers were more than 30 percent of total U. S. motor vehicle employees.[3] Detroit's centrality to the automoble industry made it the hub of a great regional complex. "Connected to Detroit through transportation and communication networks are the rubber plants of Akron, Ohio, and Kitchener, Ontario; the metal foundries of Chicago and Cleveland; the machine tool shops of Cincinnati, Ohio, and Windsor, Ontario; the steel industries of Gary, Indiana, and Buffalo, New York; and the electronics and hydraulic research laboratories of Columbus and Dayton, Ohio."[4]

Detroit was the productive heart of the American way of life. In turn, the conditions of life and labor in the Detroit region were the exemplars of the success of American capitalism. In the home of the automobile industry, a middle-income stratum of working-class Americans consumed the goods and services of what was once the highest standard of living in the world.

Understanding Detroit:
Understanding the Global System

In the early 1980s, Detroit suffered severe decline—crisis—from which it has not fully recovered. It is our view that crisis and change in the Detroit region can be situated in the context of the reorganization of capitalism on a world scale that is the central theme of this book. More specifically, Detroit's recent history is a consequence of the transformation of the automobile industry from one dominated by monopoly sector firms and the social relations characteristic of monopoly capitalism to an industry dominated by global firms and the social relations characteristic of global capitalism. As this restructuring of the automobile industry took shape, the economy of the Detroit region and the situation of its wage workers were also transformed. The crisis of Detroit was part of the transition of the automobile sector from monopoly to global capitalism.

In adopting this perspective, we do not deny that some portion of the job loss, unemployment, growing demand for public services and governmental fiscal crisis in the Detroit region was accounted for by the cyclical recession of the early 1980s. Indeed, in our view, the recent world depression was the executor of structural change.[5] For more than a decade, the rate of expansion of the capitalist world economy had been slowing, and this could not fail to have impact upon both the automobile industry and Detroit.[6] But underlying the cyclical aspects of Detroit's troubles were structural trends. The reorganization of social forces yielded a reorganization of space and change in the role of the Detroit region within world capitalism.

We proceed by analyzing changes in the capital-to-capital and capital-to-labor relations in the automobile industry as well as the capital-to-state relations in the Detroit region. In each case, we seek to illustrate the ways in which the emergence of global capitalism has transformed the relations that characterized monopoly capitalism in the Detroit region. Finally, we consider the changing economic geography of Detroit in light of these developments, the 1983–84 recovery of the U. S. economy and the U. S. automobile firms, and the trends since that time.

THE AUTOMOBILE INDUSTRY
AND THE CRISIS OF DETROIT
AS A CASE IN THE TRANSITION
FROM MONOPOLY TO GLOBAL CAPITALISM

Detroit and the Automobile Industry and the Era of Monopoly Capitalism

In Chapter 3, we outlined the basic propositions of the theory of monopoly capitalism. During the period of postwar prosperity, Detroit and the automobile industry exhibited the features described by that model:

- The industry was concentrated, and it enjoyed above average profits.
- Auto workers were protected by a powerful union and they earned wages and benefits that were above the national average and were rising in real terms.
- Detroit exhibited tendencies toward suburbanization of production and of the residences of both corporate executives and workers analyzed by O'Connor.[7]
- As the center of the industry, the Detroit metropolitan region, if not all of the central city, shared in the prosperity of the industry.

According to the monopoly capitalist conception, capital-to-capital relations are marked by the concentrated control of several large firms, the elimination of price competition, the stability of market shares among firms, the achievement of monopoly rates of profit, and the domination of the global market by U. S.-based firms. Each of these points applied to the automobile industry.

By the early 1930s, the Big Three—GM, Ford, and Chrysler—had taken control of nearly 90 percent of the U. S. domestic market, and they retained this commanding presence until the 1970s.[8] Moreover, the market shares of Ford and GM remained remarkably stable over these four decades. GM consistently accounted for between 43 and 51 percent of sales, and Ford maintained a 22 to 29 percent share.[9] With the establishment of concentrated and stable market shares came the displacement of price competition by product differentiation. Consumers were the target of dazzling and scientifically crafted advertisements for an array of different models, more powerful engines, and sundry optional accessories.[10]

The major U. S. firms also moved to a position of dominance within a growing international market for automobiles. In 1950, more than three-fourths of world production of motor vehicles took place in the United States. As late as 1960, GM and Ford together maintained a combined world market share of nearly 50 percent.

Finally, the monopoly structure and the elimination of price competition proved extremely profitable for the Big Three auto firms. GM, Ford, and Chrysler averaged, between 1946 and 1967, a return of 16.7 percent on net worth, a figure nearly twice the average rate of return for manufacturing corporations in the United States during the same period.[11]

The work force in the automobile industry and the Detroit region exhibited features consistent with the descriptions of the capital-to-labor relationship found in the theoretical tradition of monopoly capitalism. It was highly unionized, and both auto workers and others in the regional labor force received premium wages.

O'Connor's discussion of the way geographic concentration of large production facilities produces high degrees of unionization applied to the Detroit region. The spatial concentration of automobile production around Detroit produced a powerful union—the United Automobile Workers (UAW)—and a highly unionized work force throughout the region. In 1964, for example, union membership in Michigan was 42.7 percent ot total nonagricultural employment while comparable figures for Ohio and Indiana were 36.7 and 36.4 percent, each well above the 1964 national average of 29.5 percent.[12]

As the model of monopoly capitalism also suggests, the UAW was able to secure premium wages for its members. Wages of U. S. automobile workers have, since 1950, always been more than 120 percent of average manufacturing wages (see Table 7.4). And, until the late 1970s, auto workers' wages rose in real purchasing power, allowing a standard of living for manual laborers unrivalled in the world, and central to the legitimating ideology of American capitalism. In the Detroit SMSA, meanwhile, the power of the union had a drafting effect even among workers in employment categories with less powerful unions. Both unskilled plant workers and clerks in Detroit enjoyed wages well above the national average.[13]

The theory of monopoly capitalism worked well as a model for understanding the political economy of the automobile industry and the Detroit region for the period from the founding of the industry until about 1970. Both at the level of capital-to-capital and capital-to-labor relationships the data correspond well with projections which would be derived from the writings of Baran, Sweezy, and O'Connor.

But through the 1970s and 1980s the global auto industry and its Detroit center were restructured. One part of this process was broadly anticipated by all models of modern capitalism—the drastic substitution of machines for labor. But one of the central aspects of the global restructuring of the auto industry—the widespread practice of global sourcing and the employment of low cost, low-wage export platforms—was new.

Capital-to-Capital Relations
in the Automobile Industry

For most of the industry's history, competitive conditions in the U. S. automobile industry corresponded closely to those depicted by the theory of
monopoly capitalism. The U. S. economy *was* hegemonic and U. S.
automobile firms *were* dominant within the global economy. Stable market
shares and the absence of price competition *were* normal to the industry.
But none of these aspects of the capital-to-capital relation are now unambig-
uously characteristic of the world system of automobile production and
investment.

Decline of Hegemony. The era of monopoly capitalism coincided with
U. S. hegemony in the world auto industry. While this was once true, a
drastic erosion of the U. S. position has occurred over the past twenty-five
years.[14] The U. S. share of world motor vehicle production declined from
48.3 percent in 1960 to 27.9 percent in 1970. In 1980, the Japanese share
of world production surpassed that of the United States. By 1982, U. S.
domestic production had fallen to 19 percent of world production while
Japanese domestic production had reached 29 percent.[15] Even after Japan's
"voluntary export restraints" and the "recovery" of the U. S. automobile
industry, in 1984, Japanese production commanded a larger world share
than did U. S. industry, Western Europe was on a par with both, and Third
World producers had attained a world market share which Japan achieved
during the 1960s.[16]

When examined from the point of view of the world market shares of
U. S. firms, including their overseas production, a slightly different story is
indicated: the world market shares of the big two recover from their precipitous fall, even though U. S.-based production declined. From 1965 to
1970, both GM and Ford suffered sharp declines in their world market
shares. The data, show that GM's world share dropped from almost 30 percent to 18 percent while Ford's share fell from nearly 19 percent to just
more than 16 percent. After 1970, GM's situation stabilized, but Ford continued to lose ground. By 1981, Ford had fallen below a 12 percent market
share. Combined, the two largest U. S. automakers averaged a loss of more
than 1 percent of the world market per year between 1965 and 1981 as they
declined from 48.4 percent to 30 percent of the world sales.[17] From either a
country or a firm perspective, U. S. hegemony in the automobile industry
was coming to an end in the early 1980s. By 1984, Ford and GM recovered
slightly, returning to 32 percent. By then they had become thoroughly
internationalized.

Change in market share. Stable market shares were another feature of monopoly capitalism that no longer prevails in the world automobile industry. While the recent fate of GM and Ford provide some evidence of this development, world production data by corporation emphasize it. Between 1972 and 1979, eight of the twelve largest automakers significantly improved their position with Peugeot (+3.9 percent), Toyota (+1.3 percent), and Nissan (+1.2 percent) leading the way. In contrast to these gains, Chrysler (−4.6 percent), Ford (−2.1 percent) and British Leyland (−1.4 percent) lost substantial market shares. In the next three years, the decline of world market share of Ford and GM intensified (−1.8 percent and −2.3 percent, respectively), while Toyota and Nissan gained world share again (+1.8 percent and +1.3 percent, respectively); Volkswagen recovered past their 1972 share (to 7.1 percent), Peugeot was stable, and Renault gained.[18]

Through 1982, a continued churning in the world marketplace for automobiles was favoring Japanese over American producers, then it stabilized for Ford and GM. The trend was less systematically describable for Europe-based firms.

Since 1982, however, new low-end entrants have appeared: the Koreans, led by Hyundai and Daewoo, and the Yugoslavians (bringing the *Yugo* to North America). The restructuring of the market is not merely a matter of decline for North America and rise for the Japanese; it includes volatility (i.e., inconsistent changes) among the European makers and new entrants who take advantage of their low labor costs.

The decline of U. S. hegemony among competing capitals was reflected in the U. S. market. From 1970 to 1982, the foreign import share of the market nearly doubled. From a level of less than 15 percent in 1976, imports rose to more than 27 percent by 1982. Among the imports, meanwhile, changes in market share were also rapid. Between 1970 and 1982, Japanese imports moved from a position where they accounted for only one-fourth of imported passenger vehicles to a position where four out of every five imports sold in the United States were from Japan. By 1986, Korean and Yugoslavian products had replaced those from Japan at the lowest end of the U. S. import market, and Japanese makers, constrained by "voluntary restraints" had moved upscale, their share of imports falling below 78 percent. Market shares in the United States, the home base of the former global hegemonists Ford and GM and the world's largest market, had become unstable.[19]

The return of price competition. Finally, price competition, which Baran and Sweezy see as virtually absent under monopoly capitalism, appears to have returned to the automobile industry. Discussions of cost advantages and price competition dominate recent analyses of the industry. Explanations of the Japanese penetration of the U. S. market have emphasized their cost advantages in comparison to American producers—a cost advantage that was estimated in 1981 to be $1500 per automobile.[20] A major U. S. government study maintained that fuel efficiency, perceived quality, and price have been the factors enabling foreign, and in particular Japanese, firms to penetrate the U. S. market. The study concluded:

> Given the present price structure, the Japanese automakers can be assured of greater profit margins on each unit sale, giving them *significant flexibility to undercut prices* on comparable U. S. cars *to retain market share*. This is particularly important in view of projections that show a maturing world market with a potential overcapacity of auto production. *In that competitive climate, value for price will be a key determinant of world market share.* (Emphasis added).[21]

In a concentrated market, producer cost advantage may not necessarily lead to price competition. But by the mid-1980s, however, there were at least three indications that this is what in fact had occurred. First, despite the received wisdom about the difficulties of market entry in such a capital intensive and politically sensitive industry, Korean and Yugoslavian entrants had forced their way into the market on the basis of low price, based on cheap labor. Second, through major periods in 1985 and 1986, the North American market saw a ferocious round of price competition in the form of below-market financing incentives. And third, as would be predicted in a price competitive environment, profit rates among car makers declined.[22]

Summary. Dramatic changes in the relationships among automobile firms have occurred in the past fifteen years. Once a classic monopoly capitalist industry where price competition had disappeared, market shares were stable, and the U. S. economy and U. S. firms exercised market hegemony, the automobile industry now includes evidence of price competition among global firms of different national origins and change, and in some cases, instability in market shares. Capital-to-capital relations in the automobile industry no longer correspond to those depicted in the model of monopoly capitalism. For Detroit in particular, where American makers are locally concentrated, this means lower employment levels.

Capital-to-Labor Relations: Global Capital Mobility as The New Lever of Exploitation in the Automobile Industry

Throughout much of the postwar period, U. S. auto workers have been able to defend their jobs and improve their standards of living. Despite fluctuations related to short-term recessionary cycles, total nationwide motor vehicle employment expanded from 1949 to 1978, reaching a peak of more than one million employees in the latter year. Moreover, U. S. auto workers were able to improve their real wages by 48 percent between 1958 and 1978 (see Table 7.4). Auto workers' wages were also favorable relative to other workers in the U. S. economy. As Table 7.4 shows, they improved their position relative to average wages in manufacturing in this period. As monopoly sector workers, U. S. auto workers had achieved both the strategic power and the economic condition ascribed to such workers by the theory of monopoly capitalism.

For much of this period, the U. S. automobile firms agreed to or tolerated the growing material well-being of their production workers. Despite the increasing real wages of their workers and the expanding size of their domestic labor force, automobile capital was able to increase its rate of surplus extraction and maintain adequate rates of capital accumulation. As demonstrated, GM, Ford, and Chrysler enjoyed high rates of profit.

The production strategy of rationalization served U. S. automobile firms well during this era. The introduction of new technologies of production and the improvement of existing ones led to an increase of 4 percent per annum in labor productivity throughout the 1950s and 1960s.[23] Labor productivity increased even more rapidly than did wages. Therefore, capital in the automobile industry was able to increase its rate of surplus extraction despite the wage increases being gained by labor. The cost to capital of each worker may have been increasing but the labor cost per unit produced was declining.

The monopolistic structure of the industry also facilitated the economic success of the U. S. auto firms during this period. Their monopoly market power meant that GM, Ford, and Chrysler could administer or set prices in relation to costs. Their monopoly bargaining power with competitive sector suppliers provided another means for ensuring adequate rates of capital accumulation.

By the 1970s, however, the evidence suggests that the U. S. automobile industry began to experience a decline in the rate of profit throughout the industry.[24] We account for this in several ways.

That the world motor vehicle market expanded rapidly from 1950 until the early 1970s helps to explain the timing of this development. The world market grew so rapidly that U. S. auto firms expanded the size of their work force even as labor productivity was rising. Around 1973 however, the size of the world market began to stagnate. At the same time the share of that market held by U. S. firms began to shrink; U. S. auto profits declined.[25]

Among the consequences of a decline in the sectoral rate of profit is the relative withdrawal of finance capital from that industry. Banks and other lending institutions in the private sector become less willing to make capital available to firms in the ailing industry. In the auto industry, this tendency reached a crisis when private financial interests refused to continue lending to Chrysler without a state guarantee of the investment.

Concomitant with declining rates of profit, the U. S. automobile industry also faced the reemergence of price competition discussed earlier. This eroded their monopoly pricing power and further limited their ability to achieve adequate rates of capital accumulation. Foreign competition induced an emphasis upon cost-cutting and cost-control strategies as a means of recovery and survival.

By the early 1970s, costs, particularly labor costs, had to be controlled if they were to compete in price terms with foreign producers. Wages had to be controlled if profit rates were to be restored to acceptable levels. Yet the national and regional power of labor in areas such as Detroit where the industry was concentrated presented a potent obstacle. A new lever for reducing labor costs, exercising more control over labor, and increasing the rate of surplus extraction was needed.

An accelerated mobility of U. S. automobile capital within a global context became the new lever of exploitation.

Capital-to-Labor Relations: Evidence of the Global Mobility of U. S. Auto Capital

That U. S. automobile capital pursued a strategy of international mobility as a means of reducing direct labor costs can be shown in several ways. During the 1970s, U. S. automobile firms began directing substantial percentages of their investment in new plant and equipment toward foreign affiliates. They also made more frequent use of global sourcing. Proportionately larger shares of their worldwide production moved to offshore sites.

Data on foreign investment in new plant and equipment of U. S. firms making transportation equipment are a somewhat broader category than motor vehicles and equipment, but the data are suggestive.[26] In 1970, investment in plant and equipment in foreign affiliates in transportation equipment exceeded $1 billion annually for the first time in history. Even more significantly, investment in foreign affiliates rose from 13 percent of total expenditure on plant and equipment in 1966, to 18 percent in 1970, and it reached 22 percent in 1981. By 1984, the five-year average was 19 percent compared to the average of 14 percent between 1966 and 1970.

The surge in foreign investment was related to two trends in the prior years. Between 1966 and 1970, profits declined dramatically throughout the industry, and over the same period the foreign import share of the U. S. market doubled from less than 8 percent to nearly 15 percent.[27] The next marked upsurge in capital expenditures in foreign affiliates occurred between the end of 1978 and the first half of 1982, the height of the crisis for U. S. automobile capital. In current dollars, such investment grew from $1.9 billion in 1978 to $5.2 billion in 1981. As a proportion of total capital expenditures, the foreign affiliate share moved from 14 percent to 22 percent over the same years. Once again, this followed several years of rapid increase in the foreign import share of the U. S. market. Moreover, it came at the end of nine consecutive years in which the profit rates of automobile manufacturers lagged behind the national average for manufacturing corporations.[28]

By 1982, as we will see in the next section, auto capital was in a position to use their rapidly developing investment mobility to extract significant concessions from their U. S. domestic labor force. In the aftermath of this successful effort to contain labor costs in the United States, they then slowed somewhat the relative percentage of investment devoted to overseas affiliates. Nonetheless, capital expenditure overseas by U. S. firms in transportation equipment remains historically high both in current dollar terms and as a percentage of total capital investment.

In summary, between 1970 and 1984, U. S. firms in the transportation equipment sector dramatically increased their investment in overseas plant and equipment. Moreover, by looking at the five-year moving averages (designed to smooth out fluctuations related to short-term cycles), we observe a gradual increase of capital expenditure in foreign affiliates relative to total capital expenditure. This development appears related both to a declining rate of profit and to rising price competition from foreign imports. It also provides evidence of the accelerated global mobility of U. S. automobile capital.

The 1970s shift of production by U. S. automobile capital to offshore, lower-wage sites is illustrated by Table 7.1. The data in that table show that the ratio of U. S. domestic production of motor vehicles to Latin American production—by U. S. firms—declined rapidly. Between 1973 and 1980, the U. S. to Latin America ratio of GM declined from 28.8-to-1 to 14-to-1; for Ford from 12.1-to-1 to 4.5-to-1; and for Chrysler from 14.2-to-1 to 6.4-to-1. Overall, by 1980, 37.2 percent of the total motor vehicle production of the four leading U. S. automobile firms was located abroad.[29]

Global sourcing can be understood as another form of capital mobility. Previously, we have defined it as both a cost-cutting strategy which locates segments of production in low-wage and/or high-subsidy areas, and a

TABLE 7.1
U. S. AUTOMOBILE FIRMS:
MOTOR VEHICLE PRODUCTION AND ASSEMBLY IN THE UNITED STATES AND LATIN AMERICA
1973–1980
(THOUSANDS OF VEHICLES)

Year	General Motors			Ford			Chrysler		
	U. S.	Latin America	Ratio: U. S./ Latin America	U. S.	Latin America	Ratio: U. S./ Latin America	U. S.	Latin America	Ratio: U. S./ Latin America
1973	6,514	226	28.8	3,443	284	12.1	2,217	156	14.2
1974	4,673	280	16.7	3,098	327	9.5	1,789	176	10.2
1975	4,650	259	18.0	2,500	299	8.4	1,508	174	8.7
1976	6,234	266	23.4	2,942	305	9.6	2,105	176	12.0
1977	6,700	243	27.6	3,745	300	12.5	2,038	156	13.1
1978	6,876	294	23.4	3,790	338	11.2	1,870	157	11.9
1979	6,445	318	20.3	3,075	395	7.8	1,429	169	8.5
1980	4,753	340	14.0	1,888	417	4.5	883	137	6.4

Latin America Percent Big Three U. S. Production: 1973 — 5.5 percent; 1980 — 11.9 percent.

Source: United Nations Centre on Transnational Corporations, *Transnational Corporations in the International Automobile Industry* (New York: United Nations, 1983), pp. 102, 191.

response to local content requirements created by governments.[30] By creating options throughout the globe for the production of components and parts, global sourcing becomes a strategy for controlling labor costs. That the practice of global sourcing became the norm in the late 1970s is suggested by a sampling of decisions by U. S.-based automobile firms to manufacture components in foreign subsidiaries shown in Table 7.2.

These examples are amplified by the history of automotive exports from Argentina, Mexico, and Brazil. Over a fifteen year period ending in 1979 to 1980, the value of exported parts from these countries grew by over 1,200 percent.[31] By 1979 to 1980, the value of automotive parts exported from

TABLE 7.2

FOREIGN SOURCING: COMMITMENTS BY U. S. AUTO MAKERS
TO MANUFACTURE COMPONENTS IN FOREIGN SUBSIDIARIES
FOR USE IN DOMESTIC PRODUCTION: LATE 1970S

Auto Maker	Component	Components per Year	Source
GM	2.8 liter V–6	400,000	GM de Mexico
GM	1.8 liter L–4	250,000	GM de Brazil
GM	THM automatic transmission	250,000	GM Strasbourg
Ford	2.2 liter 1–4	400,000	Ford–Mexico
Ford	Diesel L–4	150,000	Toyo Kogyo[a]
Ford	2.3 Liter L–4	50,000	Ford–Brazil
Ford	Manual Transaxles	100,000	Toyo Kogyo[a]
Ford	Aluminum Cylinder Heads	———	Ford–Mexico
Chrysler	L–6 and V–8 engines	100,000	Chrysler de Mexico
Chrysler	2.2 Liter L–4	270,000	Chrysler de Mexico
AMC/Renault	Car components, power train	300,000	Renault in France and Mexico
VW of America	Radiators, stumpings	250,000	VW de Mexico
VW of America	L–4 diesel, gas	300,000	VW de Mexico

[a]Ford Motor owns 25 percent of Toyo Kogyo.

Source: U. S. Department of Transportation, Office of the Assistant Secretary for Policy and International Affairs, *The U.S. Automobile Industry, 1980*, (Washington, D.C.: U. S. Government Printing Office) January 1981, p. 56.

these three countries totalled more than 470 million.[32] Forecasts projected a further dramatic increase in the flow of parts and components from Mexico to assembly sites in the United States.[33]

As a consequence of the internationalization of production, capital expenditure, and sourcing, the work force of the U. S. automobile firms had become global in composition. A 1977 survey by the U. S. Department of Commerce reported that 38 percent of the employees of the U. S. multi-nationals that produce motor vehicles and equipment were employees of their foreign affiliates.[34]

These data are a glimpse of the internationalization of U. S. automobile firms as they entered the 1980s. They provide evidence that U. S. auto capital became increasingly mobile during the 1970s. We infer that this accelerated mobility was a strategic response to both falling profits and a resurgence of price competition in the world motor vehicle industry.

Together the decline in profit rates and the need to compete in price terms translated into a need for U. S. auto firms to devise strategies for containing labor costs. Moving phases of the production process (for example, the fabrication of engines and transmissions) to lower-wage sites such as Brazil, Mexico, and Argentina provided a direct means of labor cost control. In older sites of production this resulted, as we shall see, in plant closings and job loss. The global shift in the location of auto capital was converted into a lever for extracting concessions from labor in the old industrial heartland of the United States. That perhaps 40 percent of their employer's work force was already offshore by 1982 could not fail to affect the strategic position and bargaining power of U. S. auto workers.

Capital-to-Labor Relations: The Use of Capital Mobility as a Lever of Exploitation in the 1982 Labor Negotiations in the Automobile Industry

Faced with an imperative to lower direct labor costs and armed with their enhanced global mobility as a strategic lever, both Ford and GM moved during 1981 to pressure the UAW to agree to an unprecedented early opening of both national contracts. Building on the position that had been advanced during the Chrysler bailout negotiations, Ford and GM demanded concessions from their production workers. They claimed these were needed in order to protect their market position in relation to foreign producers who enjoyed lower labor costs. The negotiations with GM provide a clear instance of the use of capital mobility as a lever to extract concessions despite the determined resistance of the UAW.

After resisting for almost a year, UAW's executive council finally capitulated in December 1981 and voted to open talks with both auto companies.[35] Negotiations with Ford proceeded fairly rapidly, and in March 1982, a new Ford contract granting $1 billion of concessions in exchange for a two-year guaranteed freeze on plant closings was signed.[36] In contrast, GM's efforts to realize even greater concessions were resisted.

In January 1982, talks with GM were suspended amid strident disagreement. The union's attitude at this point was expressed by UAW President Douglas Fraser as follows, "It's almost unethical to make greater concessions to a company that made $333 million than to one that lost $1 billion."[37]

Yet on March 11, 1982, UAW's GM Council voted overwhelmingly to once again open talks with the industry leader. What happened to bring about such an abrupt reversal in the union position? In February 1982, GM, citing lower labor costs abroad, announced plans to close eight more plants in the United States. With 145,000 workers on indefinite layoff, the vote was 299 to 15 in favor of resuming negotiations.[38]

In late March, the talks between GM and the UAW again stalled. As if to remind union leaders of their strategic leverage, GM chose this time period to announce that it was considering plans for building a new engine plant in Mexico.[39] By the end of April, a new contract, containing greater concessions than had been granted Ford, was ratified. These included the elimination, for two and one-half years, of the annual wage increases that have been a standard feature of UAW contracts for more than three decades; the deferral of three quarterly cost-of-living adjustments (COLAs); and the elimination of nine paid holidays. In addition, the union conceded to GM new procedures allowing the company to open, unilaterally, work-rule and wage agreements with local unions. For its part, GM agreed not to close four of the plants it had announced in February as well as to some limitations on future plant closings. In effect, the union and its members traded some limited job security for reductions in total compensation and workplace power.[40]

In the period leading up to the ratification of the contract by the UAW, there emerged an effort by dissident local union leaders—Locals Opposed to Concessions—to organize against the proposed concessions. They had limited success. As Douglas Stevens, a leader of the dissident group, recounts, the global mobility of GM and the consequent threat to move was quite effective in convincing workers to accept the preferred terms:

> In the Parts Division, there was a lot more pressure on, and our work was much harder. We'd go to them and say, "Look, concessions are not the answer." But GM had scared them to death already. It is mostly parts work which has been leaving the country, rather than car assembly, and so these locals felt rather vulnerable and panicked. GM would say to them, "Look,

we can build what you build anywhere. We can build it in Taiwan, with cheap labor. We can go to Brazil, to Mexico, to any other place we want to go. There's no way you can stop us, unless you agree to concessions."[41]

As Steven's comments make clear, union leaders and rank-and-file members perceive the way in which GM's enhanced global mobility undermines their bargaining power.

The 1982 negotiations in the autombile industry have been termed historic by many commentators. As these observers correctly note, they marked both the first time that UAW members agreed to give back benefits previously won and an effort by the U. S. automobile industry to adjust to competition from foreign producers. In our view, the historic significance of the 1982 negotiations goes even deeper. They provide evidence of the restructuring of the U. S. automobile industry from an industry where the social relations of monopoly capitalism prevailed to one where the social relations of global capitalism predominate.

Capital-to-Labor Relations: the Impact of Global Capitalism on U. S. Auto Workers

The 1982 negotiations were symptomatic of the enhanced strategic power of auto capital in its relations with production workers in the industry. As the automobile industry made the transition from monopoly capitalism to global capitalism, the relative balance of class power between capital and labor was transformed. Labor became less able to defend and capital became less willing to tolerate the wage bill characteristic of the primary segment of labor during the monopoly era. This shift in the balance of class power had at least two observable forms: a loss of job security and a stagnation/ decline in real wages.

Job loss and rising rates of unemployment both translate into a loss of job security for workers. As Table 7.3 shows, in the motor vehicles industry, job loss since 1978 in the United States has been severe. From 1978 to the depth of the crisis in 1982, nearly 270,000 *production* jobs (not shown in the table) in the industry disappeared. Unemployment in the motor vehicle industry averaged 17 percent between 1980 and 1983.[42] Perhaps one-half of this job loss must be attributed to the national and worldwide depression of these years. However, by 1984, U. S. auto firms were earning all-time record profits while employing 140,000 fewer workers in the United States than had been employed during the previous boom year of 1978. Through 1986, employment was down by 160,000 workers, 16 percent fewer than the previous high.

Not only have U. S. automobile workers experienced a loss of job security in recent years, they have also been unable to defend effectively

TABLE 7.3

MOTOR VEHICLE EMPLOYMENT IN THE
UNITED STATES AND DETROIT (SMSA): 1956-1986
(000S)

Year	U. S.	Detroit	Loss from 1978 U. S.	Loss from 1978 Detroit
1956	792.5	252.0		
1957	769.3	252.0		
1958	606.5	183.0		
1959	692.3	194.0		
1960	724.1	198.0		
1961	632.3	168.0		
1962	691.7	177.0		
1963	741.3	192.0		
1964	752.9	208.0		
1965	842.7	227.0		
1966	861.6	236.0		
1967	815.8	219.0		
1968	873.7	233.0		
1969	911.4	246.0		
1970	799.0	210.0		
1971	848.5	216.0		
1972	874.8	224.0		
1973	976.5	248.0		
1974	907.7	232.0		
1975	792.4	199.0		
1976	881.0	221.0		
1977	947.3	239.0		
1978	1,004.9	252.0		
1979	990.4	232.0	− 14.5	−20
1980	788.8	192.0	−216.1	−60
1981	783.9	178.0	−221	−74
1982	699.3	167.0	−305.6	−85
1983	753.7	175.0	−251.2	−77
1984	861.7	195.0	−143.2	−57
1985	876.4	207.0	−128.5	−45
1986	843.0	206.0	−161.9	−46

Sources: For the United States, to 1976, U. S. Department of Labor, Bureau of Labor Statistics, *Employment and Earnings*, United States, 1909–1978, (Washington, DC: U. S. Government Printing Office), 1978; 1977–1983, *Supplement to Employment and Earnings*; 1984–1986 *Employment and Earnings*, vol. 34, no. 1 (January 1987). For Detroit, Detroit Planning Department, "Historic Labor Force Levels and Unemployment Rates," unpublished, 1982; for 1982, Michigan Employment Security Commission, mesc 3221, unpublished; 1986 preliminary (January 1988).

their real wages. As Table 7.4 shows, from 1951 to 1969, during the monopoly era of the motor vehicle industry, production workers never suffered an annual loss in their real wages. Since 1970, during the automobile industry's transition to global capitalism, there have been four years in

TABLE 7.4

REAL WAGES (1967 DOLLARS): MANUFACTURING AND MOTOR VEHICLES
FOR THE UNITED STATES AND DETROIT

Year	*All Manufacturing* Detroit	*All Manufacturing* U. S.	*Detroit* % U. S.	*All Motor Vehicles*	*Motor Vehicles* % Manufacturing
1958	$3.09	$2.42	128%	$2.94	121%
1959	$3.25	$2.51	129%	$3.10	124%
1960	$3.29	$2.55	129%	$3.17	124%
1961	$3.33	$2.59	129%	$3.19	123%
1962	$3.40	$2.64	129%	$3.30	125%
1963	$3.47	$2.67	130%	$3.38	127%
1964	$3.52	$2.72	129%	$3.46	127%
1965	$3.59	$2.76	130%	$3.53	128%
1966	$3.64	$2.79	130%	$3.54	127%
1967	$3.64	$2.82	129%	$3.55	126%
1968	$3.77	$2.89	130%	$3.73	129%
1969	$3.74	$2.91	129%	$3.73	128%
1970	$3.77	$2.88	131%	$3.63	126%
1971	$3.96	$2.94	135%	$3.89	132%
1972	$4.21	$3.05	138%	$4.09	134%
1973	$4.19	$3.07	136%	$4.10	134%
1974	$4.07	$2.99	136%	$3.97	133%
1975	$4.03	$3.00	134%	$4.00	133%
1976	$4.24	$3.06	139%	$4.16	136%
1977	$4.43	$3.13	142%	$4.33	138%
1978	$4.48	$3.16	142%	$4.35	138%
1979	$4.28	$3.08	139%	$4.17	135%
1980	$4.12	$2.95	140%	$3.99	135%
1981	$4.09	$2.93	140%	$4.05	138%
1982	$4.11	$2.94	140%	$4.03	137%
1983	$4.11	$2.97	138%	$4.08	137%
1984	$4.14	$2.95	140%	$4.09	139%
1985	$4.16	$2.96	141%	$4.17	141%
1986	$4.18	$2.96	141%	$4.12	139%

Sources: See Table 7.3, and for Motor Vehicles (SIC 371), *The Handbook of Basic Economic Statistics*, January 1987, vol. 41, no. 25 (Washington, D.C., Economic Statistics Bureau).

which the real wages of auto workers have declined from the prior year. In 1986, automobile workers' real wages were about what they had been thirteen years earlier, 5 percent lower than their 1978 historic high.

Figures 7.1 and 7.2 illustrate clearly the recent fate of manufacturing workers' real wages. Both 1972 and 1984 were periods of economic recovery for the auto industry, and yet from 1972 to 1986, workers' wages have stagnated in real terms, increasing by only one percent. This contrasts strongly to the 28 percent gain registered between 1958 and 1971.

These wage data also provide some evidence about the privileged status that monopoly workers have enjoyed in relation to other workers. As discussed in chapter 3, O'Connor's model of the labor markets of monopoly capitalism included "high and increasing" levels of living for monopoly sector workers. Table 7.4 shows that to have changed. However, the *differential* between auto workers wages and average manufacturing wages has *not* decreased at all. However stagnant the purchasing power of auto workers, things have been worse for others.

The logic of the theory of global capitalism leads us to expect that monopoly sector wage premiums would erode. This development is not yet apparent. Job loss and loss of control over work rules and technological change seem to have been enough, to date, to maintain the relative wage premium for those still working. There may be an historic trade-off involved: many fewer jobs at wages relatively higher than average wages versus declining wage premiums and more jobs. Because unions respond to members, not potential members, we would not be surprised if the first alternative is the path taken. The precedent was the longshore industry and containerization: guaranteed high wages in return for *many fewer jobs*.

U. S. automobile workers no longer enjoy the job security and rising real wages associated with monopoly sector workers in the theory of monopoly capitalism. In our view, these developments are linked to the transition of the motor vehicle industry from monopoly to global capitalism. As the monopoly auto firms transformed themselves into global firms, they acquired a new lever of exploitation in their relations with U. S. auto workers—global capital mobility. The balance of class forces between auto capital and auto labor shifted in favor of capital. For labor, this meant less job security and stagnating/declining real wages.

Transition or Cycle
in a Monopoly Sector

Some might argue that our analysis has made too much out of a normal cyclical event in monopoly capitalism. In their view, the recession of 1980–1982 represented just another of the periodic downturns that have plagued the automobile industry and the national economy during the postwar

FIGURE 7.1

MANUFACTURING WAGES IN DETROIT AND THE UNITED STATES: 1958–1971

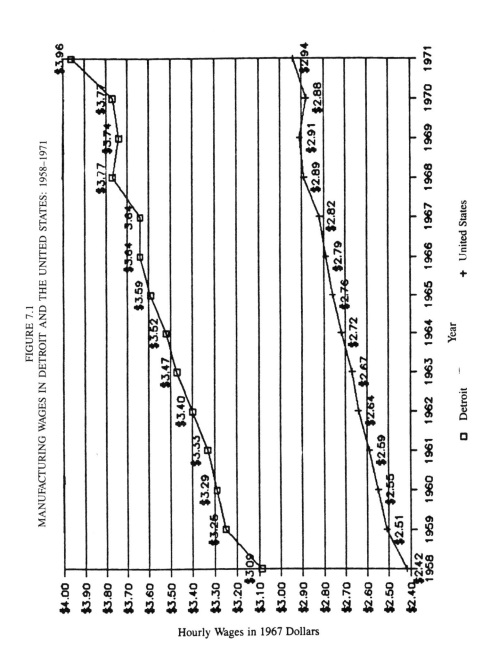

Hourly Wages in 1967 Dollars

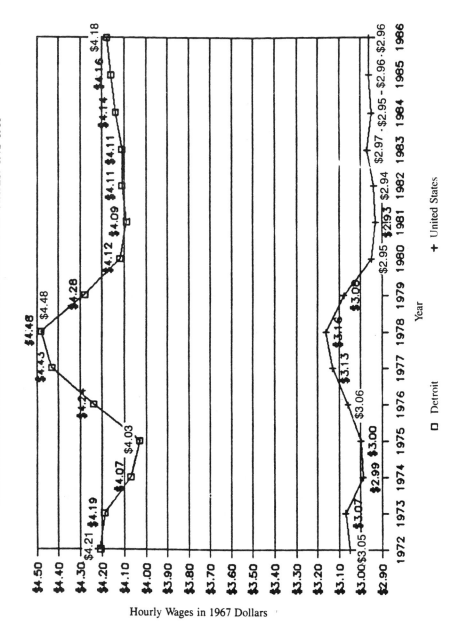

FIGURE 7.2

MANUFACTURING WAGES IN DETROIT AND THE UNITED STATES: 1972–1986

period. They would accept that the recession was of considerable magnitude and caused massive job loss and unemployment among auto workers. But they maintain that this was cyclical, signifying no major structural event; temporary job loss and unemployment hardly constitute grounds for declaring the end of monopoly capitalism and the beginning of a new era.

Such an argument ignores several essential features of the data. Figure 7.3 displays the data in Table 7.3 from 1979–1986. Nationally, only slightly more than one-half the job loss was recouped after four years of "recovery"; the same is true in Detroit.

More importantly, the recent period evidences a definitive shift in the balance of power as between capital and labor in the industry. None of the periodic downturns prior to the 1970s brought with it decline in the real wages of autoworkers.[43] The 1982 negotiations were the first time in postwar contract talks that labor was coerced into give-backs.

Furthermore, the particular form and pace of internationalization of U. S. auto capital during the past two decades has been unique.[44] Finally, capital-to-capital relations have also been transformed as indications of price competition emerged and drastic changes in world market structure occurred.

The cyclical crisis of the auto industry had passed by 1986; but employment levels in the nation and in Detroit were permanently lowered, and auto wages were still lagging. The structure had changed, and so had Detroit.

Capital-to-Labor Relations in the Detroit Region

The first part of this chapter presented an image of the Detroit region as prosperous: its workers received premium wages and enjoyed relative job security during the monopoly era of the motor vehicle industry. Given the dependence of the Detroit region upon the motor vehicle industry (motor vehicle employment accounts directly for two out of every five of Detroit's manufacturing jobs), it is no surprise that its workers have shared the experience of insecurity and wage decline/stagnation comparable to that of auto workers nationwide.

Tables 7.5 and 7.6 present data on employment in the Detroit region. Between 1978 and 1983, the Detroit region lost 193,000 (32 percent) of all manufacturing jobs. Of these jobs, 78,000 (about 40 percent) were lost in the motor vehicle industry between 1978 and 1983. Unemployment in the Detroit SMSA averaged 14.1 percent from 1980 to 1983, a figure that was 170 percent of the national average during the same years.

By 1986, employment in manufacturing in Detroit remained 117,000 jobs (about 20 percent) below that of 1978. Similarly, motor vehicle employment in the region in 1986 was 47,000 jobs (19 percent) less than

TABLE 7.5

ASPECTS OF EMPLOYMENT

DETROIT SMSA 1958–1986

Year	Total Nonagricultural Employment (000)	Total Manufacturing Employment (000)	Total Motor Vehicle Employment (000)	Total Service Employment (000)	Manufacturing Percent of Total	Motor Vehicle Percent of Manufacturing	Services Percent of Total
1958	1138.8	473.9	183.0	141.4	41.6%	38.6%	12.4%
1959	1182.0	506.8	194.0	143.6	42.9%	38.3%	12.1%
1960	1199.5	515.4	198.0	145.9	43.0%	38.4%	12.2%
1961	1127.6	455.5	168.0	148.1	40.4%	36.9%	13.1%
1962	1165.3	480.2	177.0	155.7	41.2%	36.9%	13.4%
1963	1212.5	506.1	192.0	162.2	41.7%	37.9%	13.4%
1964	1277.0	535.8	208.0	170.0	42.0%	38.8%	13.3%
1965	1366.4	576.0	227.0	178.0	42.2%	39.4%	13.0%
1966	1441.2	601.7	236.0	193.0	41.7%	39.2%	13.4%
1967	1451.1	577.3	219.0	206.4	39.8%	37.9%	14.2%
1968	1491.9	596.9	233.0	215.0	40.0%	39.0%	14.4%
1969	1553.7	613.5	246.0	217.9	39.5%	40.1%	14.0%
1970	1551.0	569.9	210.0	229.5	36.7%	36.8%	14.8%
1971	1531.8	548.8	216.0	232.2	35.8%	39.4%	15.2%
1972	1582.2	562.0	224.0	254.1	35.5%	39.9%	16.1%
1973	1669.9	610.0	248.0	273.3	36.5%	40.7%	16.4%
1974	1659.1	581.6	233.0	282.8	35.1%	40.1%	17.0%
1975	1567.6	505.5	199.0	282.4	32.2%	39.4%	18.0%

Source: See Tables 7.3 and 7.4.

TABLE 7.5 (Continued)

Year	Total Nonagricultural Employment (000)	Total Manufacturing Employment (000)	Total Motor Vehicle Employment (000)	Total Service Employment (000)	Manufacturing Percent of Total	Motor Vehicle Percent of Manufacturing	Services Percent of Total
1976	1628.4	544.4	222.0	293.6	33.4%	40.8%	18.0%
1977	1729.0	583.0	240.0	320.9	33.7%	41.2%	18.6%
1978	1799.8	608.9	253.0	335.7	33.8%	41.6%	18.7%
1979	1791.8	580.6	232.0	341.2	32.4%	40.0%	19.0%
1980	1688.3	494.1	191.0	349.9	29.3%	38.7%	20.7%
1981	1637.6	470.5	178.0	348.7	28.7%	37.8%	21.3%
1982	1554.2	419.5	167.0	352.1	27.0%	39.8%	22.7%
1983	1539.3	416.0	175.0	356.4	27.0%	42.1%	23.2%
1984	1679.2	469.5	195.0	391.1	28.0%	41.5%	23.3%
1985	1790.1	493.4	207.0	427.8	27.6%	42.0%	23.9%
1986	1840.6	491.8	206.0	447.1	26.7%	41.9%	24.3%

Source: See Tables 7.3 and 7.4.

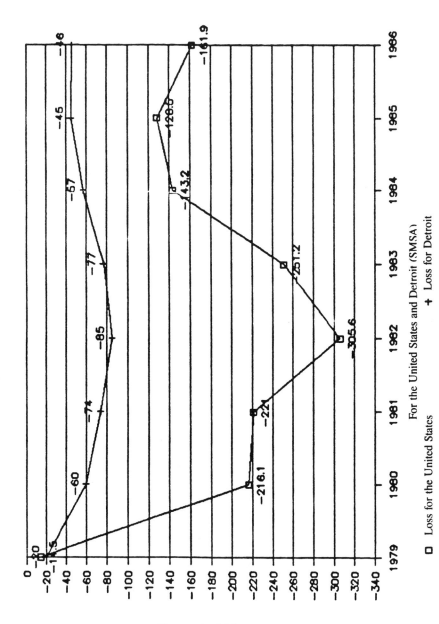

FIGURE 7.3

JOB LOSS IN MOTOR VEHICLES INDUSTRY SINCE 1978

Thousands of Jobs

For the United States and Detroit (SMSA)

□ Loss for the United States   □ Loss for the United States and Detroit (SMSA)   + Loss for Detroit

TABLE 7.6

UNEMPLOYMENT RATES: DETROIT AND THE UNITED STATES: 1970–1986

Year	Unemployment Detroit	Unemployment United States	Percent of United States
1970	6.4%	4.90%	131%
1971	7.5%	5.90%	127%
1972	6.9%	5.60%	123%
1973	5.4%	4.90%	110%
1974	6.8%	5.60%	121%
1975	11.8%	8.50%	139%
1976	9.0%	7.70%	117%
1977	7.8%	7.10%	110%
1978	6.6%	6.10%	108%
1979	7.8%	5.80%	134%
1980	13.1%	7.10%	185%
1981	12.9%	7.60%	170%
1982	15.9%	9.70%	164%
1983	14.6%	9.60%	152%
1984	10.8%	7.50%	144%
1985	9.1%	7.20%	126%
1986	8.2%	7.00%	117%

Source: See Table 7.3.

1978. Unemployment continued at depression levels through 1985, and was still more than 8 percent by the end of 1986.

These data indicate that only about one-half of the dramatic crisis of Detroit in the early 1980s was meliorated when the business cycle turned upwards; the other half is part of a structural change.

Much like those of auto workers nationally, the real wages of manufacturing workers in Detroit have stagnated in recent years. The real wages of Detroit manufacturing workers in 1986 were lower than they had been in 1973. Manufacturing workers in Detroit continue to earn real wages considerably higher than the national average for production workers in manufacturing; indeed their wage structure and its temporal movements precisely parallel those of the auto industry.

Capital-to-State Relations in the Detroit Region

The theory of monopoly capitalism highlighted the expansion of the state's role as a regulator of conditions of capital accumulation. In performing this role, the state devoted an increasing share of its budget to the assumption of

the social (i.e., legitimation) costs of accumulation. Of particular importance were programs such as unemployment compensation, disability benefits, and others that constituted additions to the social wage.

The expansion of the social expenditures of the state depended politically upon an uneasy accord between monopoly capital and monopoly labor.
To some extent, although monopoly capital exercised relative domination
over the state, the expansion of such government expenditures also reflected
a relative increment in the capacity of organized monopoly sector labor to
influence state policy. In short, under monopoly capitalism, the state was
relatively autonomous from the interests and political power of capital—
even its dominant fraction, monopoly capital.

Under global capitalism capital has altered needs for state policy; its
view of public policies toward labor hardens and its leverage over state
expenditures is heightened. We refer to this as the relative decline of the
relative autonomy of the state.

This change is based on the perspective of the global firm in which the
regions of the world form a mosaic of differentiated sites of potential investment. Wage rates and labor militancy are two important dimensions of that
mosaic. The policy output of state or substate bodies of government are
another. The political environment of a given locality may become an
important variable in a firm's location calculations.

Part of this political environment is state policy with regard to industrial
relations—policies and laws that mediate the capital-to-labor relation. No
longer held hostage to unique local agglomerations of infrastructure and
labor, global capital can now threaten to withdraw investment from localities
or nation-states whose governments adopt policies relatively favorable to
labor. They are also in a position to demand the repeal or rollback of
programs adopted during the monopoly era but which global capital no
longer regards as necessary.

In Michigan, there are many recent examples of changes in public
policy in response to the locational discretion of investors. One will illustrate the point. During 1982, Batelle Memorial Laboratories was asked to
perform a consultant contract to advise the state and Detroit of the way
robotics could be attracted to the region as a replacement industry. Batelle
proposed that reduced workers' compensation awards and insurance rates
would improve Michigan's attractiveness. Subsequently, then Governor Mil-
liken introduced such reforms.[45]

The demands of capital in the new era are not restricted to those aspects
of state policy which affect directly capital-to-labor relations. In Detroit,
this can be illustrated through a brief contrast of two eras of the city's political history.

In the late 1960s, Detroit's mayor was the liberal Jerome Cavanaugh. In
response to the civil disorders and black insurgencies of the late 1960s and

decay of the inner city, Cavanaugh became an advocate of a federal Model Cities Program. This program sought to replace a purely physical sense of urban renewal with social planning and concentrated federal resources large enough to effect the housing, training and income needs of impoverished inner city people, especially black Americans.

In 1982, Detroit's mayor was Coleman Young. Few politicians in Detroit's—or Michigan's—political history had a more progressive record. Yet Mayor Young's administration became involved in that year in the razing of an inner-city neighborhood, Poletown, so that GM could construct a new ultramodern assembly plant.[46]

During the crisis of 1982, GM announced that it would be closing both of its plants that remained in downtown Detroit. After some outcry from the city's political leaders, the company then forwarded a new proposal. While it would still be closing its older facilities, GM said it would be willing to build a new assembly plant in the city—in fact, right in the middle of an inner-city residential area surrounded by the Polish community of Hamtramck. GM made its plan contingent upon the city's cooperation in land assembly, site preparation, and the provision of a substantial tax abatement.

Given the conditions of Detroit in 1982, Mayor Young and the city council felt they had no choice but to accede to GM's demands. The city used its power of eminent domain to force 3,200 people from their homes and 160 local businesses to close. Scarce fiscal revenues were used to build highway on-off ramps upon which the company insisted. GM was also granted a twelve-year tax abatement worth as much as $240 million in foregone revenues.

Our understanding of this contrast between Cavanaugh and Young does not presume that Young was less favorable to the working class, poor people, or neighborhood interests. Rather, Young came to municipal power at a moment when capital had become less tolerant of the welfare state and more demanding of national and local governments. Having been compelled by declining profit rates and international competition to transform themselves into more globally mobile firms, the automobile companies appear to local actors to be free of any particular commitment to the Detroit region: their leverage has increased accordingly.

THE RESTRUCTURING OF THE ECONOMY OF DETROIT

A State of Emergency

The link between Detroit and the world status of the American automobile industry was made dramatically in January 1983, when Mayor Young declared that a state of emergency existed in Detroit.[47] On March 7, 1983, the *New York Times* reported that "the . . . [Michigan Department of Health] . . . said recently inadequate care of infants attributed to high unemployment has manifested itself in the increase in the state's infant death rate from 1980 to 1981 after a decade of steady decline. . . . The infant death rate increased in no other states besides Michigan."[48] With the auto industry in crisis, Detroit was gripped by a state of economic distress which rippled through the local region and the lives of its working people.

The severity of Detroit's economic crisis was an indicator of the strength of its ties to the automobile industry.

Indicators of Decline in Detroit

Detroit entered into economic difficulty during 1979, and the situation reached its worst levels early in 1983. One dimension of this economic crisis was job loss. Between 1978 and 1982, overall manufacturing employment in the Detroit SMSA fell from 609,000 to 420,000—a precipitous 30 percent loss.[49] Over the same period, motor vehicle employment declined by 35 percent and resulted in more than 85,000 lost jobs.[50] Metropolitan area employment in the primary metal sector, a key supplier to the automobile industry, fell 45 percent from 47,000 in 1978 to 26,000 by the second quarter of 1982.[51]

Job loss, of course, produced unemployment. By January 1983, official figures had reached 17.6 percent in the Detroit SMSA.[52] Workers in the region were thus jobless 69 percent more frequently than U. S. workers as a whole. Meanwhile, Detroit's black population, which is a majority in the city, was, in 1980 suffering from an incredible 27 percent rate of unemployment.[53]

Another sign of Detroit's economic crisis were changes in median family and household income levels.[54] From 1978 to 1979, Detroit's median family income declined by one percentage point from $17,931 to $17,788. More drastic was a plunge in median *household* income from $15,623 to $13,170. During the same year, U. S. median family and household income levels rose respectively by 11 and 10 percent.

With plants closing and incomes falling, it is not surprising that Detroit's municipal government faced a fiscal crisis during this period. A study of the city's budgetary policies, in fact, revealed substantial reductions in expenditures for human services, public services, and economic development.[55] Between 1978 and 1981, municipal expenditures in health services declined from $136 million to $60 million. Economic development appropriations fell by $33 million and those for public transportation by $15 million between 1980 and 1981. More than 4,000 workers, or 17 percent of the city's employees, were laid off between 1977 and 1981, with the greatest reductions coming in the police and fire, municipal parking, airport, streets and traffic, and housing divisions.

Concurrently, the need for city and human services was at a postwar high. Substantial proportions of the region's population were increasingly dependent upon public support for survival. In 1982, the Michigan Department of Human Services reported that more than 400,000 people, fully one-third of the city's population, were collecting welfare payments.[56] Louis Fermin claims that upward of 60 percent of the population received some sort of transfer payment. Nowhere in the modern history of cities, he observed, had an urban population had to depend on nonwork income to such an extent.[57]

What is the Future of Detroit?

We began this chapter by locating Detroit at the center of the industrial heartland of America. The special role of the metropolitan region as the home of the U. S. automobile industry was also described. Having just shown that the auto industry has undergone a transition to a global industry, it now becomes appropriate to ask, what is the economic future of Detroit?

Will the apparent revival of the U. S. automobile firms mean an economic recovery for Detroit? Will Detroit continue to be one of the world's leading industrial locations? Or, will Detroit follow the course of New York City—once the home of apparel production, but now the home of substandard sweatshop conditions in a shrunken industry (see chapter 8). Will Detroit lose its place among the great industrial regions of the world?

The delinking of Detroit and the automobile industry. There is a substantial probability that Detroit will be progressively delinked from the automobile industry. Despite the stagnation in manufacturing wages in Detroit analyzed above, the metropolitan region remains one in which the cost of labor is high in both global and national terms. The logic of the global era suggests that, while the automakers will, in the short run, continue their efforts to control or drive down the wages of production workers in Detroit, in the long run, the proportion of world motor vehicle production located in Detroit will continue to decline. U. S. automobile firms may never entirely abandon Detroit, but it will never again be as dominant in their production operations.

Data we discussed earlier are the basis for this estimate. First, Detroit has lost motor vehicle jobs relative to other locations within the United States. Over the entire period since 1949, the Detroit share of U. S. motor vehicle employment fell from about 42 percent to about 24 percent.

Yet Detroit's loss of automobile jobs since 1978 cannot be entirely, or even principally, attributed to relocation of automobile production within the United States. Clearly, even with a lower national share, if motor vehicle employers had not decentralized their production off-shore and had thus maintained a larger base of U. S. employment, the Detroit region's employment would have been significantly higher than it was in 1986.

Looked at in historical perspective, in 1958 motor vehicle employment was about 16 percent of Detroit jobs; in 1986 it was 11 percent. These data indicate that Detroit is gradually delinking from the U. S. automobile industry. Indeed, the contrast between the record profits of the motor vehicle firms in 1983 and 1984 and after, and the continuing high levels of unemployment in Detroit dramatize this point. What then will be the future of Detroit?

Signs of Transition in Detroit

The next chapter shows that New York City has been transformed from a light manufacturing to a service economy. Noyelle and Stanback have uncovered a comparable structural transition for seven other former manufacturing centers in the United States.[58] Bluestone and Harrison, among others, have shown that a similar transition is occurring for the U. S. economy as a whole.[59] The structural data for Detroit provide some evidence that a similar fate may await the Detroit metropolitan region.

From 1958 to 1986, the percentage of nonagricultural employment in Detroit accounted for by jobs in manufacturing has fallen from 42 percent to less than 27 percent. Earlier, we reported the decline in the percentage of jobs in the motor vehicle industry. Meanwhile, the service sector in Detroit has experienced growth almost commensurate with the shrinkage in manufacturing. From 1958 to 1986, the percentage of employment in Detroit located in the service sector increased from 12 percent to 24 percent. (See Table 7.5)

The pace of structural change in the nature of Detroit's work force quickened during the 1980–1982 depression. While the number of manufacturing jobs declined rapidly during the depression, absolute employment in the services increased slowly. The post-1984 recovery did little to reverse this development. Once again, we see a cycle as the executor of structural change.

Yet, arguing that Detroit has been or soon will be restructured into a "service" economy is premature. Unlike New York City and some other former manufacturing cities, in Detroit, the manufacturing sector still employs more workers than the service sector. In New York City, in 1984, manufacturing was less than 13 percent of total employment; in Detroit, in 1986, it still accounted for almost 27 percent of all jobs. Indeed, despite the relative decline, Detroit's figure remained well above the proportion of workers nationwide employed in manufacturing.

Predicting the precise fate of Detroit remains elusive. It depends upon many contingencies such as the future direction of local and national state policies and further transformations of the world economy. But changes underway in Detroit entail more than loss; they involve a restructured local economy. Central to an understanding of this process in Detroit and elsewhere is the heightened ability of capital to extract from workers and the local state concessions commensurate with its new freedom and power.

SUMMARY AND REPRISE

The theory of monopoly capitalism as developed by Baran, Sweezy, O'Connor, and others has been a great influence on political economy during the past twenty-five years. As a set of theoretical propositions and empirical descriptions, it provided a persuasive view of twentieth-century American capitalism. In our estimation, the theory provided a descriptively accurate model of contemporary capitalism until the advent of the worldwide crises during the 1970s. That restructuring crisis marked the onset of a transition to a form of capitalism dominated by a global variant.

In this chapter, we have sought to illustrate the transition to global capitalism through an analysis of the metropolitan region of Detroit and the motor vehicle industry. We began by showing that the prosperity of Detroit and the relative well-being of Detroit workers during the first two decades after the World War II were tied to the social relations characteristic of monopoly capitalism. We then explored the impact of global change on that industry and region.

Our conclusions are summarized below.

1. Capital-to-capital relations in the auto industry no longer exhibit the characteristics posited by the theory of monopoly capitalism: an absence of price competition, market share stability, U. S. global hegemony, and monopoly profits. Rather, elements of price competition have returned, both world and U. S. national markets have been restructured, the U. S. economy and U. S. firms have lost their hegemonic position, and the U. S. firms had to respond to declining rates of profit.

2. Capital-to-labor relations in the motor vehicle industry no longer produce a relatively privileged primary work force that is relatively immune to efforts by capital to control direct labor costs. The bifurcation of the work force into a primary and secondary segment no longer functions as the sole lever of exploitation. Rather, in response to rising international competition and a declining sectoral rate of profit, U. S. auto firms have crafted a new lever of exploitation—global capital mobility. By investing in new plants and equipment overseas and by engaging in a global sourcing strategy, these firms have shifted substantial proportions of their production and their work force off-shore. This has eroded the relatively immunity of their primary labor force. By utilizing the threat of global mobility, employers have been

able to extract concessions from auto workers. For those workers, the result has been declining or stagnating real wages and a loss of job security.

3. The recent experience of the local state in Detroit indicates a new vulnerability to the demands of investors—a decline in the relative autonomy of the state. Much as in its relations with labor, the accelerated mobility of auto capital has enabled capital to extract changes in public policy and to increase its claim upon public revenues.

4. In Detroit, the reorganization of the motor vehicle industry produced in the late 1970s and early 1980s a "state of emergency." Elevated unemployment, increasing need for public support, and shrinking fiscal revenues led to enormous human suffering.

5. The historic role of Detroit as the production center of a geographically concentrated motor vehicle industry and a major site of worldwide manufacturing is attenuating. While it is too early to be certain of Detroit's precise fate, the signs of a regional restructuring rooted in the transition of the auto industry from a monopoly to a global variant are unmistakable. The world motor vehicle industry has begun its transition to an industry characterized by the social relations of global capitalism.

The new era of the world motor vehicle industry offers opportunity and challenges for the auto firms. The record industry profits in 1983 and 1984, built in large measure upon the billions of dollars in concessions obtained from U. S. workers as well as the savings engendered by employing more low-wage Third World workers, are indicative of their "successful" restructuring.[60] For U. S. auto workers and Detroit residents, a less attractive future awaits. Whether they can craft strategies and influence policies that effectively restrain the "new leviathans" remains problematic. Their fate and that of the next generation of American workers has become a socioeconomic issue of urgency facing American society. Thus far, it is one that our political leaders have failed to confront.

New York City and Detroit: Regional Differences under Monopoly Capitalism

Choosing Detroit and New York City as case studies illustrates the argument of this book in two quite different regional economies. As O'Connor pointed out, within an economy dominated by monopoly capitalist firms, remain industries and regions where competitive capitalist social relations continue to prevail. New York City, in contrast to Detroit, is a region where competitive manufacturing sectors such as apparel never evolved into monopoly industries. Similarly, New York City has been a center for the world headquarters of both manufacturing and finance capital while Detroit, apart from the automobile firms, has not been such a global command and control center.

Distinctive differences among the working classes in the two regions also exist. Despite the venerable histories of the International Ladies Garment Worker's Union (ILGWU) and the Amalgamated Clothing Workers Union (ACWU),[61] labor in the apparel and garment industries, has never been able to obtain material gains comparable to those realized by the UAW during the 1950s and 1960s. While Detroit has not been without its migrants seeking employment, the number of unemployed migrants swelling the reserve army of labor in Detroit pales in comparison to the New York City's role as an immigrant portal.[62]

New York City-area manufacturers have been driven by competitors located in lower-wage regions where they are unrestrained by union bargaining power or state enforced standards of labor relations. O'Connor's description of the competitive sector under monopoly capitalism would lead us to expect that their real wages would be declining. Given the ease of entry into the garment industry, the option of low-wage Caribbean labor, and the vulnerability of illegal migrants, the rebirth of sweatshops in New York City may be offensive to standards of human decency, but it has not been startling to labor market segmentation theorists. The fate of New York City's manual workers is reasonably explained within the theoretical confines of the theory of monopoly capitalism, *if* the internationalization of production were restricted to labor-intensive, low-wage, competitive industry.

However, the Detroit region is different. Given their characteristic and concentrated market power and the difficulty of market entry, the U. S. auto firms might have been expected to resist the rise of competitors and to maintain the geographic concentration of production that was the hallmark of monopoly capitalism. Utilizing the relative strength of their union, automobile workers might have been able to defend their jobs and their wages and maintain a standard of living associated with monopoly-sector workers. If the era of monopoly capitalism continued, it should still be an apt description of the social relations of Detroit and the automobile industry.

Thus, while Detroit and the automobile industry were appropriate ground to illustrate the usefulness of the global perspective, in comparison to the theory of monopoly capitalism, New York City and the garment industry test a somewhat different perspective—the world systems approach to the structure of relations between rich and poor countries.

8

Global Cities and Global Classes:
The Periphery comes to the Core
in New York City

GLOBAL CITIES IN THE WORLD-SYSTEM OF CAPITALISM

The Concept of a Global City

All analyses of the global system of capitalism reserve a special place for those cities and regions that are the command centers of financial and corporate decisionmaking. Referred to as *world cities*, or *capital cities*, or, as we prefer, *global cities*, these are the location of the institutional heights of worldwide resource allocation. They also concentrate the production of cultural commodities that knit global capitalism into a web of material and symbolic hierarchy and interdependence.

Located in New York City, London, and Tokyo are the headquarters of the great banks and multinational corporations. From these headquarters radiate a web of electronic communications and air travel corridors along which capital is deployed and redeployed, and through which the fundamental decisions about the structure of the world-economy are sent. In these global cities work, but not necessarily reside, the cadre of officials and their staffs who, in their persons and their official capacities, embody the concentration and centralization of capital that now characterize the global system.

The global cities are specialized places. Indeed, as New York City is, they are increasingly specialized in economic functions such as the location of the international and financial institutions and their necessary support services, including large law and accounting firms.

The concentration of the institutional forms of capital in banks, financial institutions, and global enterprises, and the centralization of their headquarters in global cities, are widely understood and noted in the political economy of global capitalism. What is not so widely acknowledged or understood is the paradox, the contradictions, of the existence of such physical concentration of control over capital and the conditions of the working-class residents in such places.

In contemporary theory, global cities have been misunderstood in the context of the global capitalist system. At the empirical level, the conditions of labor, and capital-labor relations in the so-called rich or core countries in general have been erroneously assumed to obtain for the working class in these apparent centers of power and privilege.

We begin with a glimpse at the images one might obtain from examining prominent work in this area.

Images of the Global Cities

One tendency sees the global city as a nested entity of privilege within the privileged national community of a core industrial state. Stephen Hymer, justly appreciated for his early contribution to understanding the internationalization of productive capital, is in this case a cautionary example.

Hymer points out that world cities, which he also refers to as capital cities, are the sites of the headquarters operations of the global enterprises.[1] These operations—"goal determination" and "planning"—are the command and control functions in the world-economy. Such functions are performed in cities such as New York, London, Paris, Bonn, and Tokyo because their executive cadre must have access to face-to-face contact with other executives in the capital markets, media, and government.

But in a passage that neglects a thoroughgoing class perspective on these regions, Hymer adopted a homogeneous view of labor in the global city. He wrote:

> The occupational distribution of labor in a city or region will depend on its functions in the international economic system. The "best" and most highly paid administrators, doctors, lawyers, scientists, educators, government officials, actors, servants, and hairdressers, will tend to concentrate in or near the major centers.

> The structure of income and consumption will tend to parallel the structure of status and authority. The citizens of capital cities will have the best jobs...and will receive the highest rates of remuneration....[2]

That the executives and technical staffs of multinational capital are well-paid and live (or, at any rate, work) in the world cities is not disputed. But that high pay and good jobs are the characteristic conditions of workers in world cities is not, as we demonstrate, supportable.

Cohen also understands the role of global cities as "centers of corporate control and coordination for the new international system."[3] He emphasizes the "advanced corporate services" that develop around corporate headquarters. Cities that were previously important centers for business (e.g.,

Cleveland, St. Louis, and Boston) lose out to globally-oriented cities as the operations of large enterprises become more far-flung.

Cohen shows that New York City, London, and Tokyo are the main centers of international finance. Within the United States, only San Francisco is as internationally oriented as New York City. While in 1974, New York City was headquarters to Fortune 500 firms controlling 30 percent of all the sales of the 500, those firms headquartered in New York City controlled 40 percent of all *foreign* sales of the top 500. Along with New York City's dominant position in banking, it holds a similar position in the location of the "advanced corporate services" (e.g., major accounting and law firms).[4] Presumably New York City, along with Los Angeles, would show similar importance in the worldwide production and control of mass culture and news dissemination.

In contrast to these images of peak level privilege, Sassen-Koob and Soja, Morales, and Wolff, pay more particular attention to the diverse mosaic of economic functions and life chances in the Global City.[5] Sassen-Koob contrasts New York City's advanced service sector to the peripheral conditions of the city's legal and illegal immigrants. In Sassen-Koob's analytic structure, the internationalization of production capital induces demand for the command-and-control functions at the centers of the system. This function supports the growing advanced service sector observed by Cohen and others. Market demand for residences and services to be purchased by high-income office cadre follows. The gentrification of certain residential areas occurs as the upper income cadre of the headquarters industry bid up rents in selected areas. Similarly, says Sassen-Koob, this sector induces the employment of large numbers of low-wage workers in industries that service the needs of the headquarters complex: eating and drinking places, janitorial services, and so forth. The combination of a large, low-wage opportunity structure, and an expanded reserve of labor, she says, creates conditions propitious for the emergence of sweatshops in the otherwise decimated garment industry.

Sassen-Koob's work differs from those previously mentioned because of her attention to the differentiated effects of a Global City's transformed world functions. In the work we will report on New York City, we find good evidence for her assertions. Her conception of the circuits of capital is compatible with our understanding of the dynamics of restructuring.

Soja, Morales, and Wolff adopt a similarly differentiated but global framework for their analysis of change in the Los Angeles Basin.[6] The systemic context for their analysis is the "long waves" of capitalist accumulation and devalorization as explicated by Ernest Mandel, the Belgian Marxist. In the expansion of World War II and after, they say, Los Angeles became a major center of manufacturing and took on its characteristic decentralized morphology. In the contraction of the late 1970s and early

1980s, Los Angeles was undergoing a *selective deindustrialization* that was obscured by its continued aggregate growth in manufacturing. The internationalization of production and finance made Los Angeles a major global financial and administrative center, rivalling San Francisco as the West Coast headquarters for Pacific Rim financial control.

Employment in manufacturing in Los Angeles also grew. A major aerospace-defense electronics industrial complex became the area's most dynamic industry. About one-fourth of all the manufacturing jobs added to the U. S. economy from 1970 to 1980 were located in the Los Angeles area. To most observers, Los Angeles fits the Sunbelt-boomtown image, but Soja, Morales, and Wolff do not stop there. They point out that 75 percent of Los Angeles employment in automobile and other heavy industry was lost during the same period. They present a map of plant closings and job loss sites that could have been drawn for a central northeastern city. While acknowledging that employment in the high-wage aerospace-defense electronics sector has risen, the authors note that the low-wage service sector has also grown rapidly. Most dramatically, they observe growth in the garment industry and in its illegal sweatshop component. The consequence, they point out, is that devastation of areas of the city is similar to that found in areas of Detroit or the South Bronx. They say:

> ... [T]he Los Angeles region appears ... to combine the contrasting dynamics of both "Sunbelt" and "Frostbelt" cities, adding to this mix many of the features of intensified industrialization characteristic of Third World export processing zones. This has created a peculiar composite metropolis that resembles an articulated assemblage of many different patterns of change affecting major cities in the United States and elsewhere in the world—Houston, a Detroit, a lower Manhattan, and Singapore amalgamated in one urban region.[7]

Conceptualizing Change and Its Consequences for the Working Class in Global Cities

Hymer; Cohen; Sassen-Koob; and Soja, Morales, and Wolff advance the analysis of global cities by placing them in the context of the broader system of capitalism and the function that those cities perform in an elaborate international division of labor. Yet, there is an interesting distinction among these four contributions. The first two tend to attribute to the global cities characteristics the authors understand to correspond to the international role of the nation within which the cities are located. Conditions of life are depicted as more or less homogeneous extensions of the images of the relative privilege of core countries within the international system. We have indicated our skepticism about this approach.

The latter two articles are more analytical. While the global functions of the world cities are discussed, they include both the selective deindustrialization and the concomitant restructuring of the local and national economies. In particular, Sassen-Koob and Soja, Morales, and Wolff show the way in two aspects of their work. First, they link changes in New York City and Los Angeles to changes and crisis dynamics in the capitalist system as a whole; and second, their analysis of working-class conditions disaggregates the particular industries, migration streams, and areas of the city.

A theoretically consistent analysis of the working class and its conditions in a global city, the project of this chapter, cannot limit its conceptual horizons to the urban, regional, or national economies. Capital in these cities operates on a world scale, and therefore capital-to-labor relations in global cities must be analyzed from a perspective that conceives of capitalism as a global system.

THE WORKING CLASS IN GLOBAL CITIES: ALTERNATIVE THEORETICAL SOURCES

Theories of Unequal Exchange: The Working Class in Core Regions

Among the prime candidates for deriving predictions about the working class in a global city are the various structural analyses of the world system and world accumulation of capital.

As we saw in chapter 4, in the work of Amin, Emmanuel, and Wallerstein, the rich or core countries are understood to benefit from unequal exchange with poor or peripheral countries.[8] Each of these authors emphasizes that commodity exchange produces a flow of value to the core. They also claim that this has a positive impact upon the conditions of labor in core regions.

While none of the world system analysts have provided a detailed analysis of the conditions of workers in a global city, they have articulated a view of the general status of the working class in core regions. If such descriptive statements were to be extended logically and applied without qualification to the conditions of workers in global cities, these hypotheses would follow:

1. The working class in global cities should be engaged in comparatively high-wage and high-skilled activities. If the core is characterized by such an occupational structure, one assumption could be that the core of the core (the global city) is the site of the highest-wage and highest-skilled working class.

2. The working class in global cities should enjoy a high and improving standard of living. Capitalists in global cities are at the center of value flow in the world-system and should be most able to buy off their resident labor force.

3. The reserve army of labor in the global city should be nonexistent (or small) and declining in size. According to Amin, a characteristic of the core is an industrial sector that has been able to absorb the reserve.

Deriving hypotheses from structural analyses of the world-system in this manner poses a problem. Because neither Wallerstein nor Emmanuel explicitly addresses the question of subnational, regional, or metropolitan divisions of labor, they do not in their work explicitly exclude the possibility that certain urban regions could be uncharacteristically poor or at any rate diverse in conditions of working-class life.[9] However, Amin's argument is direct, and the proposition that the core is no longer the site of a reserve army is an appropriate application of his views.

The Perspective of Global Capitalism

In our view, conditions in a global city can be derived from an analysis of capitalism as a system of global production. This entails methodological differences with those structural analyses of position in the world-economy based upon notions of exchange. In the first instance, the characteristics of the working class in the core (and, by extension, the global city) need to be derived from the direct relations of its various segments to capital in all its complex forms. This focus on production relations leads to two particular methods that have strategic bearing on the situation of labor in global cities. They are sectoral disaggregation and the analysis of capital mobility.

Neither Amin nor Emmanuel directly addresses the possibility that subnational, regional, or urban differentiation might exist in a nation-state with core status. In contrast, as discussed in chapter 5, we explicitly conceive of a capitalist social formation at a given point in time as the articulation of several variants of capitalism: competitive, monopoly, global.

This articulation involves relations of dominance understood as flows of surplus value from subordinate forms of capitalist organization to more dominant ones. It leads logically to the disaggregation of a given formation into different types of relations between capital and labor.

In particular, although the economy of a core state or a global city may be dominated by monopoly or global capital, this does not mean that its economy is composed of a homogeneous monopoly sector of capital-to-labor relations. Rather, a competitive sector, in which the conditions of labor are typically and dramatically different than those depicted in images of core regions as a whole, has not disappeared despite its subordination. Labor in this competitive sector is neither well-paid nor powerful. But, more than that, in the competitive sector, the existence of large pools of unemployed or underemployed workers acts as a depressant on wages and autonomous organization.

Chapter 5 also emphasized the centrality of capital mobility to the contemporary era of capitalism. Specifically, we consider that two related movements of capital are decisively altering the conditions of class struggle in the core. One of these circuits has been the redeployment of productive facilities from core areas to Third World and backward European sites. This first circuit may then reestablish the conditions for profitable accumulation in the older areas and thus a second moment in the circuit of investment. This second circuit favors economic sectors where working-class organization is underdeveloped or especially vulnerable.

The entries of at least two kinds of capital, in the wake of the exit of some types of manufacturing capital, are of particular importance for global cities. The first type is attracted by the administrative specialization of the global city; office and janitorial workers, clerks and computer operators are employed in increasing numbers. A second kind of capital finds niches in the manufacturing structure where low barriers to entry and a pool of cheap labor allow for high rates of exploitation. Both forms of capital employ women, minorities, and other vulnerable or unorganized workers in proportions larger than many of the jobs that have been lost.

Together, these circuits represent aspects of capital flow and the emergence of global capitalism as a phase in the continuing evolution of the capitalist mode of production.

The spatial mobility of capital also contributes to a worsening of the situation of workers in the sphere of reproduction. State units experiencing capital outflow suffer an erosion of their tax bases and are forced to adopt austerity budgets that reduce the scope of government services and allow for the deterioration of the physical infrastructure of public transportation, roads, energy, and so forth. This deterioration then becomes exacerbated as these regions compete to retain capital investment and attract new investment through the extension of subsidies to investors. As a result, the public budget is further strained and revenues available to government for other functions further reduced. Capital mobility also negatively affects the general living conditions of the resident labor force.

Once a region has been the victim of capital outflows, the conditions for some kinds of profitable accumulation may be reestablished. First, the bargaining power of the resident labor force has been weakened. Second, as a result of complex historical precedents the site often becomes the recipient of labor migration from the periphery. Both these segments of the labor force become vulnerable to offers of employment from new capital investing in sectors where the conditions of production are favorable to capital.

The internationalization of production under the current phase of capitalism, we contend, fosters a peripheralization of segments of the working class in global cities. A reserve army of labor may expand. The material conditions of laborers are not improving, but rather stagnating or declining. Standards of reproduction of the working class may be high in comparison to that of the periphery, but the changing conditions of class conflict under global capitalism may erode that comparison.

We expect that the acceleration of international capital flows away from the core regions and toward the peripheral and semiperipheral formations will erode the bargaining power and ultimately the level of living of formerly privileged labor in global cities.

This approach can be applied to an analysis of New York City. In particular, we contend that there is a local reserve army of labor in New York City and that it is joined in a global reserve, any national or local fraction of which capital can choose to favor with investment. Furthermore, the restructuring of New York City as more specialized in global administrative functions has a negative impact on its numerous vulnerable workers. We should be able to observe this in certain specific ways.

1. Labor should be more vulnerable to capital. This would be a product of both job loss and the restructuring of industry. At downturns in the business cycle, elevated unemployment resulting from job loss indicates this vulnerability; in general, lower relative wages in manufacturing are also an indicator. This results from the first circuit of capital mobility—capital flowing out of the city. It contrasts with Amin's expectations that a reserve of labor is absent in the core as well as with other expectations implied by the picture of high wages, high skills, and similar imagery found in descriptions of labor in core regions written by theorists of unequal exchange.

2. Even while some wages are driven relatively downward, the particular kinds of job formation that does take place are apt to be low wage and nonunion jobs. This is the second circuit: new conditions of accumulation attracting new forms of capital. It, too, contrasts with the hypothesis of a high-wage and highly-skilled labor force.

3. These relations of production should also be evident in the sphere of consumption as indicated by direct measures of standards of living, such as relative housing cost and quality, and more comprehensive measures, such as infant mortality. For these latter measures, aggregate averages are less critical than the location of segments of the labor force that are, inferentially, engaged in low-wage work or dependent economic roles. Such segments of the labor force may live at standards of reproduction more typical

of peripheral or semiperipheral locations. Again, this contrasts with image of the working class as enjoying a high and improving standard of living.

One set of expectations would predict that workers in New York City constitute a relatively privileged working class that shares in a global appropriation of value and enjoys a rising standard of living. We anticipate, by contrast, a complex working class, sizeable fractions of which are vulnerable to recent structural changes in the deployment of global capital. These fractions suffer from low levels of wages and of reproduction. They are also threatened by the insecurity implied by growing reserves of unemployed or marginalized labor.

NEW YORK CITY

The Empire City

Throughout this century, New York City has been the financial capital of the nation and, certainly by the end of World War I, the world. Indeed, one of the intentions and triumphs of New York's financial leadership was the use of the mechanism of the Federal Reserve Bank system to maintain that position.[10]

Despite some departure of corporate headquarters, New York is still the leading headquarters city of the nation by quite a margin. In particular, New York specializes in corporations and banks at the center of the international command and control network.[11] Yet, for large segments of New York's residents, New York as the Empire City means New York as a place having within it all the variations in conditions of labor that can be observed on a world scale.

New York City's Manufacturing in Decline

Along with its historic role as the center of finance and corporate administration, New York was a major industrial location for manufacturing, particularly of nondurable goods. Clothing and apparel were the most obvious of these, but all types of light and not-so-light manufacturing were located in the city through the mid-twentieth century. But the high prices of land, of some labor, and of services and housing, among other factors, first made other U. S. locations preferred, and now make off-shore locations even more desirable.

This holds particularly for competitive-sector capital. Apparel production, for example, typically takes place in small enterprises, and has never been among the more highly-paid manufacturing industries despite the relative length of union history and the mythology of the clothing and garment unions. These industries are in flight from New York in their legal forms, although, as we shall see, the industry is vigorous in its illegal form.

Operating a vast network of business services, retail and eating places, and the labor-intensive industries, New York has always been home to a stream of immigrants. Extremes of poverty and wealth are part of the city's history and culture. What is new in the current situation is that what might once have been an accepted standard of minimum reproduction, what Katznelson has called the "social democratic minimum," now appears to have collapsed.[12]

Circuit One: Capital Mobility and the Vulnerability of Labor in New York City

The movement of capital from core regions and core cities to alternative sites, has altered the structure of power relations between core workers and core capital. Workers have become more vulnerable to the strategies, plans, and interests of globally mobile firms. Several empirical indicators of this vulnerability can be suggested:

1. If labor has become more vulnerable to spatial mobility of capital, we should expect a decline in employment levels, especially in manufacturing.

2. A shift in employment opportunities from higher-wage, more unionized manufacturing industries to lower-wage, less unionized, and/or competitive-sector firms and service-sector activities would also indicate a labor force less powerful in relation to capital.

3. A rise in the general level of unemployment, as well as the presence of large numbers of undocumented migrants, would suggest an increase in the size of the reserve army. This would present capital, particularly in the competitive sector, with another lever to utilize against labor.

Workers in New York suffered an extraordinary loss of job opportunities in the manufacturing sector in the last several decades. More than 60 percent of all jobs in manufacturing, approximately 648,000 employment opportunities, disappeared between 1950 and 1986. Significantly, even as New York's fiscal situation improved from its mid-1970s bankruptcy (i.e., public revenues exceeded expenditures and its debt payments were reduced), the erosion of manufacturing continued: from 1984 to 1986 31,000 manufacturing jobs were lost.[13]

The dramatic decline in New York's manufacturing base has been particularly strong in the historic apparel industry. In 1950, jobs in this industry accounted for one of every ten positions in the city (340,700 jobs).

By 1983, the apparel industry provided only 3.6 percent of New York's total employment. In this industry alone, 221,000 jobs were lost.[14] Overall, the shift of capital to other sites of production has played a major role in the loss of 62 percent of all manufacturing jobs and 65 percent of all apparel industry jobs to other areas.

While jobs in the more unionized, manufacturing sector have been decreasing, growth has been occurring in less unionized, lower-wage industries such as retail trade and services. Employment by financial, insurance, and real estate firms, hospitals, and the service sector has been rising.

More and more of New York City's visible workers are waiters, clerks, secretaries, janitors, chambermaids, and bookkeepers, while fewer and fewer are skilled machinists, garment workers, and construction workers. In 1950, 30 percent of New York's workers earned their living in manufacturing industry; fewer than 15 percent were employed in personal and business services. A generation later, the positions were reversed: less than 13 percent of New York workers were employed in manufacturing, and 29 percent worked in these service sectors.[15]

The workers in the growing service sector frequently lack protection afforded by unions, and they must accept lower wages and face competition from those who are either unemployed or underemployed.

The Reserve Army in New York City

Contrary to Amin's analysis, the global city in the core can be the site of a large reserve army of labor. The official unemployment rate in New York rose from 4.8 percent to 9.4 percent between 1970 and 1983. By 1986, unemployment was reduced to an official 7.4 percent, 236,000 people.[16]

Moreover, real unemployment and underemployment, which has been estimated at 50 percent higher than recorded figures, would yield a reserve army of about 400,000 people. This would still ignore unemployment among the hundreds of thousands of illegal residents, and it would not account for aggregate unemployment (i.e., the proportion of persons ever unemployed in a given year) as a factor in labor's vulnerability.

Two factors account in large measure for the size and growth of the reserve army in New York. First, capital migration has led to the disemployment of many of the resident labor force. Second, immigration, both legal and illegal, has played an important role.

We previously showed that some 650,000 jobs in manufacturing in New York were lost in the decades since 1950. Not all of these workers remain unemployed; some substantial fraction were absorbed by the expansion of the retail and service industries and other, competitive-sector manufacturing. Others located elsewhere, and New York's population has declined.

Still, capital migration from New York has added considerably to the size of the reserve army.

Immigration has also increased the size of the reserve army in New York. Sassen-Koob has documented the expansion of labor immigration from Third World areas.[17] She estimates that New York received at least 500,000 legal immigrants in the 1970s. Illegal immigrants, meanwhile, probably number between 750,000 and 1,500,000.[18]

As with the disemployed, not all of the immigrants enter the ranks of the unemployed. Many of the legal immigrants obtain employment in the service sector. Businesses such as messenger services, hand laundries, restaurants, food stores, and repair and domestic services are examples of those that frequently employ legal migrants. Similarly, thousands of illegal immigrants are absorbed by the illegal underground economy of sweatshops, gambling, and the like. Nevertheless, migrants, legal and illegal, have swelled the ranks of the reserve army in New York.

New York as a global city then has become a site of a reserve army of labor that is global in recruitment. The expansion of this reserve army, combined with the continuing threat of capital migration, a weakened municipal government, and declining conditions in the sphere of reproduction, alter investment conditions in New York. Precisely because the working class has been rendered less powerful in relation to capital, and the municipal authorities more pliable, New York and its labor force became an attractive alternative for reemployment by certain fractions of capital. A working class that has been peripheralized now emerges as more acceptable to both globally mobile firms and local capital in competitive sector industries.

The Reentry of Capital:
The Periphery in the Global City

In New York's garment industry, 50,000 workers toil for wages under conditions closely resembling those associated with the labor force in the periphery.[19] Moreover, the existence, expansion, and fate of these workers can be linked directly to the circuits of capital mobility outlined above.

New York was the birthplace of the garment industry in North America. In the nineteenth and early twentieth centuries, the sweatshop was the typical site of production; and, as the name suggests, the relations of production were characterized by labor's extreme vulnerability to capital. By the 1930s, however, the situation had been altered as militancy, union organization and collective bargaining, and state regulation had eliminated many of the sweatshops, raised wages, and improved working conditions.

Then, during the 1950s, both national and international outflows of production in the garment industry began undermining the position of garment workers. Jobs in the legal garment industry were lost. By the late 1970s, the number of workers employed in illegal sweatshops rose dramatically.

The apparel industry remains a competitive one. In general, this can be attributed to ease of entry. As little as $50,000 of initial capital can suffice to establish a legal shop in the industry, while considerably less is required for opening a sweatshop.[20] Furthermore, the ease with which entrepreneurial functions can be separated from productive tasks, and one productive task from another, facilitates the separation of the productive process over space. In particular, it makes apparel production a likely candidate for the export of some stages of production to other regions, while sales and management functions continue to be located in the original site.

The appearance of sweatshop labor in New York responds to pressures originating in the structure of capital-labor relations on a world scale. Indeed, the existence of a vast surplus population in dependent external economies serves as a magnet for labor-intensive stages of the production process. The free trade zone in the Dominican Republic is an example of this process. Gulf and Western Industries leads a large group of U. S.-based corporations who use this free trade zone as an export platform for the North American market.

Labor conditions in this free trade zone are quite attractive to capital. While the U. S. minimum hourly wage was, in the late 1970s, $2.90, and the average wage in the apparel industry in New York exceeded $4.50, the free trade zone hourly wage rate was $0.34.[21] As of 1978, an unemployment rate surpassing 24 percent helped maintain these low wage levels. So did the armed guards patrolling the zone's fenced-in area. Meanwhile, labor organizers are not permitted within the zones and workers feared visits in their homes as they were "terrified of being identified as pro-union."[22]

New York's garment manufacturers utilize such sites in the following way: Garments are designed, and patterns may be cut, in the northeast. They are then airfreighted to various Caribbean sites where sewing machine operators assemble them at wages that are 10 percent of official rates on the mainland. The assembled garments are then sent back to the market in North America with tariffs paid only on value-added at the foreign production site.

The global context in which New York sweatshops operate was captured in the following quotation from a sweatshop contractor in the late 1970s:

> A manufacturer will tell me he has 2,000 twelve-piece blouses he needs sewn. I tell him I need at least $10 per blouse to do a decent job on a garment that complicated. So then he tells me to get lost—he offers me $2. If I don't take that, he tells me he can have it sent to Taiwan or South

America somewhere, and have it done for 50¢. So we haggle—sometimes I might bring him up to $4 per blouse.

Now you tell me, how can I pay someone "union scale" ($3.80) or even the minimum wage ($2.90), when I'm only getting $4 per blouse? With overhead and everything else, I may be able to pay the ladies $1.20 per blouse, but that's tops. There's nothing on paper. I get it in cash.[23]

The would-be garment contractor in New York faces the choice of losing the job to overseas sources or finding means of imposing similar labor conditions on the resident labor force.

Throughout the 1960s and 1970s, the level of apparel imports to the United States grew rapidly. In 1973, one of every five garments (20.6 percent) purchased in the United States was imported. But by 1983, 45.5 percent of all garments were imported.[24]

These imports took many forms, but one that was of growing importance was firms from the United States moving some stages of production abroad in order to take advantage of cheap foreign labor and lenient tariff laws. At the same time, some firms in the northeast relocated to the southern United States for similar reasons.

In response to the competitive nature of their market, firms in the garment industry situated in New York relocated. The result, as we have noted above, was the loss of 65 percent (221,000) of New York's jobs in the industry.

Where the late 1960s and early 1970s saw fewer than 200 garment factory sweatshops in New York, by the late 1970s and early 1980s, New York had between 3,000 and 4,500 sweatshops. They employed between 50,000 and 70,000 persons, a large portion of whom were illegal migrants from the Caribbean, Latin America, and Far Eastern countries who have swelled the ranks of the reserve army in New York.[25]

The workers in the garment sweatshops are paid wages and labor in conditions closely resembling those of the periphery. As Table 8.1 indicates, New York sweatshop workers, who typically earn less than $1.75 per hour, receive wages similar to those of apparel workers in Singapore and Hong Kong rather than their counterparts in Sweden, the Netherlands, and Belgium. Their conditions have been described by New York State Senator Franz Leichter "as a form of peonage and often hazardous conditions, without the benefit of wage and safety laws—a form of labor exploitation which we thought had been outlawed for more than 50 years."[26]

There exists within New York a substantial growing segment of the labor force whose conditions of production resemble those of the labor force in the Third World. This segment cannot be considered a mere aberration. As the sweatshop owner quoted above makes clear, sweatshop labor is a

TABLE 8.1

COMPARISON OF HOURLY WAGES AND FRINGE BENEFITS
IN THE APPAREL INDUSTRY (IN U. S. DOLLARS), LATE 1970S

Sweden	7.22
Netherlands	5.68
Belgium	5.49
New York (legal)*	4.58
United States	4.35
Puerto Rico	2.57
New York (sweatshops)*	1.75
Singapore*	1.10
Hong Kong	.96
Brazil	.86
Taiwan	.56
South Korea	.41

*Does not include fringe benefits.

Sources: Sol C. Chaikin, *A Labor Viewpoint: Another Opinion* (New York: Library Research Associates, 1980); U. S. Department of Labor, *Employment and Earnings, U. S., 1909–1978* (Washington, D.C.: Bureau of Labor Statistics, 1979), Bulletin 1312-8; International Labour Organization, *Yearbook of Labor Statistics 1978* (Geneva: International Labour Office, 1978); Franz Leichter, Glen von Nostitz, and Maria Gonzalez, "The Return of the Sweatshop." (New York: Office of State Senator Franz Leichter; February 26, 1981).

necessary condition of global competition. Sweatshops in New York are the logical consequence of the globalization of production in the garment industry and the consequent competition for jobs between segments of the global reserve of labor.

The Income and Wage Implications
of New York City's Structural Shift

The outflow of manufacturing capital from New York has not been matched totally by job-creating investment in the various service sectors. From 1970 (just after the 1969 employment peak) to 1986, New York lost about 200,000 jobs.[27]

Even if the total number of jobs in the city had been maintained, however, the structural shift from manufacturing to service employment would be likely to result in lower wages and incomes because service-sector jobs are generally paid less than manufacturing jobs. Furthermore, the city's cost of living is among the highest in the country and the cost of living in New York appears to be linked to factors other than the purchasing power of its *resident* workers.[28]

Through the three mechanisms of job loss, structural shift, and a cost of living that, indeed, reflects New York's global status, relative purchasing power in the city shrank drastically during the period of manufacturing job loss, especially for its working-class population.

From 1964 to 1977, the median annual income of New York renters fell by more than 18 percent.[29] While New York renters were losing more than 11 percent of their purchasing power between 1974 and 1977, the U. S. family median increase in real purchasing power was just less than 1 percent (0.8 percent), a difference of almost 12 percent. But if we compare real purchasing power of the median renter household from 1949 to 1977 to the median U. S. family from 1949 to 1977, the gap is even more striking: the renters increased real purchasing power by 2 percent in those twenty-eight years, while the median U. S. family increased its purchasing power by 91.6 percent over a comparable twenty-seven-year period.

A number of factors contributed to this result. Clearly, the suburbanization of upper- and middle-income New Yorkers affects these comparisons, as does the relative poverty of native black and Caribbean migrants to the city as well. But, the result also stems directly from a change in the balance of power between New York employers and their workers, as compared to the nation.

Wages in the Global City

As Table 8.2 indicates, the city's workers are losing their relative wage advantage over other workers. In 1950, while New York was still the center of the garment industry and the union was relatively powerful, garment workers made 35 percent more than garment workers elsewhere in the country. By 1983, this premium had been reduced to 22 percent—for those working in *legal* shops reporting their wages and hours.

Manufacturing wages in the city appear to have suffered, on the whole, greater losses than did reported apparel wages. The other figures for manufacturing do not include areas in which a large proportion of all labor takes place in nonreporting sites (i.e., illegal sweatshops). The apparel wage reports are only the legal ones. If the actual wages paid to garment workers, including superexploited workers in sweatshops, were part of the calculated base of the apparel reports, the averages would show a much sharper decline. Indeed, we would argue that the other sectors' declines are showing the effects of the competitive pressure on wages, which has one source in the unreported low wages of the apparel sector.

We can test this view with a crude estimating technique. Estimates of the size of the sweatshop labor force in apparel in the early 1980s ranged from 50,000 to 70,000. Estimates of hourly wages for workers in sweat-

TABLE 8.2

AVERAGE HOURLY WAGES IN MANUFACTURING
IN NEW YORK CITY AND THE UNITED STATES: 1950–1983

Year	Area	Manufacturing	Nondurable Manufacturing	Durable	Apparel and Textile Products (SIC23)
1950	N.Y.	$1.57	1.60	1.47	1.67
	U.S.	1.44	1.35	1.52	1.24
	N.Y. as % U.S.	*109*	*119*	*97*	*135*
1960	N.Y.	$2.26	2.25	2.30	2.14
	U.S.	2.26	2.05	2.43	1.59
	N.Y. as % U.S.	*100*	*110*	*95*	*135*
1970	N.Y.	$3.40	3.45	3.24	3.16
	U.S.	3.36	3.08	3.56	2.39
	N.Y. as % U.S.	*101*	*112*	*91*	*132*
1980	N.Y.	$6.37	6.46	6.09	5.54
	U.S.	7.27	6.55	7.75	4.56
	N.Y. as % U.S.	*88*	*99*	*79*	*121*
1983	N.Y.	7.92	7.96	7.76	6.53
	U.S.	8.83	8.08	9.38	5.37
	N.Y. as % U.S.	*90*	*99*	*83*	*122*
N.Y. as % U.S. with sweatshop estimate (see text)					*95*

Sources: U.S. Department of Labor, *op. cit.* (1979) Bulletin 1312–8; U.S. Department of Labor, *op. cit.* (1979) Bulletin 1370–13; U.S. Bureau of the Census, *Statistical Abstract of the United States* (Washington, D.C.: U.S. Government Printing Office, 1979); U.S. Department of Labor, *op. cit.* (1981) Bulletin 1370–15; U.S. Department of Labor, *Handbook of Labor Statistics* (Washington, D.C.: Bureau of Labor Statistics, 1983) Bulletin 2175; and U.S. Department of Labor, Bureau of Labor Statistics, Current Employment Statistics Program (1983 data).

shops were in the range of $1 to $2. If we use an hourly wage rate of $1.75, and 50,000 workers, and combine this with the recorded figures for the industry, in 1983, New York's apparel workers would *average* $5.12 per hour, 5 percent below the national average, rather than $6.53 per hour, or 122 percent of the national average. Of course, a higher estimate for the sweatshop work force or a lower wage estimate for them would reduce the average city wage rate figures still further. Because sweatshop workers are an increasing fraction of all those employed, New York real average wages in this industry are *below* the reported averages in the United States.

The Sphere of Reproduction: Housing Conditions

Living at the nerve center of world capitalism, workers in New York consume goods and services in a market structure that, at its top, serves the discretionary spending of the most affluent and discriminating consumers in the corporate world. New York's cost of living, perennially among the highest in the country—and in the world—reflects the pool of buying power concentrated in a high-density market. This density also contributes to high land prices and high demand for housing.

Despite public subsidies and various degrees of rent control, and despite population decline, pressure on rental housing in the city is extremely high. This was reflected in relatively low vacancy rates and high rents through the 1970s, which claimed increasing proportions of the income of the city's renters. While overcrowding had been decreasing for a long time, responding to both population loss and smaller households, a large proportion of renters, about one in four, lived, by the late 1970s, in neighborhoods or on blocks that had boarded-up structures or units, the majority of which were derelicts.[30]

Rents in the era following World War II rose faster than the cost of living, while incomes grew more slowly than the nation's. By the late 1970s, rents had increased from almost 19 percent of renter income to more than 28 percent. Even more revealing is the distribution of this aggregate burden.

Among the city's renters, 57 percent now spend more than 25 percent of their incomes on rent (the level conventionally used to measure "excessive" rent burdens prior to 1980). There was an even more rapid increase in the number of renter-households paying more than 35 percent of their incomes in rent. The percentage of renters in this category doubled by rising from 19 percent in 1960 to 38 percent in 1978. In the Bronx and Brooklyn, the areas of the city with the lowest incomes and, as we report below, some of the highest infant mortality rates, more than one-third of renter households paid in excess of 40 percent of their incomes for rent.[31]

Part of this result was due to the much lower vacancy rates in low-rent than in high-rent units. For those spending more than 40 percent of their incomes on housing, however, about one-half lived in dilapidated structures.[32] This has occurred despite the longer-term trend in which the proportion of substandard housing in the city has been decreasing—in part due to abandonment.

Renters in the city are paying large and increasing proportions of income on housing and, for a significant fraction of renters, this purchases substandard dwellings. Subjectively, 44 percent of renter-households consider their neighborhoods fair or poor as distinct from good or excellent.[33]

Since Engels, Marxists have argued that wages and housing rents, in the long run, are part of a unitary sum that is the reproduction cost of labor.[34] This conclusion is based on the logic of production relations. It does not make any necessary assumption about the overall level of living, that is, the standard of *minimum* reproduction. If surplus exists in the labor market, a pool of reserve labor will produce downward pressure on relative wages, and an increasing proportion of income will be spent on rent. This constitutes inferential evidence that wage pressure is effectively reducing the standard of reproduction. This conclusion is bolstered when we recall the worsening relation of incomes to cost of living previously discussed.

The Periphery in the Core:
Poverty and Infant Mortality Rates
in New York City

Despite outflow of manufacturing capital, migrants continue to flow to the Empire City, from the Caribbean and elsewhere, seeking work. We have examined data indicating that substantial fractions of New York's population live in poor-quality housing that commands increasingly higher portions of their income.

Poverty has also increased. Table 8.3 shows that between 1974 and 1977 officially measured poverty increased from 16.5 percent of renter-households to 22.5 percent, rising to 27 percent in 1983, and returning to 24 percent in 1986. If one uses the more realistic measure of 125 percent of the official poverty definition, those in poverty rose from 26.3 percent in 1974 to 32.1 percent in 1977.[35]

With a somewhat larger margin of error, U. S. Census Bureau sample surveys indicated the following proportions of poverty among New York City residents:[36]

1979	20.4%
1985	23.9%
1986	20.6%

As even small-scale capital is attracted to offshore sites of production, that which remains is in direct competition with standards of reproduction typical of peripheral and semiperipheral formations. Sweatshop and sweated wages result. In turn, as capital penetrates those regions, rural to urban migration in excess of the labor absorption ability of peripheral urban economies results; some fraction of those migrants end up, legally and ille-

TABLE 8.3

DISTRIBUTION OF RENTER-HOUSEHOLDS WITH INCOMES
BELOW FEDERAL POVERTY LINE AND 125% POVERTY LINE,
BY BOROUGH, NEW YORK CITY: 1974–1986

	Total		Below Federal Poverty Line		Below 125% Poverty Line	
	1974	*1977*	*1974*	*1977*	*1974*	*1977*
All Renter-Households (percentages)	100.0	100.0	16.5	22.5	26.3	32.1
Bronx	100.0	100.0	22.1	29.1	33.8	39.6
Brooklyn	100.0	100.0	19.6	27.7	31.2	38.5
Manhattan	100.0	100.0	16.0	18.9	24.6	27.1
Queens	100.0	100.0	8.4	13.4	15.4	22.2
Richmond	100.0	100.0	9.6	13.5	18.5	19.5
			1983	*1986*		
All renter-households below federal poverty line (%):			27.1	24.0		

Source: 1974, 1977: Marcuse, op. cit., p. 32; 1983–87: *New York Times*, May 16, 1988, p. B2.

gally, in the United States, specifically, in New York. With conditions of labor and consumption now directly competitive with peripheral formations, levels of general well-being are apt to follow. One way of perceiving this is to examine variation in infant mortality rates.

Infant mortality is generally taken as a comprehensive measure of the health status of a population. This, over the long run, reflects the general level of living of a population. No surprise, then, that infant mortality rates in the high-income core capitalist countries are markedly different from those in peripheral and semiperipheral countries. New York City's overall infant mortality rate for 1980 is comparable to the U. S. average, which in turn, is at roughly the average for the rich countries. If we examine these rates for each of New York's five boroughs as in Table 8.4, the range of infant mortality rates is similar to the range found from the richest countries of the core to the poorest of the core (Bronx, the poorest borough, has a rate of 17.3, similar to Italy's 18, while Queens, at 11.8 is similar to Belgium's 12).

The story becomes much more interesting, however, if we disaggregate these borough averages to small units of health-administration data collec-

TABLE 8.4

COMPARATIVE INFANT MORTALITY:
UNITED STATES (1978), NEW YORK CITY AND BOROUGHS (1980),
AND SELECTED NEW YORK AREAS AND COUNTRIES

Area	Infant Deaths (1,000 live births)	Country with Comparable Rate (Actual)
United States	14.0	U.K.
New York City	15.0	Austria Fed. Rep. Germany
Brooklyn	16.0	Ireland Spain
Bronx	17.3	Italy (18)
Queens	11.8	Belgium (12) Canada (12)
Richmond	13.6	U.K. (14) New Zealand (14)
Manhattan	14.3	U.K. (14) New Zealand (14)
Weighted Average of Five Highest Areas in:		
Manhattan	53.5	Chile (55) El Salvador (60) Panama (47)
Brooklyn	41.8	Dominican Republic (37) Venezuela (40)
Bronx	32.9	Romania (31) Malaysia (31) Yugoslavia (34)
Queens	25.2	Taiwan (25) Cuba (25) Trinidad & Tobago (29)
Richmond	23.8	Hungary (24) Costa Rica (28)

Sources: The World Bank, *World Development Report, 1980* (New York: Oxford University Press, 1980); New York City Department of Health, *Infant Mortality 1980: By Health Areas, New York City* (New York: Health Services Administration, 1982).

tion. Of course, the variation is greater as the units grow smaller. However, these variations are systematic: The poorest areas of New York have the highest infant mortality rates, and, in each borough, these high infant mortality rates are found where minority workers who compose the reserve army of labor are concentrated in the worst physical situations. The high end of the range shows infant mortality rates similar to those of peripheral countries.

In Table 8.4 we show the borough averages and the averages for some core and semiperipheral countries. We select from each borough the weighted average of the five small areas with highest infant mortality rates for 1980. We list, next to each borough, the country or countries with comparable infant mortality rates.

However heuristic this device, inspection of Table 8.4 is fairly dramatic. At the core of the core we find indicators of social conditions which resemble those in the Dominican Republic, El Salvador, Malaysia, Costa Rica, Venezuela, and so forth. At the core of the core we find working conditions, living conditions, and well-being comparable to those in the periphery and semiperiphery.

SUMMARY AND REPRISE

In the core countries, certain cities emerge as the location of international command and control, or headquarters functions for the worldwide system. Multinational corporations and financial institutions with far-flung activities induce growth in the advanced corporate service sector and other related service industries in such global cities.

Certain structural analyses of the capitalist world-economy focus on relations of unequal exchange. On a world scale, value is understood in such analyses to flow toward rich or core states. This perspective logically expects and empirically describes the working class of the rich or core states to be relatively high-wage, high-skilled workers who share in the appropriation of value from peripheral or poor regions of the world-economy.

We have addressed the following question: Do the conditions of working-class life in the global city of New York correspond to expectations that might be derived from structural analyses of core regions in general, or some other pattern?

Predictions based on the perspective of global capitalism focus on:

1. capitalism as a global system of production;
2. the existence in capitalist development of variants in the form of dominant capitalist organization and variation in the distribution of dominant forms across industrial sectors;

3. the working class in global cities as part of a worldwide reserve of labor; and

4. mobile capital (and thus investors) joined in a global allocation system permitting investors to induce competitive bargaining between workers located throughout the world.

World systems analysis and the perspective of global capitalism have many things in common, but in this case they produce contrasting expectations about workers in a global city. To illustrate these we examined industrial structure, wage, and other indicators of conditions of life in New York.

1. Structural-exchange views characterize workers in core regions as high-wage, high-skilled, specializing in production of high technology production goods. Global-production views disaggregate by sector and place to examine characteristic forms of capital and capital-to-labor relations. Our data indicate New York has been both a center of financial control and a center of competitive-sector apparel production. The outflow of manufacturing has been high in general, with over 60 percent of all manufacturing jobs lost since 1950; but it has been heaviest in this wage-sensitive sector. Service-sector employment increased less rapidly than manufacturing declined.

2. Amin's version of unequal exchange describes worldwide reserves of labor as located in the peripheral or poor countries and as absent from core countries, thus producing upward wage pressure at the core and downward wage pressure at the periphery. We found large reserves of labor in New York, and a sweatshop sector that competes in a global market for labor based on wages and standards of living said to be characteristic of peripheral formations.

3. These contrasting perspectives are highlighted by our findings in New York, especially focussing on the decisive 1970s:

a. Manufacturing wages in the Empire City declined in their relation to the nation over the generation since 1950.

b. Among New York renters—two-thirds of the city's population—purchasing power declined and housing took increasing large proportions of income, especially for the poorest renters.

c. Increasing proportions of this large population descended toward poverty in the 1970s and 1980s.

d. As an indicator of general levels of living, New York infant mortality rates are, on average, similar to those of other industrial countries. But the highly differentiated mosaic of small area infant mortality rates reveals areas of very high rates, more typical of conditions formerly understood as the periphery than the characteristic understanding of the core.

The perspective that extends world systems analysis to New York in a homogeneous projection proves misleading. By contrast, the global perspective—focussing on capital mobility and worldwide labor markets—illustrates the variety of life and labor in the Empire City.

New York's garment industry and its traditional role as a portal for immigrants contrast sharply to Detroit's monopoly sector auto industry and its concentration of internal migrants. Nevertheless, both cities and their venerable industries have been subject to a similar process: the internationalization of capital, and the reduction of working-class standards and power this calls forth.

9

Remaking the State in Massachusetts

MASSACHUSETTS AND SOCIAL THEORY

The location of the earliest industrialization of the United States, by the late 1980s, the Commonwealth of Massachusetts had become a political, cultural, and economic symbol of "success" in the new environment of global capitalism. After decades of job loss and unemployment, Massachusetts has achieved "full employment."[1] Changes in the Commonwealth have persuaded a broad range of public officials and economic observers that Massachusetts is a case study of the "successful" transition *from* a declining, traditional or mature industry base *to* a dynamic, growing high technology, knowledge-based economy.

While the story of the Massachusetts political economy has some unique aspects, many in the declining regions worldwide look to Massachusetts for instruction.[2]

There is more than a touch of irony involved in the prominence of the Massachusetts example. For the Commonwealth and its working people, capital mobility has been a grim reality for most of this century. Once among the world leaders in textile and shoe production, the Commonwealth was among the earliest states to experience capital flight in pursuit of cheaper labor and a more permissive political environment.

However, the structural history of the Commonwealth has not been easily captured by the theories of monopoly capitalism or of world systems. As of 1950, Massachusetts was still among the most manufacturing-intensive of the United States. By contrast to Michigan and the industrial midwest, however, Massachusetts employment was concentrated in smaller firms and in competitive-sector industries. Massachusetts did not exhibit the kind of industrial structure summarized on a national scale by the theory of monopoly capitalism. Consequently, the Commonwealth's social terrain was not well portrayed by the model of monopoly capitalist social relations: wages were not high; industrial (as distinct from craft) unions were not strong; its manufacturing firms were not typically price-makers. Even when defense contractors became prominent in the post-World War II era, industrial and urban decline were the dominant themes of the economy.

World systems analysis is no more cogent than theories of monopoly capitalism. From early in the twentieth century, Massachusetts's venerable industries have been particularly affected by the availability of low-wage labor within the nation and, more recently, abroad. The geographic variation of the balance of class forces within the nation, largely ignored by world systems analysis, has been central to the history of the Commonwealth.

The story of Massachusetts's textile and apparel industries is not so very different from that of New York City's apparel industry. What distinguishes Massachusetts is the early onset of decline, and the dramatic restructuring of both the overall economy and the manufacturing sector in particular.

The industrial history of Massachusetts is, then, an instructive example of the tendency of both of these theories to aggregate and homogenize their portrayals of national systems in ways that are not helpful at a regional or subnational scale.

Massachusetts politics have been no less complex. In the mid-nineteenth century, the Irish potato famine propelled a Catholic people into a political culture dominated by their ancient ethnic and political oppressors. But in the United States, the Irish were eventually to be voters, and in Massachusetts as elsewhere, the organizers of other immigrants' votes. With their numbers and their talent for political organization, the Irish workers of the Commonwealth were able to form a plebeian political culture and to organize the Democratic Party. Joined with elements of Yankee reformism among Republicans, the amalgam produced a politics—however contentious and inconsistent—of "liberal" policies. By the late 1980s, a Greek-American lawyer, Governor Michael Dukakis, led an Irish-dominated Democratic Party in a nearly one-party state.

In this chapter, we explore the nature of the Massachusetts economic "success" and probe the transformation of Massachusetts political liberalism. Under the surface, we find a new balance of power, one vitally effected by the structure of the global system.

In previous chapters, we have focussed on the applications of the theory of global capitalism on the relative position of labor, and the human consequences of regional change. We continue these themes in this discussion of Massachusetts, with particular emphasis on the political, that is, the capital-state relation.

The discussion proceeds in stages. We examine the outflow of capital in the traditional industries, showing the job loss, wage stagnation, and unemployment that accompanied the erosion of the traditional manufacturing base of the state. Then we examine the rise of the new industries and firms. In both cases we emphasize the role of capital mobility and the global economy. We compare the structure of employment in the decade of the 1980s to its 1950 structure. This context prepares the way for an analysis of Massachusetts politics and power.

RESTRUCTURING MASSACHUSETTS

The specific developmental path of Massachusetts (or New England) is not fully predictable nor is it likely to be duplicated elsewhere. But there *are* systemic forces common to this case and the others; similar forces produce different results under different local conditions.

In the advanced capitalist countries, no indicator of well-being is more politically sensitive than unemployment; few other measures rival unemployment as a quick indicator of working-class material conditions. We therefore begin with a look at the "miracle" of Massachusetts—its low unemployment rate.

Full Employment in Massachusetts: The Aftermath of Decline

"This state was called the Appalachia of the North," Massachusetts Secretary for Economic Affairs Evelyn Murphy said. "Now, due to high tech, there's hope for the future."[3]

Since 1978, Massachusetts's unemployment rate has been below the nation's. Figure 9.1 shows the relationship of Massachusetts unemployment to national unemployment from 1951 to 1986. Through 1988, the same relationship has been maintained.

The relief expressed by business and political leaders about these developments is understandable. Massachusetts unemployment was higher than the national average in seventeen of the twenty-eight years from 1951 to 1978.[4]

An extended period of disinvestment, industrial decline, and elevated unemployment rates produces an environment of insecurity. This is to what Harrison and Bluestone refer when they discuss the "disciplining effect" of unemployment on New England workers.[5] Most typically, the recent record of Massachusetts is attributed to the growth of the high tech industry.[6] Some observers acknowledge that business and other services are the fastest-growing sectors of the economy. But business service growth is frequently ascribed to the computer industry, as software application consultants and the like "ride" the high tech "updraft."

High tech employment is the most significant growth area in an otherwise declining manufacturing sector. But the growth of high tech employment did not replace the jobs lost from the mature industries. The manufacturing base of Massachusetts has dramatically eroded. Even service

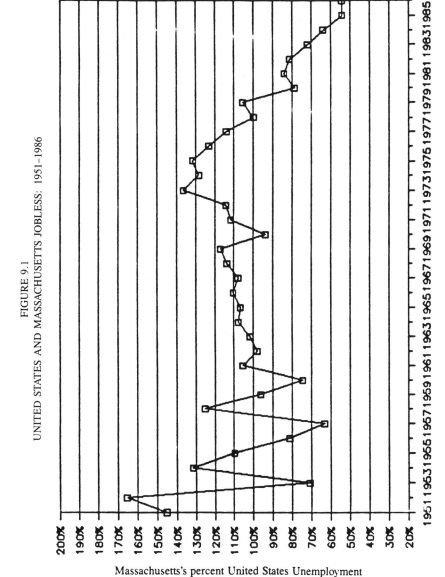

FIGURE 9.1

UNITED STATES AND MASSACHUSETTS JOBLESS: 1951–1986

growth does not account for the Commonwealth's dramatic decline in unemployment.

The underlying force that produced the apparently favorable rates of joblessness in the Commonwealth is low growth in population and labor force. This is demonstrated in Table 9.1, which performs a simple shift-share analysis of labor force and job growth in Massachusetts and the United States from 1950 to 1986.

Table 9.1 shows that Massachusetts had a *lower* rate of job growth than the nation since 1950. Logically, this would lead to the prediction that it would have *higher* unemployment than the nation. But the table shows that the labor force in Massachusetts grew even more slowly when compared to

TABLE 9.1

MASSACHUSETTS AND UNITED STATES

LABOR FORCE AND EMPLOYMENT: 1950–1986

		United States	Massachusetts
Labor Force (000s):	1950	54986	1924
. . . .	1986	117834	3051
Labor Force Percent Increase:	1950–86	214	159
Employment (000s):	1950	51758	1812
. . . .	1986	109597	2934
Employment Percent Increase:	1950–86	212	162

Shift Share Analysis:

A. Massachusetts's projected 1986 Labor Force at U. S. rate of labor force growth, 1950–86:
212% × 1,923,989 =   4,078,857

B. Massachusetts *actual* 1986 Employment: 2,934,000

C. Massachusetts potential unemployment if labor force had grown at U. S. rate (A − B):   1,144,857

D. Potential unemployment rate:

potential unemployment (C)
─────────────────────────
actual labor force (3,051,000):   37.5%

Note: Employment is nonagricultural employment.
Prior to 1980, labor force included those over 14 years of age; after 1980, labor force includes those over 16 years of age.
Source: See Table 9.2

the nation.[7] *If the rate of growth of job-seekers in Massachusetts had equalled that of the nation's, given the actual job growth Massachusetts recorded in the period, unemployment would be much higher.*[8]

Slow growth in the labor force in Massachusetts is traceable to slow and stagnant population growth.[9] The effect had two sources. First, Massachusetts fertility has been lower than the nation's. Second, there has been little or negative net migration to the state. Apparently young families have chosen to leave, or to defer or restrict their fertility.

The relative supply of labor shrank with decline in the supply of jobs. The climatic moment came in 1975. While the nation was in a deep recession, the effect in New England was devastating. Unemployment in Massachusetts climbed to 11.2 percent. The dwindling textile, apparel, and shoe and leather industries experienced a hurricane of plant closings.

Just as the sweatshops returned to New York City under the particular set of conditions there, so, too, has Massachusetts seen the growth of certain kinds of industries. This second circuit of reentry capital was predicated on the "disciplining effect" of two generations of decline.

The Effect of Job Loss and Capitalist Competition in Traditional Industries

The traditional or "mature" industries of Massachusetts were particularly vulnerable to relocation. Early in the century, textile production began its long-term shift to the southeastern United States. In the postwar era this continued at an accelerated pace; in the 1970s and 1980s, the routines of textile, shoe, and simple metalworking production diffused throughout the Third World. A significant internal change in the composition of Massachusetts industry resulted. In 1950, the so-called mature industries, which include shoe and leather, apparel, industrial machinery, paper, and furniture industries, as well as others, composed 86 percent (85.5) of manufacturing jobs. By 1982, they accounted for 62 percent of a shrinking manufacturing employment base. The change entailed the loss of 200,000 jobs in the older industries.[10]

In the last two decades, many of the traditional manufacturing industries which have declined were heavily effected by import penetration, which included both competition from external capital, and from "captive" imports of U. S. investments abroad. These industries included shoe and leather, textile machinery, textiles, and apparel.[11] Except for textile machinery, the price advantage of these imports is based upon low-wage labor, frequently from NICs. The flight of textile production from the region, however, began earlier in the century, as a regional shift to the southeastern United States.

With job loss and unemployment chronically high, manufacturing wages in the region fell relative to the national average. Table 9.2, and Figure 9.2 show that as of the late 1970s and early 1980s, Massachusetts manufacturing wages hit postwar lows relative to the nation. Then the state's average wage in manufacturing improved somewhat, fluctuating around 94 percent of the national averages, with internal variation among the metropolitan regions of the state.[12] By 1987, full employment *had* improved the relative wage in manufacturing to 98 percent of the national average.[13]

The restructuring process was painful. As entry level jobs in the older industries disappeared, umemployment was chronic, and poverty rates grew. Between 1969 and 1979 statewide, official poverty in Massachusetts *grew* by 11.6 percent, while nationally poverty was *reduced* by 9.5 percent. The aggregate poverty rates that resulted from the crisis of the 1970s were mitigated by the rising employment levels of the 1980s, and the relative trends of state and nation were reversed. Between 1969 and 1986 however, family poverty had increased from 6.9 percent to 8.6 percent.[14]

The restructured labor force and industrial structure of the Commonwealth redistributed poverty: children, in particular those in female-headed households, had grown in their proportion of the poor. By the mid-1980s, the poverty rate amongst all children had grown by 60 percent since 1970.[15] Female-headed households held most of the poor, while husband-wife families with two earners had negligible poverty rates. The implication is that second incomes, rather than high wages, were central to poverty reduction in the Commonwealth.[16]

Underlying the growth of poverty in the 1970s was the rapid erosion of older manufacturing industry. Bluestone and Harrison reported their analysis of job creation and job destruction in *The Deindustrialization of America*. Between 1969 and 1976, 731,000 Massachusetts jobs were lost by plant closures and relocations. For every 100 jobs created by openings and immigrations, 114 were destroyed.[17] The state fared somewhat better in its balance between expansions and contractions among existing facilities. Nevertheless, an average of more than 100,000 jobs were lost each year by workers whose employer was closing or leaving.

The most ruthless of the job destroyers, according to Bluestone and Harrison, were the conglomerates. Working on a relatively short-term financial investment paradigm and practicing global investment "scanning," this form of business ownership tended to acquire and then close facilities more rapidly than the others.[18]

These are all indicators of the competitive situation facing Massachusetts firms: beaten out or bought out, the small-scale and traditional activity of Massachusetts manufacturing made it vulnerable to the changing structure of worldwide production. In turn, Massachusetts

TABLE 9.2
AVERAGE HOURLY WAGES IN MANUFACTURING
IN THE UNITED STATES AND MASSACHUSETTS: 1950–1986

Year	U. S.	Mass.	Mass. as % of U. S.
1950	1.44	1.38	96
1951	1.56	1.50	96
1952	1.64	1.57	96
1953	1.74	1.65	95
1954	1.78	1.67	94
1955	1.85	1.71	92
1956	1.95	1.80	92
1957	2.04	1.88	92
1958	2.10	1.95	93
1959	2.19	2.03	93
1960	2.26	2.09	92
1961	2.32	2.17	94
1962	2.39	2.24	94
1963	2.45	2.29	93
1964	2.53	2.37	94
1965	2.61	2.45	94
1966	2.71	2.57	95
1967	2.82	2.70	96
1968	3.01	2.86	95
1969	3.19	3.04	95
1970	3.35	3.23	96
1971	3.57	3.42	96
1972	3.82	3.65	96
1973	4.09	3.89	95
1974	4.42	4.16	94
1975	4.83	4.48	93
1976	5.22	4.79	92
1977	5.68	5.13	90
1978	6.17	5.54	90
1979	6.70	5.98	89
1980	7.27	6.51	90
1981	7.99	7.01	88
1982	8.49	7.58	89
1983	8.83	8.01	91
1984	8.82	8.50	96
1985	9.16	9.00	98
1986	9.34	9.24	99

Sources: For the United States, 1950–1959, 1960–1982: *Handbook of Labor Statistics*, Bureau of Labor Statistics, 1970 and 1983, Bulletins 1666 and 2175; for 1983: *1985 Statistical Abstract of the United States*, Bureau of the Census, Department of Commerce; for Massachusetts, 1950–1982: *Employment, Hours, and Earnings, States and Areas, 1939–1982*, Bureau of Labor Statistics, January 1984, Bulletin 1370–17; 1983: *Supplement to Employment, Hours and Earnings*, August 1984, Bulletin 1370–18; 1984–1986: *Employment and Earnings*, Bureau of Labor Statistics, vol. 34, no. 5, May 1987.

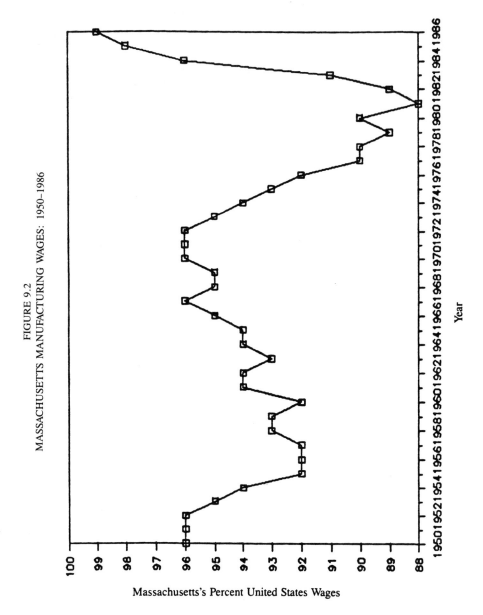

FIGURE 9.2

MASSACHUSETTS MANUFACTURING WAGES: 1950–1986

manufacturing workers and their families were relatively vulnerable to the changes of the postwar era.

The Capital to Labor Relation: Unionization

Among the expected mechanisms of labor's vulnerability would be declining rates of unionization. By the early 1980s, although unionization had declined, it had not done so more rapidly than in the nation as a whole. As of 1980, 25 percent of Massachusetts workers were members of unions, the same as the nation. Underlying these aggregate figures was a structural shift in unionization. That shift involved increased public sector unionization—among teachers, for example—and a decline in the relative proportion of manufacturing workers who were represented by unions.

After 1980, however, the continuing aggregate decline of manufacturing, in particular its unionized sectors, was not compensated by further increases in white collar or public sector union gains. (For example, the property tax limitation passed by referendum, see below, caused the lay-off of thousands of teachers, police, and fire fighters—all union members.) From 1984 to 1986, the Massachusetts work force declined from 23.5 percent unionized to 16.5 percent; a steeper drop than the national fall from 18.8 percent to 17.5 percent.[19]

These changes in the structure of capital and the vulnerability of labor can be traced to the second moment of capital mobility: change and reentry.

Job Growth in High Technology and Services: Discipline Yields Reentry

In the generation from 1950 to 1987, manufacturing declined from more than 40 percent (40.7 percent) of total Massachusetts employment to less than one-fourth (22.1 percent). Growth in the trade and service sector was similarly dramatic, increasing from 20 percent and 12 percent to 23.5 percent and 25.5 percent in the same period.[20]

In the meantime, however, the high tech sector has grown to about four in ten of all manufacturing jobs, and about one in ten of total jobs in the Commonwealth's economy. About 300,000 jobs are in this sector—although estimates vary according to which definition of "high technology" is used.[21]

The largest of the high tech sectors is electronics. A substantial portion of that sector is composed of the computer industry. Within the Massachusetts computer industry the minicomputer producers have the greatest prominence.

The high tech sector has been the only growing manufacturing sector in the state for a number of years. From its beginning in the weapons industry after World War II to its dramatic growth in the 1970s and 1980s, the industry symbolizes the hopes of the Commonwealth for a decent economic future.

These hopes are initially borne out by a superficial look at conditions in the industry. The high tech sector has higher-than-average wages. This appears to be the result of its higher-than-average proportion of professional and technical personnel. However, production workers in electronics receive *lower* than average manufacturing wages.[22]

Averages include $74,000 for the head of human resources and $271,000 for the chief executive officer. The production, clerical workers, and technical workers in the high tech sector do not earn salaries in that range. In electronic components, for example, average annual income for production workers, in 1981, was $13,563. The authors of the *High Tech Report* point out that "The annual earnings of the 60 percent of high tech workers in clerical and production jobs is barely sufficient to support a family of four at the U. S. Labor Department's lower budget level." In Boston, in 1981, this was $16,407.[23]

Industrial location studies for the high tech industry emphasized two factors in its pattern of geographic distribution and concentration: the availability of skilled labor, especially scientific and engineering personnel, *and*, less frequently mentioned, the availability of low-wage production labor.[24] The attractive force of Massachusetts Institute of Technology (MIT) as a world center of engineering is widely understood. Another important clue to the location of high tech industry in the Commonwealth lies in the fact that Massachusetts production workers in electronics earned 13 percent below the national average for their industry, in 1981—the high tide year for high tech expansion in the Commonwealth.[25]

In her examination of the concentration of high tech employment in the Lowell, Massachusetts area, Flynn showed that "Lowell's production workers remain a considerable bargain." As of 1979 (the last year for which such data were available for Lowell), Flynn reports that "production workers in the Lowell area were earning less than two-thirds the national average for production workers in the nonelectrical machinery and the electrical and electronic equipment industries."[26]

High tech industry is two worlds, according to the High Technology Research Group: a world of expansion, good pay, and stock options for professionals and executives; and a world of low pay and little union protection for others.

High tech is basically union-free. Only the communications equipment segment is unionized, and workers in that sector make a good bit more than others in the industry.[27] But the computer executives are clear and forceful in their opposition to unions. Not one of the computer producers in the state is unionized. As a personnel officer in one of the large firms told one of us, "Basically, I do union evasion."

In the early 1950s, New England unions won almost 70 percent of union representation elections. By the 1970s, this had been reduced by almost one-half. The high tech record is worse. Unions have won less than one-fourth of the elections in high tech firms since 1975.[28]

Business economists are relatively forthright in their observations about the industry's determination to remain union-free.[29] They ascribe Massachusetts's success in attracting high tech industry to the weakness of the local labor movement. Conversely, the same authors suggest that other declining regions (e.g., the auto-industrial Great Lakes states) would not be as attractive to the industry because of their combination of high wages and high rates of unionization.

Employer concerns about labor and unionization are not simply quantitative, not only tied to the wage bill. Employers, perhaps especially the aggressive enterpreneurs of this or any other new industry, wish to preserve their "management prerogatives"; that is, their control over labor and the work situation. Beyond wage issues, therefore, are other matters in high tech industry that concern both labor and management. These are issues about which management does not wish to bargain, but over which laborers would like some control. One example is the formidable list of dangerous chemicals used in the industry, primarily as solvents and cleaners. These have given rise to forbidding reports of contaminated water supplies in communities affected by the industry, as well as workplace hazards.[30] Another example is the industry's determined resistance to regulation of conditions of safe or healthful use of video display terminals (VDTs).[31]

Thus, the high tech electronics industry grew within a regional context of depressed employment and wages, promising a new future to a work force and a local political leadership frightened by a long period of industrial decline. The industrial terrain was favorable to a new industry which saw the possibility of escaping the constraints that labor's postwar strength had imposed upon other industrial sectors.

For many, these hopes were illusions. Harrison found that in the period from 1958 to 1975 workers who left the declining mill-based industries did *not* find reemployment in the high tech industries. They retired or found jobs in government or the service sector. Less than **3 percent** appeared on the rolls of the high tech sector.[32] High tech industry has grown with a new, young labor force. But now, even that growth may be coming to an end.

The Global Dimension of High Tech Growth

High tech industry, especially the computer makers, have demonstrated a high propensity to create branch production plants out of state and out of the region. In the 1970s, about 60 percent of New England's high tech firms' branch plant growth took place outside of the region.[33] This aggressive internationalization of production included global sourcing of components. As of 1983, 28 percent of the employees of six major electronics firms in the state were employees of foreign affiliates. The most typical foreign plants performed routine assembly operations. These plants tended to be in low-wage, high-subsidy locations (e.g., the Pacific Rim); or medium-wage, high-subsidy, large market access sites (e.g., Ireland and the Development (depressed) Areas in the United Kingdom). By 1985, the top five computer firms employed about 35 percent of their total payrolls in such areas, and the other high tech firms were following. During the 1985 to 1986 slowdown in the computer and electronics industry, fully one-third of a sample of large firms planned to expand overseas even as they were laying off workers in the Commonwealth.[34]

The worldwide availability of the manufacturing technology in this sector has eliminated the dependence of the producers on the local labor force. For manufacturing, *and* for testing and assembly, the low-wage rates of the Asian export platforms are now substitutable for Massachusetts and New England skills.

Since 1981, the state's employment growth in high tech has been outpaced by national growth. In the first five and one-half months of 1985 the prominent high tech firms in Massachusetts laid off more than 4,200 employees.[35] From 1979 to 1984, high tech employment in Massachusetts grew by 6 percent annually; from 1984 to 1988 its growth has been negligible.[36]

One small, young firm, Davox, announced in 1985, that it would have no domestic production, choosing Hong Kong's $1.25 per hour wages to Massachusetts $9 or $10 per hour.[37] Examples among the more established makers abound. This book was begun using a Digital Equipment Corporation (DEC) personal computer (PC)—the Rainbow. An examination of the components reveals that the printer was made in Japan and the video display monitor was made in Taiwan. The High Technology Research Group quotes DEC as stating that the disc drive was made in Singapore, the memories were made in Hong Kong and Singapore, and the integrated circuits were cut in Taiwan.[38]

Thoroughgoing global sourcing in the computer industry is not, of course, unique to Massachusetts makers. *Business Week* of March 11, 1985, reports that of a manufacturing cost of $860 for the IBM PC, $625 (72 percent) was made overseas, and about 36 percent of that portion was made in U. S.-owned plants.[39] This book was completed on an IBM-compatible PC, and *none* of its parts were manufactured in the United States.

Earlier in the decade, Ira Magaziner had pointed out that "U. S. companies in electronics have created 500,000 jobs in Singapore, Korea,

Taiwan, Japan, and Hong Kong in the past five years. . . . [F]ar more jobs than they created in the United States and most of those overseas jobs are in manufacturing."[40] In 1983, total sales by "the major Massachusetts electronics companies increased between 20 and 25 percent and net profits grew by 15 to 20 percent, but their Massachusetts employment increased by only 6.5 percent," the *High Tech Report* warned.

The logic of the global system is working its way through even booming Massachusetts. Wherever routine manufacturing functions can be performed, a ferocious labor cost-cutting decision process ensues. In Massachusetts, nonunion and relatively low-waged electronics workers find themselves in competition with even cheaper and more repressed workers elsewhere. As the high tech firms enter a new moment in the maturation of their industry, the prospects for continued manufacturing employment growth are dim.

A Note on the Pentagon Connection

In the early 1980s, the Carter-Reagan rearmament program proved a boon to Massachusetts industry. The high concentration of electronics in modern armament and missiles positioned the Commonwealth to reap large contracts, as did the political protection of the Speaker of the House, the venerable Thomas "Tip" O'Neil. While the Commonwealth received far more than its share of militiary contracts, given its population, estimates vary as to the magnitude of the local employment effect of these prime contracts. As little as 4 percent of total employment and 16 percent of high tech employment may be involved; other estimates are higher.[41] The slowdown in new prime contracts after 1984 contributed to the state's manufacturing slowdown, but it is likely that the competitive realities of the world system were more significant than military spending.

After the Storm:
A Restructured Economy

The fastest-growing sectors of the Massachusetts economy in the late 1970s were the lowest-wage sectors: wholesale and retail trade, and services.[42] Despite the rapid growth of high tech employment, 72 percent of the increase in jobs, from 1976 to 1982 were in the service and trade sectors. Wages in these sectors were lower than the average state wage.

The growth of high technology within manufacturing has not forestalled the general shift of the local economy toward a lower-wage service employment structure. There are several ways to examine this structural change.

Table 9.3 and Figure 9.3 show the comparative employment structure of Massachusetts from 1950 to 1986. In absolute terms, 81,000 fewer

TABLE 9.3
THE STRUCTURE OF MASSACHUSETTS EMPLOYMENT:
1950–1986
(%)

Sector	1950	1965	1982	1986
Construction	4.2	4.3	3.0	4.1
Manufacturing	40.7	33.1	24.3	20.8
(Mature Industries)**	(34.8)	(25.5)	(15.1)	N/A
Transportation and Public Utilities	6.7	5.2	4.6	4.2
Wholesale and Retail Trade	20.1	20.7	21.9	23.6
Finance, Insurance and Real Estate	4.4	5.4	6.4	6.8
Services (including Mining)	12.1	17.3	25.9	27.6
Government	11.8	13.8	14.1	13.0
Total*	100%	100%	100%	100%
Total in Thousands	1,757.1	2,015.8	2,638.0	3,051.0

N/A: Not applicable.
 *Totals vary from 100% due to rounding.
**Estimated
Sources: For 1950–1982, *Report of the Governor's Commission on the Future of Mature Industries*, Commonwealth of Massachusetts, 1984, Appendix A, Exhibit 9; for 1986, Division of Employment Security, *Employment Review*, Employment Supplement for 1985 and 1986, n.d.

manufacturing jobs existed in the Commonwealth than had been found a generation earlier. If Massachusetts manufacturing had grown at the same rate as the number of jobs did there would have been 412,000 more manufacturing jobs! This structural illustration is dramatic, but highly exaggerated, however, for the national economy was decreasing its proportion of manufacturing jobs.

By 1987, however, the restructuring of the Massachusetts economy had been more rapid than the nation's. If Massachusetts had merely maintained its relatively higher concentration in manufacturing as compared to the nation (41 percent compared to 34 percent in 1950), it would have had 31,000 more manufacturing jobs than it had in 1982; by 1987, the gap was 77,000 jobs.[43] The relative gap with the nation continued through 1988.[44]

These labor market developments have reflections in wages and incomes within industrial sectors. The engineer/enterpreneur in a BMW, the white-smocked technician, the word processor, and the punch-press operator live in increasingly different worlds. Harrison earlier developed trend data

FIGURE 9.3

STRUCTURAL CHANGE IN MASSACHUSETTS, SELECTED SECTORS: 1950–1986

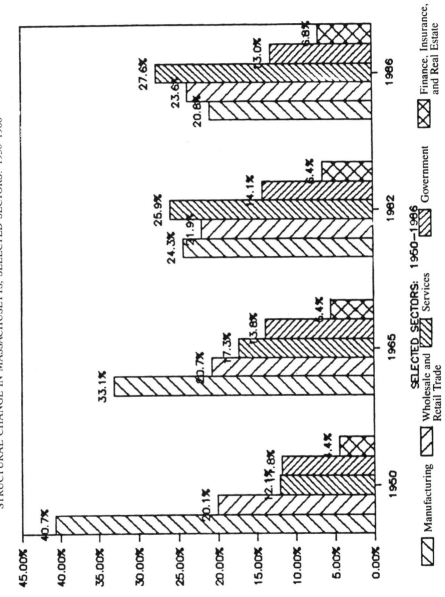

Percent Total Nonagricultural Employment

that showed increasing levels of inequality among wage-earners in Massachusetts industry, through 1976, and increasing inequality among wage-earners in high tech industry.[45] In more recent work, Harrison and Kluver found that wage inequality grew through 1986 (though somewhat more slowly than in the nation as a whole).[46]

In summary, the lower-wage sectors, which are also those with higher part-time employment and with high seasonal volatility, are the fastest growing. The only growing manufacturing sector is nonunion and pays production workers below the average for manufacturing nationally. Employers' bargaining power is increasing.

The industrial decline, unemployment, and poverty of New York City and Detroit are almost universally abhorred. By contrast, Massachusetts is often the model for successful transition from declining older industry to growing, new era, "knowledge-based" economic structure. That new era is analytically similar in Massachusetts and in the more obviously distressed Detroit and New York City.

At the bottom of the labor market, a job will not support a family. Families are disrupted; childhood poverty increases. Here we find the part-time and seasonal jobs in fast food and discount retail chains. Weak traditions and employer resistance deters the growth of unions. Simultaneously, middle-level positions are now vulnerable to the new wave of "office" and other technical automation; they are mainly "new collar." Unions find it hard to organize in these regions, so while wages are middle income, job protection erodes. The symbols of "success" in this new economy are engineers and technology enterpreneurs.

In this environment, working-class families cannot survive on one income. The attendant service costs—from child care to social support—are borne by families under much economic and social stress. Communities are difficult to knit together as family units work more total hours and geographic mobility increases.

Global restructuring as experienced in Massachusetts has changed both the calculus of employment and therefore the balance of power. In the new dispensation, state policy is made in the context of new contending parties. Despite the political "liberalism," which ethnic and reform constituencies had created, the political environment of the 1980s reveals a shift in the political constellation of the Commonwealth. This shift restricts the discretion that liberal political leaders had up to the mid-1970s; it produces more direct attempts by the state to court investment and more reluctance to defy dominant business interests. The relative autonomy Massachusetts political leaders had has been undermined by the global context of investor discretion.

THE ASCENDANCE OF HIGH TECH

Introduction

The generation-long restructuring of the Commonwealth's political economy has come to political fruition in the 1980s. A new alignment of power is now apparent; change in the structure of capital has thrown up a political cadre representing new fractions of capital. This cadre is supported by a culture and ideology of politics and new political leaders who are being molded by the new realities of work and power.

The structural and cultural realities that mold the new political alignments are moderately complex. The political result is nevertheless before us: The emergence of global capitalism has brought high tech into political ascendance in Massachusetts.

The politicized leadership of the high tech sector has organized a bloc. The vanguard of this formation is defined by the interests of capital created and invested in the high tech sector. Neither all-powerful nor totally monolithic, nor without challenge, the high tech bloc is nevertheless strategically positioned and prevails more than it loses. A new player in the games of state politics, high tech has advanced the interests it has carefully defined with great success. In itself, this topic is worthy of a separate monograph. We set out here but a framework and some examples.

In the Commonwealth, as everywhere in capitalist democracies, two kinds of political influence are exercised by capital. Although neither is "pure" or "ideal," one is more nearly indirect, implicit, and "structural." The other is more direct, explicit, and "instrumental." An example of the first is Boston's Coordinating Committee, widely known as "The Vault."[47] The Vault exercises its structural power through its direct control and indirect influence over fiscal affairs. While ostensibly a Boston group, along with manufacturers and utilities centered in the city, the Vault's membership is led by the major banks and insurance companies; that is, it represents a significant portion of the region's finance capital.

The Vault's direct influence is measured by its ability to influence budgets and tax policy of the capital city, Boston, and the state. It sometimes accomplishes this by stating its views on taxes and budgets. When it clearly opposes a given tax or budgetary proposal, it is almost never unsuccessful. (The Vault is rarely clear and explicit—in public—about anything.)

The Vault's base of power, however, is not its policy pronouncements. The Vault is not a "popular" institution; it does not deploy its forces in visible array. The ability of the Vault to influence policy is fundamentally based on its position as the voice of those who control lending and interest rates—the financial community.

The member institutions of the Vault may decline to extend loans to the public sector, as they did during Michael Dukakis's first term as governor. When Boston needed financing to cover an extraordinarily large tax abatement case, the Vault had virtual veto power over the city's budget and consequently, decisive influence over state legislation that packaged the rescue scheme.[48] Under such circumstances, the Vault gets its way.

Such explicit episodes are rare. Apart from crises, such as that of the mid-1970s, the Vault, and finance capital in general, find that their views and preferences are anticipated by "responsible" public sector actors. "Risky" fiscal policies are penalized (read, taxed) by the financial community through higher interest rates on public sector loans. Standard and Poor's or Moody's municipal and state bond ratings swing many votes in the legislature.

The 1960s and 1970s witnessed fiscal problems for all metropolitan cities and urbanized regions; Boston and Massachusetts were not different in experiencing the increment of power to financial institutions. Indeed, New York City's fiscal crisis was the paradigm. It resulted in official veto power for banks over the city's budget, and in interest rates for all municipal paper. Anticipation of such penalties is *the* major aspect of financial capital's power over public policy.

Such influence is a gross weapon in political warfare. Its arena of effectiveness is literally bottom lines rather than specific policies or regulations. Other groups are more "surgically," more directly, and instrumentally effective.

Three should be noted: Associated Industries of Massachusetts (AIM); the Massachusetts Business Roundtable (the Roundtable); and the Massachusetts High Technology Council (MHTC or the High Tech Council). Each lobbies about specific policies; the members of each are highly active in making financial contributions to political campaigns. Although each has a different style, they all agree about certain essentials of public policy: Massachusetts should remain "competitive" as a location for business enterprise. Operationally and politically, this means minimizing business costs imposed by the state, whether in the form of taxes, regulations, or a generous and emboldening social wage.

Despite similarities among the business associations, the big winner in the last decade is the High Tech Council. The council's influence and power is measured by its legislative and political victories, and partial victories. It is also measured by the centrality of focus the mass media and the political process place upon the needs and views of the industry. For example, while high tech employment, as we have seen, remains but 10 percent of the state's job market, the industry's news dominates *The Boston Globe's* business section. The pronouncements of its business leaders are afforded the exposure usually reserved for statewide elected officials.

The council, as do AIM and the Roundtable, emphasizes the comparative status of Massachusetts as a location for business investment. But there are important distinctions in the weight given to such pronouncements from the various groups. AIM represents manufacturers of all kinds. Most of its approximately 2,600 members, therefore, are relatively small firms, representing both declining and growing industrial sectors. AIM has a long history of opposition to all social legislation which regulates business. It is notorious for its opposition to child labor laws earlier in the century.

AIM's complaints about taxes or regulatory matters are more or less understood by political actors as crude business self-interest. Enraging AIM incites business people in an elected official's local constituency, which may, in turn, create a financial launching pad for an opponent. This is U. S. politics as usual; when AIM bemoans a policy as bad for the local "business climate," this is understood as speculative and general.

As one state representative put it, if the High Tech Council is "like a fast halfback looking for a long gainer, AIM is more like a grind it out, one-yard-at-a-time fullback."[49]

The Roundtable represents the sixty largest employers in the state. These include financial, industrial, and service enterprises; total employment of member firms is about 360,000, or about 14 percent of all jobs in the state. Given the size of its constituents, the Roundtable does not reflect the ideological conservatism of small or local capital. It is more pragmatic and "responsible" than AIM. Along with its interests, for example, in controlling such cost factors as taxes and workers' compensation insurance rates, the Roundtable is mindful of the need for the state to invest in public higher education.[50] Its members, however different from AIM's typical members, are in some sense bound to the local scene.

By contrast, the High Tech Council's members are part of a notoriously footloose industry. Its members as individual firms, and the council as collective spokesperson for the industry regularly remind policymakers that they have a world to choose from in their location decisions.

Former Senator Paul Tsongas is an example of a political leader who became quite responsive to high tech's political agenda. Indeed, he became a chief spokesman for their line of attack in public policy. This line is terrifyingly succinct. As Tsongas said in a speech to the Massachusetts Legislature, "We must demonstrate that we care about the health of the goose, even as we prepare to distribute the golden eggs. No goose; no golden egg.... "Defeat the business community in a thrilling emotional battle, and what happens? A plant opens up in North Carolina or California or New Hampshire or Minnesota instead of Massachusetts."[51]

The intense interstate and international rivalry for high tech locations puts the council in a highly leveraged political situation. That there are many more potentially suitable locations in the world than there are high tech facilities, means that there is a buyer's market in industrial sites. So, when a spokesman for a high tech firm says that legislation requiring advance notification for plant closures would forestall expansion in the state, or even force a move out of state, the threat is: (1) taken seriously; and (2) given the very special political-symbolic significance of the industry as a hope for the future. A hope—a goose—that must be courted lest it lay its golden eggs somewhere else.

That any given pronouncement of "job blackmail" may be a bluff or an exaggeration about the actual factors in a business location decisison is both widely understood by political decisionmakers, and ineffective as a political reply. The propensity of the industry to move both routine and not-so-routine functions to alternative sites lends enough force to its threats to produce a high degree of political compliance.

These structural factors in high tech political clout are backed up by a tough, aggressive, "outsider" political style. Speaking for a young industry, whose executives carry the confidence of entrepreneurs who have made young fortunes, the council and its spokesman do not play the political game within the rules of middle-level pluralism. They insist on getting their way with little compromise. And they back up their uncompromising policy positions with intense activism.

Two recent policy issues illustrate high-tech's clout, and its ideological conservatism: tax limitation and plant-closing legislation.

Proposition 2½:
Developing a Mass Base

Massachusetts cities and towns are dependent upon property taxes for local revenue to a greater degree than other cities. There are no city income taxes, nor city sales taxes. And, until 1979, state government paid for a smaller proportion of local education than most other states.

By the late 1970s, local property taxes were extremely high compared to the nation, and the combined state and local tax burden was among the highest in the nation.[52] Conservative political figures and the business community referred derisively to "Taxachusetts" in their view of Massachusetts' business climate.

Between 1978 and 1979, the High Tech Council took property tax limitation as its primary political mission. They were instrumental in the erection of a political front—Citizens for Limited Taxation (CLT)—to which they made the greatest and most important financial contributions.

Propelled by the California tax limitation success, and supported by high inflation and increasing tax burdens, the High Tech Council and CLT led a referendum to restrict property tax collections. The limit proposed was 2½ percent of assessed value, with a rate of increase of no more than

2½ percent per year. The legislation further required that any program mandated by the state (e.g., minimum standards of teacher pay) would have to be paid for through the state budget. Building on the perceived self-interest of homeowners of all classes, the campaign was successful.

While the biggest winners were public utilities and other large business property owners, the overall effect of the legislation was to reduce the relative burden of state and local taxes in the Commonwealth.[53]

The reasons that the High Tech Council undertook this campaign—or, at any rate, the arguments they used—are revealing.

The competitive market for engineers and executive personnel was chief among the claims made by the High Tech Council in support of Prop 2½. The argument was we need highly trained and relatively well-paid engineers and managers. We are, effectively, in a national market. If competing states have lower property and income taxes, then our engineers will demand higher salaries in order to live in Massachusetts. This will erode our competitive position, thereby constraining our growth in the Commonwealth. If we are to continue to provide new employment in the state, taxes must be lowered.

This appeal had a number of political virtues. First, it established the industry council as spokesperson for the interests of its upwardly mobile cadre of managers and engineers. Second, it allowed the industry to present itself as protector of broader middle- to upper-income interests; that is, it put high tech in a leadership role beyond its sectoral borders. Third, the argumentation for the proposal was a significant platform for molding the political climate around the council's preferred template—the need to protect job formation by currying favor with the new industry.

The High Tech Council and its political front, CLT, played St. George to the dragon of taxes, slaying the negative "business climate." The campaign and the political agenda were a success. The accuracy of the claims made on its behalf, however, are a different matter.

Industry claims about the relative importance of state and local taxes to location are not supported by the data. For example, from 1975 to 1980 high tech growth among the states with significant high tech employment had little relation to the level of taxation in a given state.[54] The attractions of the Commonwealth far outweighed its relative tax disadvantage—within the borders of the United States.

Another way to examine the reasoning behind the High Tech Council's claims is to examine salaries within the industry on a comparative basis. Massachusetts's high tech employers do not offer engineers higher salaries than other states with significant high tech employment. Indeed, for both production workers, as mentioned above, and for professional personnel, Massachusetts employers pay less than their prime competitors.[55] However burdensome Massachusetts taxes are or were, they do not seem to have forced employers to pay a premium to obtain the talent they need.

The federal tax system allows state and local tax deductibility from taxable income. Thus, local variation in taxes borne by individuals is significantly buffered. After deducting one's state taxes from federal income tax returns, the effect of higher local tax profiles is not substantial.

Ecker and Syron estimated that in the late 1970s (the years when Massachusetts was at its peak in comparative tax burden) an engineer earning $50,000 per year in California would have lost but $700 after Massachusetts *and* federal taxes.[56] It seems unlikely that this 1.4 percent differential would occasion East to West moves, or particular resistance to West to East moves. The fact that salaries were not and are not higher in Massachusetts than in lower tax jurisdictions supports this conclusion.

Tax limitation caused a good bit of distress in the larger, poorer cities. Government payrolls sank and major service cutbacks were implemented in Boston and in school systems elsewhere. The predicted and potential disasters were limited, however, because the state drastically increased its contributions of local aid to cities and towns. In some ways, the legislature, in particular, the Senate, turned a potential urban disaster into a rather interesting restructuring of fiscal burdens. The statewide income tax, arguably a more progressive way of raising revenue, now supports a substantially larger share of local education and other services.

There has been a significant cost to this damage control: the billions of extra dollars in state aid that now protect services in cities and towns are *ipso facto*, not available for other programs of income maintenance or regulatory enforcement (see below). It is here that the more fundamental agenda of the High Tech Council is revealed.

Distinguished as it is by both a Darwinian social philosophy of market relations and hostility to the social program of labor, High Tech Council leaders look to low-wage export platforms as the ideal alternative for much of their production. Their general view is that a given location must be "internationally competitive."[57] Prop 2½ and its aftermath severely constrain the ability of the Commonwealth to continue an activist, high social benefit profile. Behind lower taxes is a program for less government.

By mid-1985, this program had become more clear. The High Tech Council called for repeal of a mid-1970s income surtax (i.e., the basic rate on "earned" and "unearned" income from Massachusetts banks was 5 percent, plus a 7.5 percent surtax, for a total tax rate, after deductions of 5.375 percent. The High Tech Council also wanted a cap on the increase of tax collections, the limitation to be linked to the growth in personal income in the state. The CLT prepared another referendum campaign with this objective. It was a sign of the times, and of the clout of the High Tech

Council, that the ("liberal" Democratic) Governor-sponsored the surtax repeal that laid the groundwork for the fiscal crisis that awaited Dukakis after his defeat in the Presidential campaign.

Even after a complex courtship with the High Tech Council and persuading the legislature, especially a reluctant Senate, to pass a more moderate tax cap, the governor was unable to prevent the council (i.e., its CLT front) from passing a 1986 referendum which embodied its position. The High Tech Council's playing of tax politics, and its success in making tax politics central, does distinguish it from the other business lobbies. The Roundtable, representing more financial institutions and large employers with basic infrastructure concerns, was not able to form a consensus in favor of Prop 2½. Its Boston members were concerned about bond ratings and basic services that might be hurt by sharp contraction of its tax base. Even AIM, which usually opposes most any tax or business regulation, had enough Boston members to restrain its support of the "meat-ax" approach of Prop 2½. But the High Tech Council has few members with facilities in Boston; it persevered and continues to do so.

Plant Closing Legislation: The Politics of Consensus

Michael Dukakis was first elected governor in 1974. Succeeding a "liberal" Republican who had pioneered in such social policies as deinstitutionalization, Dukakis had run as a liberal reformer who would not raise taxes. Within days of his election, Dukakis found that state's deficit was about to explode. The government was engrossed in a budget crisis throughout the next year. Anticipating unprecedented fiscal pressures, the governor submitted a budget requiring large-scale lay-offs, major cuts in services, diminished support for the poor, *and* major new taxes. By November, five months after the start of the state's fiscal year, the budget had not yet passed. The governor was unhappy with the extent of the service cuts; the legislature balked at the tax increase.

In order to break the stalemate, Richard Hill, president of the State Street Bank and chairman of the Vault, and other banker-members of the Vault visited the leadership of the House and Senate, and met with the governor.

The state was about to sell a $131 million bond issue. The proceeds of the issue would "roll over" $120 million of short-term borrowing held by leading members of the Vault and others. The bankers' delegation told the legislature's leadership and the governor that they would declare the state in default of its short-term notes. They said that they could not sell the bond offering unless the state eliminated its more than $300 million deficit and improved its revenue position.

By threatening to withhold further loans, the banks obtained fiscal restructuring. Dukakis was forced both to cut services and to raise taxes. The hardest hit portions of the state budget were those that supported the poorest of the poor. For example, Medicaid was withdrawn from recipients of General Relief and General Relief payments were cut.[58]

In the ensuing four years, Dukakis was battered by the restructuring of the state's economy. The 1975 recession was much worse in Massachusetts than the national average, and plant closings reached very high levels. Recalling the Bluestone and Harrison data, more than 100,000 jobs each year were being lost through business failures, closings, and relocations. The governor's administration, in the meantime, took a relatively strong consumer protection stance. It became known as antibusiness, even though its austerity policy had alienated social service professionals and advocates for the poor.

In 1978, Dukakis was beaten by Edward J. King in the Democratic primary for the gubernatorial nomination. King ran as a conservative, pro-life, pro-death penalty, pro-business Democrat. Having aliennated labor and many in the liberal citizens groups, Dukakis lost.

As our data showed, 1978 was the hinge of Massachusetts development. After that year, unemployment has consistently been favorable in relation to the national rate. Tax receipts increased, allowing the state to assume the slack in local revenues.

King, who became known as Ronald Reagan's favorite governor, and who has since joined the Republican Party, was burdened by poor appointments, incompetent and corrupt in a number of cases. King lost the rematch in the Democratic Party primary of 1982, and Dukakis was elected for the second time.

As 1983 began, the structural inheritance of the hard times of the 1970s (and earlier) were to have a strong impact on the political agenda of labor, working-class neighborhood activists, and the new business activists as well. Dukakis's first administration had been frustrated by what O'Connor identified as the fiscal crisis of the state under monopoly capitalism: an inability of state expenditures for "legitimation" functions (i.e., social programs, the social wage), to keep pace with state revenues. Financial interests had compelled Dukakis to take steps that estranged his labor and liberal allies, and activated his business community opponents. By 1983, however, the restructuring process in Massachusetts had changed the terrain.

The "new" Dukakis ("Duke II" to State House insiders) had apparently resolved to form a new political persona. The first aspect of this was to hold the line on taxes. The second was to ensure that he would never again be vulnerable to the label of being antibusiness. The methodology for accomplishing this while maintaining his basically liberal political base was to seek "consensus" for each major issue. The stage was set for the contending claims of Dukakis liberal and labor allies to be tested against the new ascendancy of high tech.

The AFL-CIO and community activists (especially in Massachusetts Fair Share, an outgrowth of the community organizing populism of the movements of the 1960s) had campaigned in the late 1970s for plant closing legislation. With a governor more sympathetic to their concerns than King, they had reason to believe that their time had come.

A bill requiring advance notice of plant closings was filed in the legislature, as it had been in each session since 1979. It had broader support from legislators, especially in the House than ever before. But the leadership of the House in particular was especially sensitive to business pressure— House Speaker Thomas McGee was from Lynn where General Electric is the largest employer.

The plant closing bill, introduced by Rep. Thomas Gallagher and Senator Gerard D'Amico, anticipated the fierce opposition of AIM and the High Tech Council. Having failed to get it out of committee for several years, the sponsors placed their hopes on a version of the bill omitting earlier provisions requiring employers closing facilities to contribute to a community reinvestment fund; severance pay provisions were scaled down; and the schedule of advance notice (ninety days for fifty employees, up to one year for 900 employees) was widely understood to be negotiable.

The governor's response was to call for the formation of a Commission on the Future of Mature Industries. Its ostensible charge was to examine the role of traditional manufacturing industries in the state and to recommend policies that would maintain stability (i.e., employment) and that would deal with the problems of workers dislocated from them. The commission was provided with a small but excellent research staff (whose research we have used extensively in this chapter).

Whatever the broader mandate, and however sincere the governor's desire for a comprehensive look at industrial policies for the state, the commissioners and the legislature knew from the start that their real job was to deal with the plant closing issue. The strategy was to give the governor time to work out a solution that preserved his political base *and* kept business, especially high tech leadership, from going into open opposition.

The commission members included representatives from the AFL-CIO, Fair Share, and bankers and members of both high tech and the traditional manufacturing firms. Executive agencies were amply represented, but advocated no particular view until the governor's negotiators had "cut the deal." While not a numerical majority, a large bloc of the regular commissioners were from the business community. No matter: from the outset, the governor and his staff made clear that he would support recommendations only if they were consensual. This gave the business bloc close to veto power. In time, the governor further made clear that he preferred "voluntary" measures, "mandatory" advance notice would be seen by him as too confrontational.

In a negotiating situation in which consensus is the object, the hardest bargainer, the most extreme position, the player willing to let the process fail for want of consensus has the most power: veto power. They made clear that they would insist on a "voluntary" scheme.[59]

High tech leaders backed their position with explicit threats. High Tech Council President Howard Foley wrote, in *The Boston Globe*,

> "...the way in which these two issues are resolved [unitary taxation and plant closing notification] will provide either positive or negative signals for decisionmakers to consider as they make expansion and location decisions that will affect job growth in Massachusetts for years to come. They may not seem important to others, but they are of the utmost importance to the high technology industry in Massachusetts. Each will be a major factor in every plant-siting decision made by high tech company presidents in 1984.[60]

In the midst of the process, Teradyne's representative to the Commission told *The Boston Globe* that if the mandatory notice law was passed, Teradyne would reconsider building a [second] plant in Boston. A front page headline carried the news: "*Teradyne may call off expansion if closing bill passes*.... Fred Van Veen [a member of the Commission], Teradyne's vice-president of corporate relations, said any measure requiring companies to give advance notice to employees of closings or lay-offs is 'antibusiness' and would 'definitely' force the firm to reconsider expanding in Boston."[61]

Foley and Van Veen were articulating a persuasive line of argument. The long shakeout in the textile industry that climaxed in the 1970s made such threats thoroughly plausible. The threat of capital mobility has not been idle in the past. While declining unemployment was easing the pain of plant closings (underestimated by the commission staff as affecting only 5,000 to 10,000 workers annually in the early 1980s) the economic history of the Commonwealth was haunting its politics. Dukakis's secretary of economic affairs (to become, in 1986, his lieutenant governor), Evelyn Murphy, aligned herself closely with the high tech community and its argument about the necessity of preserving "the business climate." Testifying against the bill, to a chorus of union members' "boos," she said, "The state's competitive edge would be quite damaged by this bill."[62]

Grassroots support for the bill declined in intensity as unemployment did; the AFL-CIO Secretary-Treasurer began to emphasize obtaining benefits instead of, as he explained to us, "sticking it to the employer."

After a year of work, the commission's 1984 compromise conformed to a relatively narrow structure of choice which the business community and the governor had previously announced.

The state's group insurance laws were amended so that all future contracts would include a ninety-day continuation of employer contributions to insurance premiums.

The state further declared that ninety days' notice or severance pay equalling thirteen weeks pay, or any combination thereof, was to be considered a standard of good corporate citizenship. This was embodied in a "social compact" signed by the commissioners, and announced in the law eventually passed. This standard was voluntary. If workers were dislocated without these protections, the state was committed to making job finding and retraining services available. Dislocated workers would be eligible, subject to legislative appropriation, for supplements to unemployment compensation which would bring them up to 75 percent of their gross pay for thirteen weeks, minus whatever period of notice or weeks of severance pay they had been given.

The "Labor Caucus" of unions, legislators Gallagher and D'Amico, and the community members of the commission, had originally understood that the supplemental unemployment benefit (Reemployment Assistance Benefits or RABs) would be financed out of a fractional payroll tax (about 0.1 percent) and that employers with big lay-off records would suffer unemployment insurance ratings increases. The governor's final message on the matter financed the package through general appropriations. By 1989, during the state's fiscal crisis, RABs were no longer available.

The closing standards were not to be voluntary for those firms that had accepted one or another of the state's variety of economic development subsidies, the largest program of which is the below-market financing of industrial revenue bonds. No enforcement mechanisms were provided.

Finally, added to the state's unusually diverse economic subsidy agencies were two new ones: a fund to help finance buy-outs of firms threatened with closure but which might be viable (the Economic Stabilization Fund); and a product development fund which would subsidize new products in older industry (the New Product Development Corporation). Both of these were quite small, with initial pools of $2 million. Neither was actually part of the compromise: they were too interventionist for the industry members of the commission and were the major changes in the package made by the legislature.[63]

The new benefits obtained union support for the package. But Rep. Gallagher said that "socializing" the cost of irresponsible plant shutdowns offended his sense of fairness. Senator D'Amico, the other primary sponsor of the original notification bill expressed his sense of limited choice in a radio interview: "I'm tired of hearing from Samuel Gompers one week and Adam Smith the next. The debate on this issue has been long, tired, acrimonious, and predictable. We need new ideas."

When the compromise was discussed by the Labor Caucus, as time was running out in the legislative session, a particular flaw in the package was identified by one us (Ross) acting as D'Amico's representative. The RABs, funded by the general taxpayer rather than employers, and embodying no "punishments" for behavior contrary to the "voluntary" standards, gave no incentive for firms to change their behavior. The original intent—protecting families and communities from sudden job loss—was not likely to be achieved unless the "social compact" was made the subject of a massive public campaign aimed at changing the very definition of "decency"; that is, that "historical and moral" standard of material reproduction to which Marx referred. Absent such executive leadership, the benefits package, it was argued, would probably not effect advance notice behavior.

As it turned out, the package actually embodies *perverse* incentives for an employer *not* to give advance notice. One indication of this is a report issued by the state on "partial closings" or large-scale layoffs, including data on the first six months of the law's operation. There is no evidence of increase in amounts of notice given, and the report contains evidence that the proportions of employers giving formal notice or severance pay may have actually fallen. The report also establishes that many more workers are effected by such lay-offs than the early 1980s data had indicated.[64]

By late 1987, however, another dimension of the problem had surfaced. Through mid-1987, *no* workers had collected RABs, because the state account was insolvent, and the legislature was balking at supplemental appropriations. The fund had been depleted in 1985–86 largely because of a single closing—General Dynamics's Quincy shipyard, where no *written* notice had been given to several thousand workers, accounting for 22 percent of the $7.5 million given to 28,000 workers from January 1, 1985 through September 30, 1986. In fact, the impending closing, accomplished in several large waves of lay-offs was widely discussed in the press beforehand. But the law encouraged a collusive withholding of formal notice between employer and union. The Massachusetts House "balked at further funding for fiscal year 1987 because of the lack of corporate accountability written into the law." The Ways and Means Committee of the House unsuccessfully attempted to direct the state to obligate employers to repay costs incurred under the system.[65] In short, the legislature is objecting to a system in which an employer who wishes to give notice can do so in such a manner that still obligates the state to fund benefits. In the meantime, thousands of workers are registered as eligible for, but unable to collect, these benefits.

High tech activists were not alone in the business community in opposing a mandatory advance notice statute. But they were the key actors—and they won.[66]

The cases of property tax limitation and plant closing notification are far from unique in the recent past. As 1988 closes, the Commonwealth's unemployment rate is still much lower than the nation's and potential tax revenues could have funded major innovations in such crisis laden areas as housing and welfare poverty, worker health and safety, or hazardous and solid waste. But the High Tech Council, in 1986, was successful in resisting regulatory initiatives (such as Visual Display Terminal, or VDT, health standards), and in leading a referendum campaign for a tax revenue cap. The latter is another brilliant stroke of "popular" position and strategically effective policy. New initiatives in public policy have been choked off at the fiscal source.

Conclusion

Decades of elevated unemployment made the Commonwealth particularly vulnerable to a political formulation (the relative business climate), which maximized the advantages of a geographically mobile industrial segment: high tech electronics producers.

Summary: Strategic Relations in Massachusetts

Capital-to-capital.   Both older and newer branches of Massachusetts industry have been price competitive, making low-wage labor for routine production a particularly credible alternative for location. Older industry was forsaken by investment capital, and conglomerates actively divested local facilities. Reentry capital has been in services and high tech manufacturing.

Capital-to-labor.   A "disciplining" effect on labor was apparent. The reentry of high tech was supported by low-wage rates, and employers in this sector were determined and successful in resisting unionization. Excess labor was soaked up into a burgeoning, diverse, nonunion service sector. Major parts of this sector, such as eating and drinking places, fast-food restaurants, contract housecleaning services exist because two-worker and single-parent families must purchase more services outside the home. Manufacturing wages were below national averages, but powered by a very tight labor market in the late 1980s, gradually caught up with those nationwide.

To the extent that the Commonwealth had been "progressive" in many aspects of its public policy environment, the declining power of labor in the economy has been particularly reflected by the increasing power of employers in their relation to state policy.

Capital-to-state.   The interaction of reformist, higher status, political forces, and working-class politicians, accommodated the new international discipline with a pro-business liberalism. The ability of elected officials to maneuver between factions of capital, depending on a plebian electoral base, was thus highly constrained.

The reality of capital mobility has given its threat an irresistible political force. All branches of the business community benefit from this source of leverage. Wherever a policy may be argued to impose differential costs or perceptions between jurisdictions, the "golden goose," business climate argument creates the context of all discussion. Particularly by exerting pressure on taxes and expenditures, limits are placed on other distributive or regulatory possibilities. Many policies are the subject of explicitly targeted threats of investment withdrawal. High tech activists have been particularly prone to use this approach.

The political turning point in the Commonwealth's recent past was nearly coincidental with its economic pivot. In the mid-1970s as traditional industry was being decimated, a liberal Governor Dukakis was forced by the financial community to reduce services, especially to the poor, and to raise taxes simultaneously. From then on, the state's politics have been dominated by the contradictions that inhere in a reform-minded executive leadership explicitly adopting the rhetoric and policies designed to propitiate aggressive threats of capital withdrawal.

Elected political officials have faced more unity among business political leadership and therefore less discretionary ability to adopt policies opposed by this leadership. Business leadership has passed to the High Tech Council and the financial sector; working-class interests are more fragmented. The upshot is that Massachusetts "liberal" leadership presents itself as pro-business, and is constrained to those policies that approximate consensus among business political leaders. The "autonomy" of state policy declines.

Reinforced by an ambience in which they are the culture heroes, the new rich of the high tech community are riding high.

Part IV
Politics and the State

10
The Strategy of Classes in the Older Regions

Introduction

This chapter examines the strategic political responses to structural change made by capital and labor in the United States. Particular attention is paid to the initiatives of the local capitalist class, labor unions and local populist groups, and public policy planners. We close with some reflections upon the limitations of any political response that focusses principally upon the local, or even the national arena. While our examples are primarily based upon the North American experience, our contention is that wherever the boundaries of state jurisdictions offer investors viable choices, the process of global competition among those jurisdictions will give investors a political advantage in the struggle for state policies and benefits.

The politics of transition have been most turbulent at the local level. Cloaked in a mask of regional change for more than twenty years, the global transition has become apparent in highly uneven ways. At the centers of decisionmaking, the international context is taken to mean trade competition and currency exchange rates. This is echoed in local conflicts, but the locational choice of investors is nearer to the explicit strategies of both capital and labor.

Capitalist Class Strategic Initiatives

In North American federalism, the local state is the focus of political activity for the locally based business class. Those businesses dependent specifically on regional markets and land use patterns are those whose representatives are most likely to become activists. Commercial and real estate interests, locally based banks, newspaper and other media interests are examples, as is the scatter of small competitive sector manufacturing firms.[1]

Faced by local transformation, such interests, often with the support of local labor (especially in the building trades), turn to state institutions and to translocal capital for assistance in maintaining the viability of their enterprises. The booster coalition is born.

Local capital creates coalitions oriented to changing the priorities of the local state. They advocate for direct and enlarged outlays for infrastructure and for subsidies to potential investors. With such inducements in hand, local business leaders and public officials approach the controllers of large-scale investments in an attempt to attract economic activity to this juris-dictions and market areas.

Typical local strategies for attracting and retaining translocal capital investment, include a competitive and a structural strategy. The competitive strategy seeks to attract the remaining manufacturing potential of a region to a given jurisdiction. The structural strategy seeks to abet the transformation of urban economies toward characteristic retail and service-sector agglom-erations. Both of these strategic modes require the local state to subsidize in-migrant capital through a variety of tax, capital provision, and infra-structural schemes. Both require that the local state transform the political terrain in ways that will be perceived by potential investors as creating a propitious environment for new economic activity. Both have limitations in the context of global capital.[2]

The criteria by which investors judge the relative attractiveness of a geopolitical area is termed the *local business climate*. When the competitive status of a local business climate is used to justify resistance to worker or consumer interests, activists call it the *business climate argument*. When accepted by local authorities, it operates to delegitimate working-class demands on the state. When implemented, it tends to drive down the social wage of the resident working class.

From the "boom" in Houston to the restructuring of Massachusetts, the government's "consistently positive attitude towards the free enterprise system"[3] and "a healthy business climate"[4] are the summary phrases used to signal the added power that locational competition has given to local and potential investors.

When the business climate argument is writ large on the national scene it is the ideological force which prepared for and was expanded by the ascendance of the Reagan Right in the United States and of Thatcher in the United Kingdom.

The credible threat to leave a region or to curtail investments enforces capital's program. The competitive disadvantage of the relative tax burden on the salaries of executives and professional/technical workers, for exam-ple, was used by the high tech spokesmen in their campaign for the restric-tion of state taxation in Massachusetts. They then used a similar argument for the campaign to restrict state revenues, and against expenditures for those functions they do not value. Social services, and redistributive pro-grams in general, are attacked. In Massachusetts, the explicit position of the leading business group—the High Tech Council—has been that they will continue to expand employment in the state *only* if state taxation rates decrease.

Financial institutions play significant roles in the changing balance of power. Holding large amounts of local government debt, the larger regional banks can choose to exert decisive pressure on public budgets by refusing to extend further credit when the fiscal capacities of local units of government appear to be imprudently extended. The role of New York City financial institutions during that city's fiscal crisis of 1975 to 1978 is typical. In return for continued credit, New York City was forced to give legal veto power over its budget to an agency explicitly representative of the financial interests holding New York paper, the Emergency Financial Control Board.

The strategic agenda of capitalist class political activists in response to the new situation is comprehensive. As employers they seek to resist wage and benefit demands by threatening to relocate if labor is recalcitrant. As political actors, they resist and/or attempt to rescind those burdensome policies that protect the quality of life of workers and other residents through, for example, environmental or occupational health and safety regulations.

Among the early casualties of the restructuring of regional capital was been loosening of air pollution regulations. For example, the automobile industry was able to parlay its rigorous international situation into delays in the implementation of various regulations.

In Massachusetts, the High Tech Council has been successful in provoking the restructuring of public secondary and higher education, inducing plans to focus on their needs for personnel familiar with or prepared to learn the various tasks necessary to the computer and electronics industry. As the single growing manufacturing sector in the state, their political influence was rivalled only by that of financial institutions.

Such political initiatives have been broadly successful. Everywhere in the older regions, benefits and programs obtained through generations of consumer and labor activity were withdrawn as attention was focused on the desperate "need" to court investment by a business class that has a more or less clear set of prerequisites.

Often these political successes evidence the ability of translocal and local investors to convince labor that such transformations are both necessary and helpful in maintaining jobs and levels of living. This persuasion is assisted by mass media, which accept the arguments at face value, and by politicians, who act as the carriers of bad news that necessarily requires austerity.

These ideological definitions of the situation are not unopposed, nor are they perfectly efficacious. Capital's ability to affect local political change is often greater than its willingness to invest in older regions. And, however late, labor acting in its interests both as producer of value and as consumer of commodities and services has begun to develop discernible responses. These responses by labor have been primarily, although not exclusively, defensive.

Working Class Strategic Response: Organizing in the Sphere of Production

The main vehicle by which workers attempt to defend their interests is the labor union. The shift of manufacturing away from highly unionized environments has weakened the unions politically and has eroded their membership base, which is falling as a proportion of the labor force.

The acceleration of union losses has reached crisis proportions. At its peak, in 1945, union members were more than one-third (35.7 percent) of all nonagricultural employees. By 1986, less than 18 percent were members of unions.[5] Losses have been most disturbing in the bastion of union strength: manufacturing. Excluding government workers, only 15.5 percent of private employees are in unions.[6]

Nevertheless, unions attempt to hold onto the wage and benefit packages they have won and to include in collective-bargaining agreements some protection against structural shift. The more powerful monopoly-sector industrial unions (for example, automobile, rubber, and steel workers) had contract provisions that ensured notification in advance of lay-offs or shutdowns and provided severance pay linked to the years of service of employees. Auto workers have accepted some job security provisions in return for wage concessions on several occasions.

These efforts are limited in extent and in success. The real wages of U. S. manufacturing workers are stagnant. Before then President Reagan allowed the notification law to become law in the summer of 1988, only 30 to 34 percent of the major collective-bargaining agreements include notification and severance payment provisions. This means that less than 10 percent of U. S. workers are covered by such agreements.

In the political sphere, labor's primary responses have been traditional protectionism. They have called for the federal government to institute various tariffs, quotas, and other means of limiting "foreign imports." The UAW has supported a domestic content bill designed to require large-scale auto manufacturers to make in the United States up to 90 percent of the value of automobiles sold in the United States.

Before the advent of the Reagan Administration, unions also proposed the abolition of features of the U. S. tax code, which gave investors financial incentives to close older installations and to relocate. Similarly, a number of unions supported abolition of tax code provisions that treat favorably the foreign earnings of Transnational Corporations (TNCs).[7] These policies, one should note, can be evaluated for their efficacy through an analysis of the experience of the West Germany, Sweden, and the United Kingdom, which have more rigorous legal restrictions on relocations.[8]

Another approach, arguably more internationalist, is the international labor rights perspective on trade policy and union international relations. Advocates of this approach have succeeded in influencing trade legislation, which allows third parties to petition the government to remove trade preferences from those countries failing to recognize labor's right to organize.[9]

In any case, these are strategically defensive responses. In the 1980s, U. S. policy for coping with the flight of manufacturing looked to subsidies from state and local government to attract or maintain private investors in older areas. They do not propose labor or state-controlled enterprises. Some discussion has been devoted to state policy that would facilitate worker acquisition of threatened plants, but thus far experiments with such schemes have been limited. The installations turned into cooperatives and so forth have, in many cases, been marginal and technically obsolescent.

At the local level, in both industrial and political arenas, labor leaders find defending what they have obtained in past years difficult. Major advances, for example, organizing drives, have been stalemated. The conservative ascendancy contributed to union decline in two different ways: ideological and bureaucratic.

The ideological climate makes it harder for unions to convince workers that union representation will be a concrete aid. The fear of capital flight in the face of unions is part of the general culture. Reinforcing this fear is the domination of the labor relations apparatus of the state by newly energetic conservatives. Already a source of bureaucratic inertia in the 1970s, by the mid-1980s, Reaganite domination of the National Labor Relations Board (NLRB) had perforated the legal protection U. S. law had afforded to labor organizing.[10]

Working Class Strategic Response: Organizing in the Sphere of Consumption

In their role as consumers and citizens, workers have responded to the deterioration of community institutions and services somewhat more militantly and exuberantly, but still defensively. In the older regions of the United States, urban populist organizations flourished in the late 1970s and early 1980s.

These social movement organizations were independent of the political parties through the early 1980s. Although still independent, by 1985, some of them began to enter the electoral arena as insurgents in the Democratic Party.

At the heart of the new populism are employed working-class and lower-middle-class city residents. They tend to focus on consumption and public service issues such as local taxes, utility rates, arson, and bank "red-lining" (the refusal to extend housing mortgage credit in a given area).

Since 1984, many of these citizen action groups have mobilized around hazardous wastes and other "toxics."

Urban social movements. In their independent organization based on interests in neighborhood and public services ("collective consumption") the U. S. populist groups are quite similar, if not identical, to those groups Castells characterized as "urban social movements."[11]

The similarity in composition and focus suggests that their strategic situations may also be quite similar. Castells, reflecting on French experience in the late 1960s and 1970s, thought that urban social movements could be a decisive new force in capitalist society.

By contrast, our focus on the heightened mobility of capital in the global era highlights the difficult strategic situation of the new populism. We share Castells's appreciation of the energy and aspirations of such groups, yet we are struck by the mismatch of resources between consumer and neighborhood groups and the global managers of investment. The limits of local populism rests on an analysis of the global framework as distinct from Castells's view of the social formation as dominated by "monopoly capital."

The language of the populist groups expresses their political situation. Although some of the organizers are people with socialist ideas, their constituency shares the antisocialist ideology of U. S. political culture. Thus, in the late 1970s and early 1980s the political rhetoric of these groups was that of "economic democracy."

The economic Democrats projected an appeal that pitted the grassroots against corporate power and vaguely called for a redistribution of wealth and power. It condemned the callous disregard for community and human welfare evidenced by the conglomerates that remove capital from the cities and older regions while demanding subsidies. At its peak, this movement was suffused with populist militance bordering on class awareness.

By the mid-1980s, many of the grassroots and community organizations faced much more difficult organizing situations. While some had developed some stature as local political forces, the larger climate has eroded the meaning of their gains.

The limits of the new populism.   The political climate of the 1980s has had two axes. One is ideological: the conservative ascendance shrank the arena in which the new populists can successfully work. The other is material: as the system becomes more thoroughly globalized, the local arena (local public policy, the local state) is required to take ever more energetic steps to court business because the arena of investor choice has become so very large.

Together, this has meant the domination of the business climate argument in local politics. As a result, although some grassroots groups have attracted considerable municipal or statewide political influence, the defensive nature of their work has become more marked. Good will is not enough: if an initiative was broadly perceived as deterring investment, it has had to be softened; rhetoric has become less militant, too.

In assessing the limits of populist groups in the present political and strategic context, the limitations of focussing only on local issues are particularly worthy of attention. The fact that organizing is done within the sphere of consumption rather than production also produces problems that must be noted.

A populist movement organization typically takes the form of neighborhood chapters. Members become involved in issues that are quite local and immediate: abandoned buildings, traffic problems, and so forth. Chapters, once stabilized, will participate in citywide campaigns. In Worcester, Massachusetts, for example, a chapter of a prominent neighborhood-based populist organization (Massachusetts Fair Share), campaigned, in the late 1970s, to expose large developers and landlords who were tax delinquents. At the statewide level, utility rates, taxes, plant closing notification and "right-to-know" about hazardous substances legislation have been the subject of Fair Share campaigns.

The local arena.   "Victories" in such matters are rare. When won, they face two limits: they either affect but a small part of the overall deterioration of the members' material situation, or they may be subverted by investment generated and controlled at more distant levels of power and authority. Local organizing always faces the fact that the bulk of capital resources are not allocated on the basis of local welfare considerations.

At the current conjuncture, local reform is made, therefore, both difficult and more dangerous by the expanding context in which important business decisions are made. Each municipal or state/provincial reform is met with the threat of capital mobility. Some of these threats are merely attempts to discourage local activism and citizen demands. Some of them are real. Together, they compose an ideology that has become dominant.

As we have seen, long-standing features of the local terrain are compared by investors to the qualities of other and distant terrains. Even within the national arena of the United States, the fact that fifty state legislative arenas exist creates the potential for continual variation in local configurations of capital-labor relations and state policy configurations. Thus, an advance for workers in one state, if not matched elsewhere within a relevant time period, may be the occasion for the threat and reality of capital's withdrawal from the progressive state and relocation to a more retrograde domain. This will bolster the austerity atmosphere in the former locality, stiffen the opposition to local working class demands, and in general act to suppress the possibility of local success.

In summary, the local base and focus of the new populism is constrained by the disproportionality between the needs and problems of constituents and the power and resources available at the local level; by the centrifugal tendency of the many local groups, which makes national action difficult; and by the ability of capital to obviate or forestall local gains by moving or threatening to move to more propitious locations.

The sphere of consumption.   The limitations of localism are related to and highlighted by the limitations associated with organizing residents in their roles as consumers. Central city neighborhoods are infrequently populated by people with the same employer in the same industry. When they are, as, for example, in certain Chicago steelworkers' neighborhoods, community activity, union activism, and local politics may converge in a manner that facilitates class awareness.[12] Typically, however, neighborhoods are diverse occupationally although homogeneous in income and ethnic terms.

The typical job structures of modern enterprise create a diversity of occupational niches that often obscure the underlying and common class situation of the employees. Furthermore, the social and political history of U. S. labor unions has produced a relatively narrow orientation to the job as distinct from the community interests of union members. This has generated political isolation, for there is also a certain distrust—insularity, perhaps—in the attitude of local and regional union officials toward social activists based outside the official labor movement. In consequence, workers' neighborhood problems are not usually perceived as union issues; rather, they are viewed through the ideological screen of the citizen role.

In this role, the aggrieved citizen demands equity from government and resists business-class demands that make the task of maintaining a household more arduous. Thus, it is the populist movement rather than the labor movement that organizes and channels the anger and activism provoked by the deterioration of economic and environmental conditions in the neighborhoods of declining cities and regions.

In addition to the inherent limits of local action, similar limits constrain action in the sphere of consumption, collective or individual. For example, by the time the withdrawal of bank loans for housing becomes a visible public issue in an area, one has moved quite far along in the chain of resource allocation. Financial institutions have decided on regional locations toward or away from which they will direct their investments; they have also decided on a mix of housing and other forms of investment, and a mix of long- and short-term loans for the next period. These decisions have been heavily constrained by national monetary policy. In turn, this policy is heavily influenced by calculating at the level of international finance, for example, the exchange rate of the dollar. At this highly aggregated level, investment flows are determined by changes in labor's position vis-a-vis capital in a vast number of local sites.

Thus, the consumer of housing credit is at the end of a very long sequence of decisions; and the decisionmakers at whom the point-of-consumption organizers direct their demands have little left to distribute and little discretion in its distribution.

This is ever the dilemma of local populist strategies. By focusing on local, area-defined worker and consumer interests, a populist organization is able to develop a popular base even though, or because, it avoids socialist rhetoric. But by so organizing workers, it risks operating at level and in a sphere where their action is severely handicapped.

Coalition Formation

Under the regime of monopoly capital, organized workers, especially in monopoly industries had more power when organized in relation to employers than they could obtain through the more diffuse structures of neighborhood action. Currently, that power is being eroded by the global deployment of capital, and the social and local consequences of this process.

One noteworthy strategic response has been the occasional combination of the forces of labor and community-based groups, and forging of class unity around a common political agenda.

The new populists did perceive this as a desirable project. In Massachusetts, Connecticut, Ohio, and elsewhere, for example, labor-citizen action coalitions formed to support plant closing notification legislation from the late 1970s to the mid-1980s. They began the extremely difficult process of uniting the interest groups and therefore the interests of workers in their separated roles as producers and consumers.

The process of public argument and coalition formation which those legislative struggles created were a kind of challenge to business hegemony over the context of political discourse. That capital does not have the right to destroy communities, unmindful of costs; that workers and citizens do have the right to constrain capital mobility—these embodied principles to forge class unity and to resist the dominance of the business climate argument.

The activists in these coalitions reported that the "business climate" argument gave local capitalist activists a great deal of leverage in curtailing or defeating programs supported by citizens and labor groups. The plant closing controversy inevitably opened such arguments to scrutiny. In response, organizers focussed on the role of the global conglomerates in accounting for a large proportion of closings and job losses, even when local facilities may have been viable.

Coalition activists reported that the focus on conglomerates made it easier to oppose business climate arguments; for the conglomerates were readily portrayed as manipulative and not to be trusted. Finally, the activists said that although national legislation is desirable, local movements and victories will hasten it.

In other words, the organizers of these campaigns valued the benefits plant closing legislation would give workers, but they valued at least as much the political implications of forming and winning them. They pointed the way to a more conscious and unified class politics.

By the mid-1980s these initiatives had become more difficult. As we saw in Massachusetts, the result was a modest benefits program. Elsewhere, local plant closing legislation was a hostage of the expansion of the mid- to late 1980s. It was the conjuncture of the 1988 presidential campaign that won the mandatory notice law at the federal level.

The activists' discourse about multinational corporations, plant closing legislation and capital mobility was characteristically indignant. When activists learned that a conglomerate had closed a plant in an older area even as it built one abroad, the fact that this shift was profitable to the firm seemed to indict it. The implication was that highest rates of return are somehow a matter of choice, and that the global firms could, if they willed it, settle for less.

While projecting their indignation had the modest virtue of casting the conglomerates as villains, the activists seemed to imply that large-scale capitalist enterprises can thrive in the long run without seeking the highest rates of return and lowest labor militance.

As an invention of investors and employers, as with all such massive shifts in social scale, the global firm was born of necessity. As we have shown in our analyses of the apparel and textile, motor vehicle, and electronics industries, the growing control of global firms over the worldwide resource allocation process is a response to clear exigencies, not deficient sensibility.

The political form of this structure portrays U. S. capital as facing falling rates of profit and competition from global firms of different national origins. The local constituency of labor unity has absorbed the implications of this context; it has feared to pit its interests against capital's. This climate of fear subverts the coalition building project.

The national arena. The strategies of conglomeration and internationalization are designed to provide capital with strategic leverage to force labor and taxpayers to bear the burden of the conflicts and contradictions of the restructuring process. These strategies operate nationally as well as locally.

Consider the strategic implication of the takeover, in the early 1970s of the largest U. S. producer of bread and baked goods (Continental Baking) by ITT. Previous to Continental's acquisition, the union representing its workers had the strategic ability to bring a halt to all or most of Continental production. Once acquired, Continental's contribution to ITT's overall corporate profits amounted to one percent. The Bakery and Confectionery Workers Union (BCWU) was thus shifted from a situation in which it could shut down the employer to one in which it could jeopardize but one percent of the employer's profits.

Changes such as the BCWU example are changes in the relations of power at the point of production. They are paralleled by changes in relations of local political power. As the global firms deploy their capital worldwide, any national group of workers undergoes a similar erosion in power. North American workers employed by Ford, for example, work for an organization which gains most of its profits from foreign operations.

These exigencies of global capitalism are the crucible of contemporary political strategies. On one hand, capitalists in industries threatened by foreign capital are leading, or attempting to lead, corporate-labor coalitions for protectionist trade policy. This accompanies a chauvinist ideological mobilization using such pretexts as Soviet military force. The atmosphere engendered encourages national cross-class solidarity, as distinct from international-class solidarity. It asks workers to subsidize corporate profits in the name of "international competitiveness."

Alternatively, as we have seen, labor and progressive citizens groups have begun to develop policies at state and national levels to regulate or even direct the mobility of capital, that is, "industrial policy." The struggle for this program promises to unite workers in their roles as consumers and producers. But, even if successful, the strategy will confront the investor's world of choice.

Conclusion

Once one ventures beyond the moral critique of corporate behavior, the probability that national regulation of capital allocation in the global context may simply be ineffective in maintaining or enhancing the position of the working class must be confronted.

This conclusion bears on two aspects of current political developments in North America. On the one hand, the populist movement rests on a pragmatic orientation toward the defense of working people's interest in local politics. It avoids characterizing itself as socialist, but sometimes fosters both anticorporate consciousness and a programmatic demand for more regulation. (We have seen, however, that local regulatory demands can be evaded and are subject to concerted attack by business activists.)

On the other hand, social democratic perspectives on economic planning and the social control of capital gained some ground among activists, intellectuals, and a small number of elected officials in the early 1980s. Visible fractions of the Democratic Party, that is, parts of the Jesse Jackson constituency, had a social democratic agenda.

These beginnings seemed to have been nearly erased by the Reagan landslide of 1984 and then turned back once again by the Bush victory in 1988. The fiscal crisis caused by Reagan's earlier policies have created a context widely experienced as holding little possibilities for new initiatives— surely as much a part of the program as any of its apparent justifications.

In this situation, the more vigorous, mass-based populists are unable to address the question of the social ownership of the means of production, while the more elite-based democratic socialist alternative is more or less committed to pursuing its political and strategic program within a Democratic Party arena dominated by "centrist" perspectives. That arena was vitally formed by Reagan's 1984 triumph. Democratic Party elected officials hastened to align their rhetoric and their ideas with the new realities of business dominance.

The prospect of achieving a program oriented to overcoming the power of the global firms and sustaining levels of living in North America through a party that seems to be trying to shed its image as a party of blue-collar labor is not favorable. Thus, despite the renewal of genuinely working-class dissent from national policy, there is no near-term prospect of a powerful political force which can, in very practical ways, project a program of socially based solutions to capital allocation. Yet, the strategic dilemma is even more complex.

U. S. workers, and, we suspect, their European counterparts, formulate strategy and tactics very much within the confines of a national political perspective. There are exceptions in detail, but the fundamental strategic outlook of trade union, socialist, and communist movements tends to presume that each national arena offers each working class the opportunity to improve its objective conditions, and even to transform social relations.

A few years ago, a U. S. newspaper article, reflecting on the troubles of the automobile industry, revealed clearly the inadequacy of such strategic views. Discussing nationalization of the U. S. auto industry in a speculative fashion, the article pointed out that very large proportions of the assets of the Big Three auto makers were held overseas. What would be the disposal of these assets in the event of nationalization in the United States, but no corresponding initiative in Europe or South America? Clearly, without the cooperation of other states, and other national communities of workers, such a tactic would fail.

In any case, the new world order of capitalism has changed the scale of class conflict, and thus the scale of appropriate progressive responses. Often, we become aware of great changes, we gain knowledge of large systems, only as they pass into history. In the older industrial regions of the United States, the United Kingdom, France, and elsewhere, the social impacts of global capitalism were experienced far before workers and their allies understood it as a system: "The owl of Minerva," Hegel wrote, "takes flight at dusk."

11

State Autonomy and the Prospects for Socialism

'Tis the final conflict
let each stand in his place
the international working class
shall be the human race.
                    —*The Internationale*

Introduction

The heroic prospect of nineteenth-century socialism has been much delayed, and the emergence of global capitalism will delay "the final conflict" further still. The restructuring of the 1970s and 1980s not only weakened the strategic situation of the working class in the older industrial regions, it also added an adaptive depth to the systemic defenses of capitalism.

Throughout the older industrial regions, the economic difficulties of the 1970s and 1980s brought a "conservative" political trend, restraints on the social wage, and renewed dependence on market initiatives. The 1980s witnessed the triumphs of Thatcher, Reagan, and Kohl, while socialist governments in France and Sweden turned to austerity and scaled down their ambitious projects, "chastised" by the competitive pressures of the new international system of production. The emergence of global capitalism underlies these common threads of political change in North America and Western Europe over the last fifteen years.

This final chapter completes the journey begun in the discussion of power in chapter 1. Having moved to a presentation of models of capitalism, we proceeded to case studies of the impact of global change on industries and regions. Then the analysis turned to strategic perspectives on class and state policy. All the while, the central theme has been the development of new bases for power. Now, as we come full circle from our beginning, we integrate our studies by addressing two questions, one theoretical, one practical.

The theoretical proposition brings focus to our general theme of power relations and the way global capitalism changes the relation of the capitalist class and the working class to state power and policy. This chapter addresses the ways in which this has taken place, and how our view differs from those discussions of the relation of the capitalist class to state power that are framed in the context of monopoly capitalism. The thesis is that the partial independence of government from the will of fractions of the capitalist class in democratic capitalist societies has been reduced—there is relative decline of what has become known as the relative autonomy of the state.

The practical question is this: how does the emergence of the new variant of capitalism change the prospects for socialism?

The Historical Basis of Relative Autonomy

The concept. The concept of the relative autonomy of the state was elaborated in the course of debates, primarily among Marxists of various hue, about the relationship of the capitalist class to state power.[1]

However elaborate the discussion has become, the idea of relative autonomy is simple enough. It begins as a critique of a relatively unsophisticated version of Marxism:

1. The simplistic version of Marxism conceives of an "economic" base which determines a "political" superstructure. From this is derived the simple formula: change in the base yields change in the superstructure. This may be referred to as the "correspondence" thesis, or the "one-to-one correspondence" of base and superstructure.

2. Because the state in capitalism is nothing but the "executive committee of the ruling class"[2] the capitalist state: (a) is an *instrument* with which the capitalist class maintains its power and privilege; and (b) all state actions, including reforms that workers have sought, are motivated by, and often work out to serve, the interests of the capitalist class in its own continuance as a dominant class.

Both of these formulations seemed to need such extreme qualification that they fell to the wayside of intellectual discussion. Among the provocative questions we will address is whether the task of painstaking qualification and restatement would have been better than rejection. Through the 1960s and 1970s, however, scholars of a variety of views within neo-Marxism countered with the following two propositions:

1. The superstructure-base dichotomy is overly drawn, mechanical, false.

By 1890, Engels had rejected the notion that the materialist conception of history asserted that the "economic element is the *only* determining one," as "meaningless, abstract, senseless."[3] But neo-Marxist scholars went further. The very idea of an "economic" base was challenged, in the sense that the roles, norms, and values by which the category "economic" was understood were seen to be inseparably "social," therefore, participating in the very "superstructural" elements they were to have determined.[4]

Furthermore, the "correspondence" thesis, in the face of the variety of states, cultures, and social formations that were juridically "capitalist" was found wanting as well. The notion of relatively autonomous dynamics in a variety of spheres of social life was developed especially powerfully in the work of Louis Althusser. Althusser referred to "autonomous" levels of a social formation, and said the base was determinative "only in the last instance," adding that the "last instance never comes."[5]

2. State behavior that preserves capitalism as a system is determined by its embeddedness in an "ensemble" of capitalist structures. Capitalism is a "totality."

Neither capitalist class personnel, nor even capitalist parties in power are necessary to compel states, that is, governments, to act so as to preserve capitalism. They are forced to do so lest their actions produce capital strikes, inflation, and other negative economic consequences that threaten the incumbency of state officials. And, anyway, as participants in a culture dominated by capitalist outlooks ("ideological hegemony"), most politicians and state managers are prisoners of their own restricted imagination and wills. They cannot dare to do what they cannot imagine doing.

The thesis continues by arguing that while the state does act to preserve capitalism, it does so with some considerable discretion, with some autonomy from the direct intervention of capitalist class persons and their direct expression of momentary interests.

The basis of this discretion and autonomy is derived in part from the general characteristics of capitalism and in part from the specific features of capitalism as it was understood—in the 1960s and 1970s—when these matters were widely discussed.

The general characteristic is this: capitalists compete with one another at the level of the enterprise, and they strive for gain in a system of values of individual rewards. The state, within capitalism, must serve to reconcile such differences and interests so as to "manage the common affairs" of capital, essentially, ensuring the reproduction of the system as a whole. These propositions became central points of consensus within an otherwise diverse family of views known as structuralism.

Relative autonomy and monopoly capitalism. The particularities of state-society relations that were depicted by structuralism as producing a "relatively autonomous" state in the 1950s and 1960s, were the result of the strategic situation characteristic of, rather than declining under, "monopoly capitalism." Policy responsive to the needs of monopolistic firms was fundamental to state activity despite the ideological obeisance to "free markets" and entrepreneurial activity.

The regime of monopoly capitalism required management of the tensions inherent in a system in which actual dominance was exercised by monopolistic firms and the class that controlled them, within a social formation in which "individual, free enterprise" and entrepreneurial character was lionized. These tensions, with but few exceptions, have been a neglected feature of discussions of legitimation in the advanced capitalist countries.[6] Yet, they have been central to the twentieth-century history of the political right in every country of the West. The "autonomy" of state managers to impose sometimes unpopular policies on the capitalist class has rested on either the ability of large-scale capital to prevail over competitive capital, or the ability of finance capital, for example, through central banks, to impose its regulatory preferences over all others.

The imposition of state policy against partial or even majority capitalist class opposition has, therefore, been led by monopolists and financiers. Yet, the standard treatment of this matter has been deficient. Contributing to such behavior were, it has been noted, the interests large firms had in uniform standards of national law, especially in federalist systems such as North America.[7] But the upheaval of the 1930s and the World War II produced a set of pressures on large-scale capital that further impelled its concessions to the Welfare State. This was the enfranchisement of labor. Indeed, the ideological legitimation of the Western system became much more complex in the post-Popular Front/New Deal era: both small-scale capital *and* labor had to be governed. By mid-century, to take but one indicator, the most politically sensitive economic indicator in the West was the unemployment rate.

We hasten to add that the enfranchisement of labor—socially, economically, politically—was hardly automatic. It was not "granted," it was won. The social and economic policies that underlay modern workers' empowerment were almost always the occasion of terrific struggles.[8]

New variants of capitalism have had uneven effects on the political power of classes and class fractions. The transition from competitive to monopoly capitalism yielded the economic enfranchisement of organized labor, concentrated in the monopoly sector. At the same time, a stratified or "segmented" labor force structure emerged in the advanced industrial nations, yielding a far from privileged secondary labor market and its concomitant—a marginal proletariat sometimes characterized as "underclass."[9] Within the capitalist class, large firms with concentrated market power were able, more often than not, to mold state policy to their advantage, even as they made concessions—in direct negotiations, and in social policy, to unions and their political representatives. The ability of large firms to tolerate these concessions rested on their market power: costs of governmental regulation and of wage and benefit hikes could be passed on to both consumers (through administered prices) and to their smaller scale suppliers, through market leverage.

So the transition to monopoly capitalism entailed, in the long run, an increase in the political influence of organized labor in the advanced industrial nations. In all of them, the monopoly era witnessed the limited ability of unions, when well connected to potent political parties, to influence labor legislation, trade policy, and other policies surrounding the social wage.

The result included expansion of the social expenditures of the state, driven in part by the uneasy political accord between monopoly capital and monopoly labor.[10] This accord entailed a relative increment in the capacity of organized monopoly-sector labor to influence state policy, for itself, and for its allies.

Competitive-sector capital, and especially small firms, did not participate fully in this accord. In a price-competitive environment, without the ability of larger firms to pass on the costs of labor legislation, taxation, or regulatory burdens, competitive industries and small firms opposed the social policies and regulatory environment of monopoly capitalism. But the secular trend was toward concentration of capital and the apparent marginalization of the national political influence of such force.

Labor had won a fragile, minority stake in politics: accommodation with labor was a *political* requisite to governing in North America and Western Europe in general. The mechanism of this process was labor's influence in the popular parties of the West: the Democratic Party in the United States, the social democratic parties of Western Europe. This bridgehead allowed the organized working class to participate in the struggles for reforms which it defined as central to its interest.

Examples include the ferocious struggles in the United States over social insurance and medical benefits, health and safety regulation, and labor law. In Europe, nationalization and income policies saw uneasy, often temporary, compromises between capital and labor.

Thus, under monopoly capitalism, the state was relatively autonomous from the momentary interests and direct political intervention of particular fractions of capital. But autonomy from the more "conservative" preferences of competitive capital was a function, in large part, of the relative dominance of monopoly capital within the capitalist class, and the relative ability, in turn, of monopoly capital to make concessions to labor. Labor's enfranchisement was both the predicate and the motivation for these concessions.

The original concept of the relative autonomy of the state under monopoly capitalism denoted relative autonomy of state behavior from:

1. the transient will of fractions of the capitalist class; and

2. the direct intervention or influence of incumbency by capitalist class personnel.[11]

As Ralph Miliband put the first proposition: "while the state does act... *on behalf* of the 'ruling class,' it does not for the most part act *at its behest*."[12]

In this context, "autonomy" implied discretion for decisionmakers who were compelled objectively and subjectively to preserve the social order of capitalism. Preserving that social order required state action that conferred legitimacy on its claim to be something more than "instrument" of a privileged capitalist class; and it often required state action that labor won through "democratic class conflict" and "forced" on capital regardless of capital's momentary preferences.

The zone of discretion produced state policy that, under the conditions of monopoly capitalism, appeared to be "imposed" on various fractions of capital.

The "test" of the first of these assertions were those instances where "enlightened" capitalist class leadership implemented or merely tolerated policies rejected by that class's numerical majority, for example, many Progressive Era and New Deal reforms in America, and a variety of social and industrial policies in Western Europe.

The test of the second assertion has been the relative continuity of state policies when governments have been formed by social democratic and labor parties, while cabinets have been recruited from outside the ranks of corporate leadership.

In addition to these two widely accepted aspects of relative autonomy noted above, therefore, this analysis includes a third:

3. relative autonomy also entailed discretionary power of state managers to accommodate some of the needs/demands of labor in the political system.

The Transition to Global Capitalism

The monopoly variant of capitalism was dominant through the 1960s and throughout the advanced countries. But the constellation of forces were not static. Two kinds of forces disrupted the stability of this moment. Inherent contradictions of capitalist accumulation appeared in new forms; and new entrants to world capitalism's competitive system forced change in the political behavior of the older oligopolists.

During the last twenty years, the social system of capitalism has undergone crisis and change. As noted earlier, the crises of the 1970s and 1980s, however, have not been of the apocalyptic "breakdown" nature which Marxist theory long anticipated. Rather, similar to the structural crises of the late nineteenth century, the recent period has been one of "restructuring."[13] The political turmoil of the earlier period witnessed the emergence of monopoly capitalism out of the shell of competitive capitalism. The political events of this era are underlain by the succession of global capitalism from monopoly capitalism.

Recall that in regard to *class-state relations*, the principal theorists of monopoly capitalism share the view that monopoly capitalism brings about new forms of state activity. In particular,

1. working-class people are seen as receiving a rising portion of rising state outlays, while
2. monopoly capital is viewed as adopting a positive or tolerant attitude toward the expanding role of government in the economy.

Again, the Reagan, Thatcher, Mitterand, and Kohl governments, to mention just a few, however different, do not justify this view of the last ten or fifteen years.

Global Capitalism and Relative Autonomy

Under global capitalism, the expectations that capital has of state policy are altered, its attitude toward public policies favorable to labor hardens and its leverage over state expenditures is heightened. This leads to the relative decline of the relative autonomy of the state.

From the perspective of the global firm, the regions of the world form a mosaic of differentiated sites of potential investment. Wage rates and labor militancy are two important dimensions of that mosaic. The policy output of national states or subnational bodies of government are another. The political or policy environment of a given locality become an important variable in a firm's location calculations.

Part of this political environment is state policy in regard to industrial relations, policies and laws that mediate the capital-to-labor relation. No longer held hostage to unique local agglomerations of infrastructure and labor, global capital can now threaten to withdraw investment from localities or nation-states whose governments adopt policies relatively favorable to labor. They are also in a position to demand the repeal or rollback of programs adopted during the monopoly era but that global capital no longer regards as necessary.

This view of contemporary capitalism results in a thesis distinguished from both recent extensions of structuralism, and from the "orthodox" criticism of that work.[14] Our conclusion is that the emergence of global capitalism shifts the balance of class forces toward capital, and one of the results is decline in the relative autonomy of the state from transient capitalist class will and ideology.

Theories of the state should include a response to the fundamental questions of "why, how, and with what effect states change." The concept of relative autonomy implies that if autonomy is not absolute, but relative, then it may vary. The possibility of variation implies a historical dimension. The question of autonomy thus has a historical specificity shared by the general question of change in the state, and in class and social relations to the state. As C. Wright Mills translated Marx, "...[W]ithin [any given] historical type [of society] various mechanisms of change come to some *specific* kind of intersection."[15] (Emphasis added.)

Responses to these questions should "descend," as the level of abstraction approaches concrete social formations, toward more historically specific terms.

Global Capitalism and the Theory of the State

Some basic concepts.   Recent discussions of state theory have produced the thesis that the state itself, and state managers themselves, may, under given historical conditions, *create* changes in underlying social relations. States, in this so-called state-centered approach, may act not just "relatively" independent of "society" they may be, in certain respects, *determinant* in society.[16] This view is one possible extension of the rejection of the simplistic base-superstructure correspondence thesis. A full discussion of it would take our project too far afield. Nevertheless, our exploration of the implications of structural change in recent capitalism compel the view that, *at the minimum*, there is yet ample reason to maintain a major role for the "older" view of society-to-state dynamic in the direction of political change.

The study of global capitalism leads to the conclusion that important changes in the state will occur when the underlying relations among classes are transformed. The obvious caveats, too often absent from discussion that presents itself as scientific in these matters, are least two: first, while the underlying changes are *sufficient*, they may not be necessary, that is, there are other sources of state change; second, changes in the form, process, and policy outputs of states, clearly *lag* changes in underlying class relations.[17]

In theoretical terms, therefore, among the sources of change in states is structural transformation of a mode of production from one characteristic and dominant *variant* to another. The analysis of such change "descends" to a level of abstraction more specific than the mode of production in general, for example, "capitalism," and examines change among its historical variants, or *submodes*. The specification of state-society relations may then be applied to these submodes, for example, competitive versus monopoly capitalism, monopoly capitalism versus global capitalism.

States will change after the underlying balance of power between different classes or class fractions is restructured. Within capitalism, such changes *eventually* result in political responses to obstacles to accumulation. The analysis of such obstacles, we noted in the opening chapters of this book, need not focus only on a breakdown problematic, that is, the analysis of those dynamics within capitalism that will or might produce its historical termination as a mode of production. Restructuring crises will also produce state change, through the strategic class-state relationship.

Restructuring crises are the midwives of transition to a new variant of capitalism. State policy and political processes become responsive to newly dominant class fractions—or new bases of unity among them.

For example, as discussed above, in the course of the twentieth century, the elaboration of monopoly capitalist institutional structures entailed state policies that were particularly sensitive to the needs of the monopoly sector and that *also* had to accommodate the popular force generated by monopoly-sector labor.

Under global capitalism, political structures rest upon a new dimension of political unity within the capitalist class. This political unity, not so paradoxically, is formed in the face of a new dimension of competition—price competition based on a global search for appropriate, but low-wage labor.

The global scale of this competition grants and compels new strategic resources in capital's demands on state policy. The threat and practice of *global mobility of capital*, disciplines both labor and state decisionmakers, who lose discretionary power over some major matters—taxation, social policy, entitlements—lest investment decline within their areas of jurisdiction. Capital prevails over labor more frequently and more nakedly in the political realm.

The political stability of monopoly capitalism depended in part on state activity which meliorated the condition of the poor—surplus laborers concentrated in the secondary labor market and the competitive sector. The expenses of these activities both facilitated accumulation (by buffering aggregate demand) and legitimated the system by promoting social peace through welfarist policy and ideology.[18] The programs that meliorated the condition of the poor, it should be noted, bolstered the bargaining power and potential militancy of workers in general, for the consequences of striking or changing one's employment were buffered by the variety of income maintenance and social transfer programs.[19]

The Decline of Relative Autonomy

As monopoly capitalism gives way to global capitalism, all sectors of labor decline in bargaining power, in social potency and political influence. Social expenditures give way to market coercion as the mode of enforcing discipline. The threat of penury rather than the promise of social justice maintains order.

Workers (and others) support market-oriented regimes through a blend of motives. Without relinquishing their preferences for welfarist policies, they nevertheless are persuaded in some degree and previously unusual numbers, that conservative regimes can best attract the golden goose of investment which lays the egg of jobs.

The articulation of capitalist class interests with the state also changes in the transition from one submode to another. At the turn of the century, finance and monopoly capital began the construction of an institutional relation to state power that supplanted the personalistic advantages enjoyed by the entrepreneurial founders of family fortunes.[20] The institutional order that prevailed by mid-century throughout the capitalist West afforded special access and favorable policy for the monopoly sector. Small-scale and monopoly-sector capital had divergent interests in industrial relations, social wage, and taxation policies. With the power of administered pricing, monopoly-sector capital could tolerate the welfare state more equanimiously than competitive capital could.

Now, spurred by competition in the search for low-wage labor, and constrained by access to finance, large-scale capital becomes global—the multinational conglomerate replaces the monopolistic firm as the dominant form of enterprise. Politically, however, the project of producing abroad has a domestic face of coalition with competitive-sector conservatives in an assault on the social wage, and on the discretionary expenditures of the state. Class unity is reforged around resistance to the organizational and policy demands of labor. Combined, these changes can be grossly summarized as:

1. a relative increase in the power of investors and employers in relation to labor; and

2. the increasingly transparent shift from legitimation activities to those state activities that attempt to facilitate capital accumulation.

With labor in decline, and capital struggling to cope with changes in its competitive environment state managers have less "space" to take actions that meet either the long-term needs of the social formation or the demands of labor. The autonomy of the state declines in relation to the period in which national oligopolies were the dominant form of enterprise.

Relative Autonomy:
An Alternative View

The decline of relative autonomy is not a consensual inference from the facts of the current era. In an otherwise excellent essay on the politics of economic decline in the United States and the United Kingdom, for example, Krieger reaches the *opposite* conclusion.[21] Krieger claims that the "management" of decline in both the United States and the United Kingdom, which from our view is but one part of the moment of restructuring on a world scale, results in *dirigiste* regimes in both nations. Krieger deals with the politics of race and the splintering impact of decline on the working classes of both countries with sensitivity and wisdom. But his theoretical reflection on the *increase* of relative autonomy rests on the distinction between conservative rejection of macroeconomic wisdom, but concession to microeconomic lust.

Krieger notes that, at various moments, financial or industrial elites in both the United Kingdom and the United States, articulated clear opposition to Reagan and Thatcher policies.[22] His conclusion is that both regimes developed unusually high degrees of autonomy from capitalist-class interventions. This conclusion rests upon a misunderstanding of the original concept of relative autonomy and of the nature of the changes in the current global system.

Let us focus on the difference of interpretation about the United States. Krieger reports the financial community's early and articulate concerns about the massive deficits caused by Reaganomics.[23] He argues that the ability of the Reagan Administration to continue on its reckless fiscal course indicates its "autonomy" from capitalist-class intervention.

The problem with Krieger's analysis of autonomy is its neglect of the distinction between the financial community's interest in macroeconomic aggregates, and the capitalist class's interest in prevalence over labor. However "voodoo" the Reagan Administration's fiscal policies were, its gutting of the NLRB, of the Occupational Safety and Health Administration (OSHA), the erosion of the social wage, the massive redistribution of income to upper income groups through the Economic Recovery Tax Act of 1981—all of these, and manifold others, were what Krieger himself calls "policy plums" that "justifiably delighted" business elites who received "administration favors" to a "wide set of capitalist interests."[24] This indicates exactly the decline of autonomy from a "transient" will of the capitalist class in its disaggregated form of a scatter of firms and sectors, and its unified form as labor's adversary.

The idea of relative autonomy was, centrally, autonomy of the state to act, in Miliband's words, on behalf of the capitalist class, rather than at its behest. What the Reagan Administration did in its first term was to act at the behest of the common program of antilabor small-scale capital and the internationally pressured large-scale capital. This amounted to a political program of rollback of the long, social democratic march, which Krieger notes, of the Keynesian regime. Others have called this the attack on the social wage.[25]

Krieger may be right that the Reagan program was not in some putative long run interest of the capitalist class, in the sense that it sows the seeds of future instability, inflation, and so forth. But the idea of relative autonomy is one in which just such long-range interests may be imposed on the temporary will of a class whose political problem is the contradiction between firms and investor-based individual interests and systemwide or long-term class interests. That the particular advocates of lenient regulation, for example, or attacks on the social wage were able to prevail in this context, accounts for a paradox that Krieger does not discuss. Despite the notably irresponsible fiscal impact of Reagan policy, the consensus of business support for him contrasts sharply with the dissensus among large-scale elites that Goldwater faced in 1964.[26] The difference was not to be found in the policies advocated by the two political figures: it was, rather, the structural imperatives, experienced at the level of the firm, twenty years later. In this sense, then, Krieger's comments about elite concern over the Reagan program are the exception that proves (i.e., tests) the proposition about the decline of relative autonomy. The Reagan government was more sensitive to the transient microeconomic needs of capital in the global era than it was to the macroeconomic views of financial managers. The reason, from the point of view of our theory is clear: macroeconomic wisdom is abstract; but political unity in the Republican party was forged around the common program, long held by small-scale capital, but newly held by global capital: the concessions to big labor, in the global context were no longer desirable or necessary.

The Implications of the Relative Decline of Relative Autonomy

The implication of the change is a drastic loss of power and policy prerogative by labor, and the coalition of less-than-privileged interests to which it was central. The enfranchisement of labor was a central feature of the civilization of monopoly capitalism. The ideals of equality, equity, and democracy were carried on labor's advance. The new world of global capitalism challenges that civilization. It raises once again a proposition long held by the Western socialist tradition, one that is even more widely contemplated now: the coincidence of capitalism and democracy may not be permanent part of the Western legacy.

Socialism and Global Capitalism

We end where we began: the socialist project of Western labor. In the waning years of the Reagan era, one engages in such a commentary, to paraphrase Guevara, "at the risk of seeming ridiculous." The 1988 U.S. presidential election found the Democrat, Dukakis, the most pro-business nominee of that party since 1924. A man of liberal principal and good will, Dukakis, we note in chapter 9, is a political leader whose views have been formed by the rigors of the global era.

In Western Europe, the socialist aspirations of the socialist parties have also been the victims of the restructuring of the world market. The aggressive Mitterand of 1981 becomes the centrist of 1988. Even the brave Sandinistas find that there is no room for their socialism in the world system.

Not so coincidentally, the People's Republic of China has moved, in the 1980s, toward an aggressive introduction of market forces, toward an open door for Western investors, and most significantly, to a role as an export platform exploiting its "comparative advantage" of massive quantities of cheap labor.

Many of the former growth economies of the "newly industrializing countries" have been hurt badly by the burden of debt incurred in the 1970s, but the pressures of that debt pushes them even further into export strategies that depend on their cheap labor.

Not so long ago the prospect for socialism looked very different. The 1960s and early 1970s saw growing strength on the European left, and the development of "Eurocommunism" seemed to portend renewed unity among working-class political forces. Revolutionary movements in the Third World portended an enlargement of the "socialist bloc." How different our world has become.

The response to the contradictions of monopoly capitalism gave new life to capitalism. In a thoroughly globalized production system any given nation's movement toward an alternative mode of civilization is put in jeopardy by capital's ability to find willing hands elsewhere. That the number of poor hands reaches into the billions suggests the depth of reserves that capital as a system maintains under global capitalism.

The gradual incorporation of larger and larger fractions of the world's population into global capitalism's production system implies a substantial period in which the unevenness of world conditions will continue to produce tremendous leverage for capital. That nations will rise and fall in this system is certain; and not even internationalization will abolish the internal contradictions that have led millions to aspire to another way of life; but its medium-run persistence seems certain.

At time of the Russian Revolution, the problem we are now posing was foreseen. Could Soviet socialism survive in one country? Many believe that the cost of its isolated survival was the unfortunate history of Soviet authoritarianism and technical backwardness.

In the era of global capitalism, however, it is more than ever clear that international solidarity is not merely a sentiment for the socialist movement—it is its only means of birth and existence. In a world of nation-states of vastly uneven levels of living, capital has many places to "hide." To take but one contemporary metaphor: the most appropriate level of authority for a "plant closing notification" law is neither the local state nor the national state, but the world.

Amidst the complexity of everyday politics and class contentions the practice of international working-class cooperation seems hardly "realistic." Until it is, it *appears* that the "final conflict" is a long way off.

But rather than a counsel of despair, our view is more practical, and more tentative. We are only at the beginning of the global era. In everyday political and economic practice human ingenuity can be counted on to discover, over time, strategies and policies that "work," that advance their struggles for material decency and dignity. And in further scholarship, new tools, new strategies, new analytical perspectives will be found that will advance our early attempt to formulate the problem. Much is to be learned about how to tame this New Leviathan. That is the prospect before us. After all, "No one rules forever on the throne of time."

Endnotes

CHAPTER 1

1. Michael Kinsley, quoted by Lynn Hirschberg, "The Unbearable Rightness of Michael Kinsley: The *New Republic* Editor Mouths Off," *Rolling Stone*, issue 526, May 18, 1988, p. 108.

2. See, for example, Katherine Gibson, et al., "A Theoretical Approach to Capital and Labour Restructuring," in Phil O'Keefe (ed.), *Regional Restructuring Under Advanced Capitalism* (London: Croom Helm, 1984), pp. 39–68; Robert Ross, et al., "Global Capitalism and Regional Decline: Implications for The Strategy of Classes in Older Regions," Ibid., pp. 111–30; Kent Trachte and Robert Ross, "The Crisis of Detroit and The Emergence of Global Capitalism," *International Journal of Urban and Regional Research*, vol. 9, no. 2, June 1985; Robert Ross, "Facing Leviathan: Public Policy and Global Capitalism," *Economic Geography*, vol. 59, no. 2, April 1983, pp. 144–60; Robert Ross and Kent Trachte, "Global Cities and Global Classes: The Peripheralization of Labor in New York City," *Review*, vol. VI, no. 3, Winter 1983, pp. 393–431; Robert Ross, Don Shakow, and Paul Susman, "Local Planners—Global Constraints," *Policy Sciences*, vol. 13, 1980, pp. 1–25; and Robert Ross, "Regional Illusion, Capitalist Reality," *Democracy*, vol. II, no. 2, pp. 93–99, 1982.

3. Among our inspirations when we began our collaboration was the early work of Barry Bluestone and Bennet Harrison that eventuated in their influential *The Deindustrialization of America* (New York: Basic Books, 1982). We resolved that their elegant empirics and review of research required a theoretically informed accompaniment. As we completed our work, their equally influential *The Great U-Turn* (New York: Basic Books, 1988) made this need all the more apparent.

4. Harrison and Bluestone, 1988, op. cit.

5. We have been asked why so much of our work focusses on some matters about which primarily Marxists are concerned; and why we risk narrowing our audience by engaging the somewhat obscure language of that tradition. Our response is dual: we think this tradition of social science has the most powerful tools for the job at hand; but these tools are not in good repair. We thought our greatest contribution would be to assist in its renewal.

6. Paul Baran and Paul Sweezy, *Monopoly Capital* (New York: Monthly Review, 1966); and James O'Connor, *The Fiscal Crisis of the State* (New York: St. Martin's Press, 1973).

7. Joseph Schumpeter, *Capitalism, Socialism, and Democracy*, 5th ed. (London: George Allen and Unwin, 1976).

8. For example, David Gordon, "Capitalist Development and the History of American cities," in William K. Tabb and Larry Sawers, eds., *Marxism and the Metropolis: New Perspectives in Urban Political Economy*, 2nd ed. (New York: Oxford University Press, 1984) pp. 21–53.

9. See Christopher Chase-Dunn, "The World System Since 1950: What Has Really Changed?," in C. Berquist, ed., *Labor in the Capitalist World Economy* (Beverly Hills: Sage, 1984); and David Gordon, "The Global Economy: New Edifice or Crumbling Foundations?," *New Left Review*, vol. 168, March/April 1988, pp. 24–64.

10. See M. Storper and R. Walker, "The Theory of Labor and the Theory of Location," *The International Journal of Urban and Regional Research*, vol. 7, 1983, pp. 1–41; and by the same authors, "The Spatial Division of Labor: Labor and the Location of Industries," in Larry Sawers and William K. Tabb, *Sunbelt/Snowbelt: Urban Development and Regional Restructuring* (New York: Oxford University Press, 1984) pp. 19–47.

11. This is the position taken by Chase-Dunn, op. cit., and by Gordon, op. cit., 1988, in different ways.

12. See chapter 2, for a discussion of the relevance of this era of theorizing for our own. Anthony Brewer, *Marxist Theories of Imperialism: A Critical Survey* (London: Routledge and Kegan Paul, 1980); and Tom Bottomore, *Theories of Modern Capitalism* (London: George Allen and Unwin, 1985) have useful summaries.

13. Thorstein Veblen, *The Theory of Business Enterprise* (New York: Charles Scribners' Sons, 1904, 1963).

14. In some respects, the pioneering analysis of American power structure by C. Wright Mills, in *The Power Elite* (New York: Oxford University Press, 1956), was part of the same—long—process. While Mills was certainly far from Marxist orthodoxy, and was criticized by Marxists for the Weberian elements in his work, he clearly understood his enterprise as the sociological counterpart of the political economists' encounter with monopoly capitalism. See chapter 11, "The Theory of Balance," in *The Power Elite*.

15. See chapter 4 below for a discussion of Wallerstein and world systems theory.

16. The majority of the United States's chief trading partners, competitors, and recipients of manufacturing investment in Western Europe, for example, have more stringent plant closing notification requirements than the sixty-day requirement vetoed by President Reagan in the spring of 1988, but then allowed to become law by him in the summer, under the pressures of the presidential campaign.

17. See chapter 7.

18. See chapter 5.

19. Mills, op. cit., p. 9.

20. Peter Bachrach and Morton Baratz, "The Two Faces of Power," *American Political Science Review*, vol. 56, 1962, pp. 947–52.

21. Matthew A. Crenson, *The Un-Politics of Air Pollution: The Study of Non-Decisionmaking in the Cities*, (Baltimore, Md.: Johns Hopkins University Press, 1971).

22. Antonio Gramsci, *Selections from the Prison Notebooks*, Quintin Hoare and Geoffrey Nowell Smith, eds. and trans., (New York: International Publishers, 1971).

23. Most any textbook illustrates most aspects of this approach, for example, S. Stanley Eitzen with Maxine Baca Zinn, *In Conflict and Order: Understanding Society*, 4th ed. (Boston: Allyn and Bacon, 1988).

24. In a related context, Ross and Staines argued that there was a "politics" of analyzing social problems before those problems ever reached legislative or policy resolution. Robert Ross and Graham Staines, "The Politics of Analyzing Social Problems," *Social Problems*, vol. 20, no. , 1972, pp. 18–40.

25. See chapter 7.

26. Gordon, op. cit., cites a contrasting methodological summary of a general approach to historical regimes of capital accumulation in David M. Gordon, Thomas E. Weisskopf, and Samuel Bowles, "Power, Accumulation, and Crisis: The Rise and Demise of the Postwar Social Structure of Accumulation," R. Cherry et al., eds., *The Imperial Economy* (New York: n.p., 1988), vol. I.

27. For example, see Robert Ross, "Facing Leviathan: Public Policy and Global Capitalism," *Economic Geography*, vol. 59, no. 2, April 1983; and Robert Ross, Don Shakow, and Paul Susman, "Local Planners—Global Constraints," *Policy Sciences*, vol. 13, 1980, pp. 1–25, for discussions comparing U.K. and U.S. effects and policies in relation to global capitalism. See

Richard Peet, ed., *International Capitalism and Industrial Restructuring: A Critical Analysis* (Boston: George Allen and Unwin, 1987), for a number of articles which discuss internationalization and its impact on labor. Also, J. Carney, R. Hudson, and J. Lewis, eds., *Regions in Crisis: New Perspectives in European Theory*, (London: Croom Helm, 1980), and R. Hudson and D. Sadler, "Contesting Works Closures in Western Europe's Old Industrial Regions: Defending Place or Betraying Class?," in Allen J. Scott and Michael Storper, eds., *Production, Work and Territory: The Geographical Anatomy of Industrial Capitalism* (Boston: George Allen and Unwin, 1986), pp. 172–93.

28. William Kornblum, *Blue Collar Community* (Chicago: University of Chicago Press, 1974).

29. See Barry Bluestone and Bennett Harrison, *The Deindustrialization of America* (New York: Basic Books, 1982) pp. 133–39; Richard Peet, "The Relocation of Manufacturing Capital Within the United States," *Economic Geography*, vol. 59,no. 2, April 1983.

30. James O'Connor, *The Fiscal Crisis of the State* (New York: St. Martin's Press, 1973).

CHAPTER 2

1. While Marxists have welcomed their own predictions of capitalism's breakdown, non-Marxist social scientists have also, but regretfully, predicted it. See, prominently, Joseph Schumpeter, *Capitalism, Socialism, and Democracy*, 5th ed., (London: George Allen and Unwin, 1976).

2. For a succinct presentation as well as critical analysis of the contributions of Bukharin, Lenin, and Luxemburg, see Anthony Brewer, *Marxist Theories of Imperialism: A Critical Survey* (London: Routledge and Kegan Paul, 1980). For the Austro-Marxists, for example, Hilferding, and Weber and Schumpeter's non-Marxist analyses, all concurring about the structure and significance of the transition from competitive to monopoly capitalism, see Tom Bottomore, *Theories of Modern Capitalism* (London: George Allen and Unwin, 1985).

3. See Paul Baran and Paul Sweezy, *Monopoly Capital* (New York: Monthly Review, 1966). Two critical but excellent recent reviews of the work of Baran and Sweezy are Brewer, op. cit., ch. 6; and John G. Taylor, *From Modernization to Modes of Production: A Critique of the Sociologies of Development and Underdevelopment* (London: MacMillan, 1979), ch. 3.

4. Erik Olin Wright, *Class, Crisis and the State* (London: New Left Books, 1978) pp. 165–66.

5. Ibid., pp. 168–80.

6. Michel Aglietta, *A Theory of Capitalist Regulation: The U.S. Experience* (London: New Left Books, 1979), p. 381. For his criticism of Baran and Sweezy, see pp. 27, 155.

7. David Gordon, Richard Edwards, and Michael Reich, *Segmented Work, Divided Workers: The Historical Transformation of Labor in the United States* (Cambridge: Cambridge University Press, 1982) p. 19.

8. Gordon, Edwards, Reich, op. cit., p. 171.

9. This methodology is not, however, consensual. World systems analysis emphasizes continuity, not variation, in capitalism. See chapter 4, below, and Christopher Chase-Dunn, "Stages of Dependency or Cycles of World System Development?," *Humboldt Journal of Social Relation*, vol. 8, no. 1, Fall/Winter 1980–81, p. 10; and Chase-Dunn, "Cycles, Trends, or Transformation?: The World System Since 1945," in Terry Boswell and Albert Bergesen, eds., *America's Changing Role in the World System* (Beverly Hills: Sage, 1985).

10. The concept of variants or submodes of the capitalist mode of production in general, and the particular theory of the transition to hegemony by the global capitalist submode has been the characteristic contribution of an international group of political economists variously associated with Clark University. Their work, and that of others which discusses the theoretical status of the concept includes the following: Katherine D. Gibson and Ronald J. Horvath, "Global Capital and The Restructuring Crisis in Australian Manufacturing," *Economic Geography*, vol. 59, no. 2, April 1983, pp. 178–96; Katherine Gibson et al., "A Theoretical Approach to Capital and Labor Restructuring," in Phil O'Keefe, ed., *Regional Restructuring Under Advanced Capitalism* (London: Croom Helm, 1984), pp. 39–68; Julie Graham, *Economic Restructuring in the United States, 1958–1980: Theory, Method and Identification* (Unpublished Ph.D. diss., Clark University, Worchester, Mass., 1983); Katherine Gibson, *Structural Change Within the Capitalist Mode of Production: The Case of The Australian Economy* (Unpublished Ph.D. diss., Clark University, Worchester, Mass., 1982); and Paul Susman and Eric Schutz, "Monopoly and Competitive Firm Relations and Regional Development in Global Capitalism," *Economic Geography*, vol. 59, no. 2, April 1983, pp. 161–77. For a critical appreciation of this line of argument, see Richard Peet, "Introduction: The Global Geography of Contemporary Capitalism," *Economic Geography*, vol. 59, no. 2, April 1983, pp. 105–11.

11. For discussion of the concept of articulation of modes or variants of modes of production, see Nicos Poulantzas, *Political Power and Social Classes* (London: NLB, Verso ed., 1978),pp. 15, 71, 90–91, 150, 157. The dominance of a submode of capitalism within a given social formation takes the form, in principle, of a flow of value from the subordinate variant(s) to the dominant variant.

12. Cf. Gibson, 1982, op. cit.

13. On the internationalization of capital, see, Christian Palloix, "The Self-Expansion of Capital on a World Scale," *Review of Radical Political Economics*, vol. 9, no. 2,Summer 1977, pp. 3–28. On the velocity of capital mobility and "hypermobility," see Felix Damette, "The Regional Framework of Monopoly Exploitation: New Problems and Trends," in John Carney and Ray Hudson, eds., *Regions in Crisis* (London: Croom Helm, 1980), pp. 76–92.

14. Cf. Harry Braverman, *Labor and Monopoly Capital* (New York: Monthly Review, 1974).

15. For the role of class struggle (i.e., the capital-labor relation) and the structure of causation in capitalist societies, see Eric Olin Wright, *Class, Crisis, State,* op. cit.

16. Cf. Aglietta, op. cit.

17. G. William Domhoff has developed the research and theory of the *social* nature of capitalist class cohesion in a series of studies: see his *The Bohemian Grove and Other Retreats* (New York: Harper and Row, 1974); *The Higher Circles* (New York: Random House, 1970); and *Who Rules America?* (Englewood Cliffs, N.J.: Prentice-Hall, 1967).

18. For reviews of the debates among crisis theorists, see, Erik Olin Wright, *Class, Crisis and the State* (London: New Left Books, 1978); Manuel Castells, *The Economic Crisis and American Society* (Princeton, N.J.: Princeton University Press, 1980); and Julie Graham, *Economic Restructuring in the United States, 1958–1980: Theory and Identification* (unpublished Ph.D. diss., Clark University, Worchester, Mass., 1984). For a brief review and empirical evaluation, see Thomas E. Weisskopf, "Marxian Crisis Theory and the Rate of Profit in the Postwar Economy," *Cambridge Journal Economics*, vol. 3, 1979, pp. 341–78.

19. This section follows closely and is heavily indebted to Wright, op. cit., pp. 111–54.

20. Wright, op. cit., p. 112.

21. Weisskopf, op. cit., p. 341.

22. We are well aware that Marx's labor theory of value has been under sustained technical attack and is hardly consensual, even among those who adopt his general perspective on class dynamics. We explicated our views about the transition to global capitalism in terms of the contending theories based on the labor theory of value in part because we share an agnostic view of this controversy. Our position is that this transition can be understood with the aid of any one of these theories or independent of them.

23. See, for example, Andrew Glyn and Bob Sutcliffe, *British Capitalism, Workers and the Profit Squeeze* (London: Penguin, 1972), who proffer an analysis of long-term structural decline of the British economy; Raford Boddy and James Crotty, "Class Conflict and Macro Policy: The Political Business Cycle," *Review of Radical Political Economics*, vol. 7, no. 1, 1975, who present an interpretation of business cycles based on class struggle dynamics; and Gordon, Edwards, and Reich, op. cit., whose problematic is the existence of different phases or stages in the history of capitalism.

24. For a fuller explanation of this criticism and citations, see, Wright, op. cit., p. 150. See also, David Harvey, *The Limits to Capital* (Chicago: University of Chicago Press, 1982), pp. 52–57, for a review and an additional critique of the perspective.

25. Manuel Castells, *The Economic Crisis and American Society* (Princeton, N.J.: Princeton University Press, 1980), p. 48.

26. Wright, op. cit., pp. 151–54.

27. This expression is adopted from Wright, op. cit., p. 126. We are aware, as Wright notes, that this is not the traditional way in which Marxists have defined the organic composition of capital (see Wright, fn., p. 126). The normal practice has been to express it as the ratio of constant capital to variable capital. This change in definition reflects the view of a number of recent authors that the ratio c/v is not an adequate measure of capital intensity; they have substituted the ratio $c/v+s$. The adoption of the more recent language and ratio here reflects our view that it affords a more clear explanation.

28. This apparently "physical" dimension of reproduction has as we noted, from Marx, above, a "historical and moral" component; and in modern conditions of labor, where so much of the assumptive capability of the working class is dependent on skill and literacy, "reproduction costs" include the reproduction of what conventional economists call "human capital."

29. The general process is specifically illustrated when American manufacturers (e.g., in the automobile industry) invest in robots as part of their "response" to Japanese or Korean competition. Unable to drive wages down to a qualitatively lower tier on the world scale, they attempt to reduce their use of it. There are other explanations offered in the literature, including, as Wright, op. cit., pp. 132–33, notes, limits on the supply of labor.

30. Broadly, surplus value can be increased in two ways—by lengthening the working day or by reducing necessary labor. The former produces absolute surplus value, Marx observes; the latter augments relative surplus value. See Brewer, op. cit., pp. 34–36, for a detailed discussion.

31. We agree with Wright that terming the *class struggle, profit squeeze* position as circulationist is inaccurate.

32. Weisskopf, op. cit., p. 346.

33. See Wright, op. cit., p. 142.

34. Castells, op. cit., pp. 26–41, reviews a variety of these efforts. In particular, among those workers we have found particularly useful are: Anwar Shaikh, "Political Economy and Capitalism: Notes on Dobb's Theory of Crisis," *Cambridge Journal of Economics*, vol. 2, 1978, pp. 233–51; Thomas E. Weisskopf, "Marxian Crisis Theory and the Rate of Profit in the Postwar U.S. Economy," *Cambridge Journal of Economics*, vol. 3, 1979, pp. 341–78;and Ernest Mandel, *The Second Slump: A Marxist Analysis of Recession in the Seventies*, Jon Rothschild, trans., (London: New Left Books, 1978) ch. 5.

35. Wright, op. cit., p. 163, and Fig. 3.6, pp. 168–69.

36. Among the orthodox the problem with our position is that it equivocates between determinist (i.e., structural logic) and voluntarist (i.e., class struggle) views of the dynamics of capitalism. We are unable to satisfy true believers about this matter. Global capitalism is the emergent reality, and we can see the ways in which it is the result of any of these arguments. The challenge to any of the particular orthodox adherents is to show that their view of crisis dynamics better explains that reality. Our own suspicion is that the ultimate answer is not an exclusive categorical choice.

37. Katherine Gibson et al., *Toward a Marxist Empirics* (unpublished ms., 1986), pp. 7–1. See also Gibson and Horvath, op. cit., 1983; Gibson et al., op. cit., 1984, pp. 39–68; op. cit., 1983; and Gibson, op. cit., 1982.

38. For an especially lucid discussion of the nature of capitalist accumulation and crisis that has influenced this presentation, see, Gordon, Edwards

and Reich, op. cit., pp. 26–32. See also the extension of this argument by Samuel Bowles, David M. Gordon, and Thomas Weisskopf, *Beyond the Wasteland*, (Garden City, N.Y.: Anchor Press–Doubleday, 1983).

CHAPTER 3

1. Paul Baran and Paul Sweezy, *Monopoly Capital* (New York: Monthly Review, 1966), pp. 3–7.

2. See, for example, Joseph Schumpeter, *Capitalism, Socialism and Democracy* (New York: Harper and Row, 1950); John Kenneth Galbraith, *The New Industrial State* (Boston: Houghton Mifflin, 1967); and C. Wright Mills, *The Power Elite* (New York: Oxford University Press, 1956).

3. Some of the more important works in the tradition include, Paul Baran, *The Political Economy of Growth* (New York: Monthly Review, 1957); Paul Sweezy, *The Theory of Capitalist Development*, 2nd ed. (New York: Monthly Review, 1970); Paul Sweezy, "Some Problems in the Theory of Capitalist Accumulation," *Monthly Review*, vol. 26, 1, 1974, pp. 38–55; Harry Magdoff, *The Age of Imperialism* (New York: Monthly Review, 1969); and Harry Braverman, *Labor and Monopoly Capital* (New York: Monthly Review, 1974).

4. James O'Connor, *The Fiscal Crisis of the State* (New York: St. Martin's Press, 1973). O'Connor uses some concepts Sweezy does not (e.g., social capital). In his *Accumulation Crisis*, (Oxford: Basil Blackwell, 1984, 1986) he explores the American ideological and cultural contributions to national dimensions of its accumulation crisis. As noted in chapter 5, O'Connor acknowledges but does not incorporate in his analysis the international dimension of the crisis of the 1970s; cf. p. 2.

5. For examples of this interpretation of Baran and Sweezy, see, John Weeks, *Capital and Exploitation* (Princeton, N.J.: Princeton University Press, 1981) pp. 150–54; and Anthony Brewer, *Marxist Theories of Imperialism: A Critical Survey* (London: Routledge & Kegan Paul, 1980), p. 6.

6. Baran and Sweezy, op. cit., p. 6.

7. Ibid., p. 71.

8. Baran and Sweezy argue that "...unstable market conditions of this sort were very common in the earlier phases of capitalism and still occur occasionally, but they are not typical of present-day monopoly capitalism," Ibid., pp. 50–58.

9. O'Connor, op. cit., p. 16.

10. Paul Baran, op. cit., p. 111.

11. Ibid., p. 112.

12. Some theorists utilizing the monopoly capitalist framework have revised Baran's views of industrial stagnation in "backward" countries. See, for example, James O'Connor, "The Meaning of Economic Imperialism," in K. T. Fann and Donald Hodges, eds., *Readings in U.S. Imperialism* (Boston: Porter Sargent, 1971), pp. 54–57.

13. See, for example, Baran and Sweezy, op. cit., pp. 178–217; O'Connor, op. cit., 1973, pp. 151–57;O'Connor, op. cit., 1970, p. 44; and Magdoff, op. cit.

14. Baran and Sweezy, op. cit., p. 201, state that what really interests the giant corporations dominating U.S. foreign policy is "monopolistic control over foreign sources of supply and foreign markets." Magdoff, op. cit., p. 35, argues that two of the prominent features of the contemporary era of imperialism are "control over as much of the sources of raw materials as possible" and the "conquest of foreign markets."

15. O'Connor, op. cit., p. 152, writes, "Monopolistic producers need and seek foreign markets and investment outlets in order to keep aggregate demand in step with productive capacity."

16. Thus, the level of social reproduction of the working class can and has risen over the last century in the advanced capitalist countries.

17. The social wage is that bundle of state policies, such as social and health insurance, which add to the real income of workers.

18. For this argument, see O'Connor, op. cit., 1973, pp. 15–23. Baran and Sweezy are cognizant of and do offer an explanation for their apparent oversight: "We do not claim that directing attention to the generation and absorption of surplus gives us a complete picture of this or any other society. And we are particularly conscious of the fact that this approach, as we have used it, has resulted in an almost total neglect of a subject which occupies a central place in Marx's study of capitalism: the labor process." See Baran and Sweezy, op. cit., p. 8.

19. O'Connor, op. cit., 1973, pp. 15–16.

20. Ibid., pp. 22–23. In various presentations of this model of monopoly capitalism, colleagues in political science and labor history have hastened to point out that the enfranchisement of labor that resulted in this "tacit agree-

ment" was hardly a gift from capital. The conditions of the monopoly sector may have been the most favorable for labor organization—large plants, impersonal organizations, routine production processes, and class segregated neighborhoods—but capital did not yield without fierce resistance and decades of labor struggle. Ralph Miliband impressed upon us the need to emphasize labor's agency in producing its ability to create the terms of the agreement.

21. Ibid., p. 22.

22. Bennett Harrison, "Institutions in the Periphery," in David M. Gordon, ed., *Problems in Political Economy: An Urban Approach*, 2nd ed. (Lexington, Mass.: D. C. Heath, 1977).

23. O'Connor, op. cit., p. 27.

24. There have been several excellent reviews of this burgeoning literature. See, for example, David Gold, Clarence Lo, and Erik Olin Wright, "Some Recent Developments in Marxist Theories of the State," *Monthly Review*, vol. 27, no. 5 and 6, 1975; Bob Jessop, "Recent Theories of the Capitalist State," *Cambridge Journal of Economics*, vol. 1, no. 4, 1977, pp. 353–73; John Holloway and Sol Picciotto, *State and Capital: A Marxist Debate* (London: Edward Arnold, 1978);and Bob Jessop, "Accumulation Strategies, State Forms and Hegemonic Projects," *Kapitalistate*, Double Issues, vols. 10/11, 1983, pp. 89–112.

25. Baran and Sweezy, op. cit., pp. 142–51.

26. Ibid., pp. 65–66.

27. This interpretation does not mean that Baran and Sweezy view the assumption of an activist role by the state as a feature unique to monopoly capitalism. As they point out, and we agree, "to lay special emphasis on the role of the state in the present stage of monopoly capitalism may only mislead people into assuming that it was of negligible importance in the earlier history of capitalism." Baran and Sweezy, op. cit., p. 67. Rather, it is the specific function of this increased government spending, the absorption of the surplus, that is the unique feature of monopoly capitalism.

28. O'Connor, op. cit., p. 6.

29. Ibid., ch. 4.

30. Ibid., ch. 5.

31. Ibid., ch. 6.

32. Julie Graham, *Economic Restructuring in the United States, 1958-1980: Theory and Identification* (unpublished Ph.D. diss., Clark University, Worchester, Mass., 1984), p. 40. Readers may recall that in the classical analysis of value in Marx's political economy, the ratio of dead to living labor is the "organic composition of capital." It is expressed as c/v, where c is constant or physical capital and v is variable capital—wages advanced to laborers. The rate of profit in *value* terms is $s/c+v$; where s is the surplus extracted by the employer after a worker's wages have been paid. If c/v increases, $s/c+v$ must decrease.

33. For two useful and succinct summaries of "underconsumptionist" theories, see Erik Olin Wright, *Class, Crisis and the State* (London: New Left Books, 1978), pp. 138-47; and John Bellamy Foster, "Marxian Economics and the State, *Science and Society*, vol. XLVI, no. 3, 1982, pp. 257-83.

34. Baran and Sweezy, op. cit., p. 72.

35. Ibid., p. 9. The term is not used consistently. See, for example, Baran in *The Political Economy of Growth*, who defines *actual economic surplus* as "the difference between society's actual current output and its actual current consumption" (p. 22). Baran clarifies that the term "comprises obviously a lesser share of total output than that encompassed by Marx's notion of surplus value." His comments come very close to suggesting that the economic surplus is the same as "aggregate profits" as understood by conventional economists. As *Monopoly Capital* is the latter work, we will, for our purposes, accept the usage proffered there. For discussions of problems caused by Baran and Sweezy's inconsistent usage, see Brewer, op. cit., pp. 138-41;and John G. Taylor, *From Modernization to Modes of Production: A Critique of the Sociologies of Development and Underdevelopment* (London: Macmillan, 1979), pp. 71-73.

36. Baran and Sweezy, op. cit., p. 76.

37. This is approximate. Baran and Sweezy write, in their critique of Nicholas Kaldor: "Where Kaldor has gone wrong is, first, in identifying recorded profits with the theoretical 'share of profits.' The latter is really what we call surplus, the differences between total output and the socially necessary costs of producing total output. Under certain assumptions this will be equal to aggregate profits; but, as already noted, in the actual economy of monopoly capitalism only part of the difference between output and costs of production appears as profits." See Baran and Sweezy, op. cit., p. 76.

38. For the discussion of monopoly pricing, see Ibid., pp. 52-64.

39. Ibid., p. 69.

40. Ibid., pp. 71–72.

41. For the development of this argument, see Baran and Sweezy, op. cit., ch. 4.

42. Ibid., p. 108.

43. O'Connor, op. cit., p. 25.

44. Ibid., p. 24.

45. See Ibid., pp. 25.

46. See Ibid., pp. 26–28.

47. Ibid., p. 28.

48. The crisis tendencies of monopoly capitalism may differ from those offered by the theory's originators. First, distinguish between "breakdown" and "restructuring crises" in capitalist development. Second, a different account of profit rates may be offered. The evidence suggests that the transition from competitive to monopoly capitalism restored the rate of profit. This development, however, is consistent with the older analysis of the tendency for the profit rate to fall.

First, the surge of overseas investment in raw material production that accompanied the emergence of monopoly capitalism had the effect of lowering wage rates for these inputs to capitalist production in the leading countries. Through unequal exchange between the advanced countries and their backward colonies and dependencies, the aggregate rate of exploitation increased. Second, the expansion of production with the shift to larger firms also restored the rate of profit. Indeed, the purpose of restructuring the relations of production within capitalism, both from a firm and a systematic point of view, must logically be a restoration of the rate of profit.

As monopoly forms of production in various sectors matured, however, these means for ensuring adequate rates of accumulation reached their limits. Despite their ability to exercise monopoly pricing powers, firms introduced labor-saving/cost-cutting innovations. These labor-saving innovations kept costs down and ensured profit margins in the *price* sphere large enough to enable them to fund the costly forms of nonprice competition characteristic of monopoly capitalism.

But these innovations produced a rise in the organic composition of capital (i.e., the capital-to-labor ratio). Simultaneously, the organized monopoly-sector working class began to erode the *rate* of exploitation. In combination, these forces may have produced a tendency in mature monopoly capitalism for the value rate of profit to fall. In turn, falling rates of profit in a sector brought about a withdrawal of old capital and a withholding of new capital from that sector. At this point stagnation, emphasized by the theory of a rising surplus, then occurred. As always, the problem with this alternative view is behavioral: how does a capitalist class, or its investment banker proxies, know when the *value* rate of profit is declining?

CHAPTER 4

Authors' Note: "World-economy" refers, in this tradition of analysis, to an international network in which economic links between "nations" or societies are politically conditioned, while "world economy" refers to the strictly economic dimension of those relations. "World systems" (plural) refers to the analytical and theoretical school of thought pioneered by Wallerstein, while "world system" (singular) refers to the capitalist world system itself.

1. Immanuel Wallerstein, "The Rise and Future Demise of the World Capitalist System: Concepts for Comparative Analysis," *Comparative Studies in Society and History*, vol. 4, 1974, pp. 387–415; and Immanuel Wallerstein, "The Present State of the Debate on World Inequality," in Wallerstein, ed., *World Inequality: Origins and Perspectives on the World System* (Montreal: Black Rose Books, 1975). Both essays have been reprinted in Immanuel Wallerstein, *The Capitalist World Economy* (Cambridge: Cambridge University Press, 1979). For Wallerstein's terming of the approach "world systems theory," see Wallerstein, op. cit., 1979, p. 53.

2. Wallerstein now heads an important research center at the State University of New York at Binghamton, the Fernand Braudel Center. The center publishes a highly regarded journal, *Review: A Journal of the Fernand Braudel Center for the Study of Economics, Historical Systems and Civilizations*. The American Sociological Association has created a special section concerned with world systems analysis, "The Section on the Political Economy of the World System."

3. Wallerstein is in the midst of writing a several-volume history of the modern world system. Thus far, the first two volumes have been published; see, Immanuel Wallerstein, *The Modern World System I: Capitalist Agriculture and the Origins of the European World-Economy in the Sixteenth Century* (New York: Academic Press, 1974); and Immanuel Wallerstein, *The Modern World System II: Mercantilism and the Consolidation of the European World-Economy 1600-1750* (New York: Academic Press, 1980). Wallerstein has also authored singly, or with Terence Hopkins, numerous essays, explicating and developing aspects of the theory. Many of these have been reprinted in various collections of essays. See, in particular, Immanuel

Wallerstein, *The Capitalist World-Economy* (Cambridge: Cambridge University Press, 1979); and Terence Hopkins and Immanuel Wallerstein, eds., *World-Systems Analysis: Theory and Methodology* (Beverly Hills: Sage, 1982). Among the new generation of world systems writers, particular noteworthy is the work of Christopher Chase-Dunn. See, among others, Christopher Chase-Dunn, *Socialist States in the World-System* (Beverly Hills: Sage, 1982);Volker Bornschier and Christopher Chase-Dunn, *Transnational Corporations and Underdevelopment* (New York: Praeger, 1985); and Christopher Chase-Dunn, *Global Formation: Structures of the World-Economy* (New York: Basil Blackwell, 1989).

4. Wallerstein himself notes the influence of Baran; see Wallerstein, op. cit., 1979, p. 53.

5. Again, see Ibid.

6. Ibid.

7. Ibid., pp. 53–54.

8. See Christopher Chase-Dunn, "Stages of Dependency or Cycles of World-System Development?," *Humboldt Journal of Social Relations*, vol. 8, no. 1,Fall/Winter 1980–81, p. 10.

9. Wallerstein, op. cit., 1979, p. 15.

10. Wallerstein's analysis of how this division of labor first came into being is found in Immanuel Wallerstein, op. cit., 1974.

11. Terence Hopkins and Immanuel Wallerstein, "Patterns of Development of the Modern World-System," in Terence Hopkins and Immanuel Wallerstein, eds., op. cit., 1982, p. 59.Previously published in *Review*, vol. 1, no. 2, Fall 1977, pp. 111–45.

12. Ibid., p. 21; see also, Immanuel Wallerstein, "Semiperipheral Countries and the Contemporary World Crisis," *Theory and Society*, vol. 3, Winter 1976, pp. 461–83; reprinted in Wallerstein, op. cit., 1979, pp. 95–118.

13. Christopher Chase-Dunn, "Cycles, Trends or Transformation?: The World System Since 1945," in Terry Boswell and Albert Bergesen, eds., *America's Changing Role in the World-System* (Beverly Hills: Sage, 1985.).

14. For this argument, see Wallerstein, op. cit., 1979, pp. 21–23.

15. See Ibid., pp. 18–19 or Chase-Dunn, op. cit., p. 8.

16. The most extensive analyses of unequal exchange are Arghiri Emmanuel, *Unequal Exchange: A Study of the Imperialism of Trade* (New

York: Monthly Review, 1972); and Samir Amin, *Unequal Development: An Essay on the Social Formations of Peripheral Capitalism* (New York: Monthly Review, 1977). For a brief account of Wallerstein's views on the matter, see Immanuel Wallerstein, "World-Systems Analysis: Theoretical and Interpretative Issues," in Hopkins and Wallerstein, eds., op. cit., 1982.

17. Wallerstein, for example, has written, "We find ourselves at the beginning of one of those periodic downturns, or contractions, or crises that the capitalist world-economy has known with regularity since its origins in Europe in the sixteenth century." See Wallerstein, op. cit., 1979, p. 95. Similarly, Chase-Dunn has argued, "that the global system has not undergone transformative change in the period since the second World War." See Chase-Dunn, op. cit., forthcoming.

18. Chase-Dunn, op. cit., 1980–81, p. 2.

19. See Wallerstein, op. cit., 1980, ch. 2, for a discussion of both the theory and the case of the United Provinces.

20. From this perspective, all monopolies are transitory phenomena, and monopoly capitalism did not signify a structural change in capitalism, because the "structure," i.e., core-periphery relations, continued.

21. Two of the more succinct explanations of the forces driving cycles of contraction can be found in Hopkins and Wallerstein, op. cit., 1982, pp. 65–67; and Immanuel Wallerstein, "Crisis As Transition," in Samir Amin et al., *Dynamics of Global Crisis* (New York: Monthly Review, 1982), pp. 15–22.

22. This means workers paid wholly by, and dependent only on the wage. Peripheral workers may owe feudal dues or be slaves: they are part of a capitalist system, nevertheless. The *preferred* position of direct producers in this system is the "fully proletarianized" wage worker—the type most characteristic, in this theory, of labor in the core. On this key point, see Hopkins and Wallerstein, eds., op. cit., p. 68.

23. For discussions of secular trends, see Hopkins and Wallerstein, "Patterns of Development," in Hopkins and Wallerstein, eds., op. cit., pp. 54–57; Terence Hopkins and Immanuel Wallerstein, "Cyclical Rhythms and Secular Trends of the Capitalist World-Economy: Some Problems, Hypotheses and Questions," in Hopkins and Wallerstein, eds., op. cit., pp. 104–06; Christopher Chase-Dunn, "The World System Since 1950: What has Really Changed?," paper presented at the Seventh Annual Conference on the Political Economy of the World-System, Duke University, Raleigh, N.C., March 30, 1983, pp. 5–7; Chase-Dunn, op. cit., 1980–81, pp. 10–11; and Chase-Dunn in Boswell and Bergesen, eds., op. cit.

24. Wallerstein, op. cit., 1982, pp. 22–23.

25. This secular trend has not been much emphasized by Wallerstein, but has been treated by Chase-Dunn and researched by Albert Bergesen. See Chase-Dunn, op. cit., 1983; and Albert Bergesen, "Long Economic Cycles and the Size of Industrial Enterprise," in Richard Rubinson, ed., *Dynamics of World Development* (Beverly Hills: Sage, 1981), pp. 179–91.

26. This is the central argument of Chase-Dunn, op. cit., 1980–81; Chase-Dunn, op. cit., 1983; and Chase-Dunn in Boswell and Bergesen, eds., op. cit.

27. Wallerstein, op. cit., 1982, pp. 39–40.

28. See also Christopher Chase-Dunn, "International Economic Policy in a Declining Core State," in William P. Avery and David P. Rapkin, *America in a Changing World Political Economy* (New York: Longman, 1982), pp. 77–96.

29. Wallerstein, op. cit., 1982, pp. 38–39.

30. For a review of this literature, see chapter 5.

31. Wallerstein, op. cit., 1982, pp. 17–18.

32. Ibid., p. 39.

33. Chase-Dunn, op. cit., in Boswell and Bergesen, eds., op. cit.; and Wallerstein, op. cit., 1979, pp. 95–118.

34. The eagle's eye view of world capitalism which characterizes the world systems perspective on industrialization in the periphery and semi-periphery might be fruitfully compared to elements of party orthodoxy. In 1960 one of us [Ross] had a long, all-night, conversation with a Communist activist of many decades, instructing a young civil rights worker about the realities of capitalism. *"They,"* she pronounced from the Leninist orthodoxy of that era, "will never let *them* industrialize."

35. Chase-Dunn, op. cit., 1983, p. 21; Chase-Dunn, op. cit., in Boswell and Bergesen, eds., op. cit., and Hopkins and Wallerstein, op. cit., 1982, pp. 66–67.

36. Hopkins and Wallerstein, op. cit., 1982, pp. 67–69.

37. Chase-Dunn, op. cit., 1983, p. 22.

38. Wallerstein, op. cit., 1979, p. 99.

39. Hopkins and Wallerstein, op. cit., 1982, p. 70.

40. Wallerstein, op. cit., 1982, p. 19; see also, Wallerstein, op. cit., 1979, pp. 99–100.

41. See, for example, Raymond Vernon, *Sovereignty At Bay* (New York: Basic Books, 1971).

42. For these arguments, see Chase-Dunn, op. cit., 1983, pp. 16–17 and pp. 25–26; and Chase-Dunn in Boswell and Bergesen, op. cit.

CHAPTER 5

1. William K. Tabb, "Economic Democracy and Regional Restructuring: An Internationalization Perspective," in William K. Tabb and Larry Sawers, eds., *Sunbelt/Snowbelt: Urban Development and Regional Restructuring*, (New York: Oxford University Press, 1984), pp. 403–5.

2. Manual Castells, "High Technology, Economic Restructuring and The Urban-Regional Process in the United States," in Manual Castells, ed., *High Technology, Space, and Society*, (Beverly Hills: Sage, vol. 28, Urban Affairs Annual Reviews, 1985), pp. 19–20.

3. Ibid.

4. He continues: "These crucial issues, however, are by and large beyond the scope of this work." James O'Connor, *Accumulation Crisis* (Oxford: Basil Blackwell, 1984, 1986) p. 2. This is exactly our enterprise.

5. See, for example, Robert Lenzner, "Revolution on Wall Street: New Mobility of Capital is Altering Market," *Boston Globe*, July 5, 1986, pp. 1, 20.

6. Michael Storper and Richard Walker, "The Spatial Division of Labor: Labor and The Location of Industries," in Tabb and Sawers, eds., op. cit., p. 22.

7. Michel Aglietta, *A Theory of Capitalist Regulation: The U. S. Experience* (London: New Left Books, 1979), p. 381; and Alain Lipietz, "Towards Global Fordism," *New Left Review*, vol. 132, March–April 1982, pp. 33–47.

8. The purchase of intermediate inputs from contractors or subcontractors located in such export platform areas—what has been called "global sourcing"—is part of this process. See Richard Child Hill, "Transnational Capitalism and Urban Crisis: The Case of the Auto Industry and Detroit," paper presented at the Annual Meeting of the Society for the Study of Social Problems, Toronto, Canada, August 23, 1981.

9. For extensive data on wages and collective bargaining in the automobile industry, see chapter 7. For data on living conditions in New York City and working conditions in its garment industry, see chapter 8.

10. Peter Evans, *Dependent Development: The Alliance of Multinational, State and Local Capital*. (Princeton, N.J.: Princeton University Press, 1979); Folker Frobel, Jurgen Heinrichs, Otto Kreye, *The New International Division of Labor: Structural Unemployment in Industrialized Countries and Industrialization in Developing Countries* (Cambridge: Cambridge University Press, 1980), ch. 2; Raymond Vernon, *Sovereignty at Bay* (New York: Basic Books, 1971), pp. 66–77; Bob Rowthorn, "Imperialism in the Seventies—Unity or Rivalry?," *New Left Review*, vol. 69, September/October 1971, pp. 31–51.

11. Robert Goodman, *The Last Entrepreneurs* (New York: Simon and Schuster, 1979); Bennett Harrison and Sandra Kantor, "The Political Economy of States' Job-Creation Business Incentives," *Journal of the American Institute of Planners*, October 1978, pp. 424–35.

12. E. J. Hobsbawm, "The Development of the World Economy," *Cambridge Journal of Economics*, vol. 3, 1979, p. 313, as quoted by Peter Dicken, *Global Shift: Industrial Change in a Turbulent World* (London: Harper and Row, 1986), p. 3.

13. See Graham, op. cit., 1983; and Gibson, et al., op. cit., 1986.

14. For other versions of the contention that the capitalist world economy began to experience declining rates of profit in the 1960s, see: Michel Aglietta, *A Theory of Capitalist Regulation* (London: New Left Books, 1979); Giovanni Arrighi, "Towards a Theory of Capitalist Crisis," *New Left Review*, vol. 111, September/October 1978, pp. 3–24; Ernest Mandel, *The Second Slump*, Jon Rothschild, trans. (London: New Left Books, 1978); and Ernest Mandel, *Long Waves of Capitalist Development* (Cambridge: Cambridge University Press, 1980).

15. James O'Connor, *The Fiscal Crisis of the State* (New York: St. Martin's Press, 1973), pp. 125–37.

16. Among the indicators of the widening acceptance of the views of Baran, Frank, and the *dependistas* is the fact that one of the first and more popular mainstream texts for undergraduate courses in international political economy devoted considerable attention to them. See David Blake and Robert S. Walters, *The Politics of Global Economic Relations* (Englewood Cliffs, N.J.: Prentice-Hall, 1976).

17. These are discussed in some detail in chapter 4.

18. See, especially, Paul Baran, *The Political Economy of Growth* (New York: Monthly Review, 1957);and Andre Gunder Frank, *Capitalism and Underdevelopment in Latin America* (New York: Monthly Review, 1967).

19. Warren's views were first published in Bill Warren "Imperialism and Capitalist Industrialization," *New Left Review*, 81, September/October 1973, pp. 3–44. They were elaborated subsequently in a posthumous book; see Bill Warren, *Imperialism: Pioneer of Capitalism* (London: New Left Books, 1980).For reviews and assessments of Warren's work, see Philip McMichael, James Petras, and Robert Rhodes, "Imperialism and the Contradictions of Development," *New Left Review*, vol. 85, May/June 1974, pp. 83–104; Dudley Seers, "The Congruence of Marxism and Other Neoclassical Theories," in K. Q. Hill, ed., *Towards a New Strategy for Development* (New York: Pergamon, 1979);and Ronald Munck, "Imperialism and Dependency: Recent Debates and Old Dead-Ends," in Ronald C. Chicote, ed., *Dependency and Marxism: Toward a Resolution of the Debate* (Boulder, Co.: Westview, 1982).

20. Cardoso's first contribution to the debate appeared at almost the same time as Warren's; see Fernando Henrique Cardoso, "Dependency and Development in Latin America," *New Left Review*, 74, July/August 1972, pp. 83–95. An expanded version is presented in Fernando Henrique Cardoso and Enzo Faletto, *Dependency and Development in Latin America*, Marjory Mattingly Urquidi, trans. (Berkeley: University of California Press, 1979). For a concise exposition of the Cardoso thesis, the debate among *dependencia* writers, and a critique from a marxist perspective, see Colin Henfry, "Dependency, Modes of Production and the Class Analysis of Latin America," in Chilcote, ed., op. cit.

21. Robert Brenner, "The Origins of Capitalist Development: A Critique of Neo-Smithian Marxism," *New Left Review*, July/August 1977, pp. 25–92. Among others making similar arguments, see John Weeks and Elizabeth Dore, "International Exchange and the Causes of Backwardness," *Latin American Perspectives*, vol. VI,Spring 1979, pp. 62–87; and Aiden Foster-Carter, "The Modes of Production Controversy," *New Left Review*, vol. 107, January/February 1978, pp. 47–77. For Wallerstein's statement on an earlier version of the "circulationist" critique of his theory, see his "The Rise and Future Demise of the World Capitalist System: Concepts for Comparative Analysis," in Immanuel Wallerstein, *The Capitalist World-Economy* (Cambridge: Cambridge University Press, 1979), esp. pp. 8–10, 16–18.

22. Albert Szymanski, *The Logic of Imperialism* (New York: Praeger, 1981), pp. 112–13; for his detailed argument, see ch. 10.

23. Martin Landsberg, "Export-Led Industrialization in the Third World: Manufacturing Imperialism," *Review of Radical Political Economics*, vol. 2, no. 4, 1979,pp. 50–63.

24. James M. Cypher, "The Internationalization of Capital and the Transformation of Social Formations: A Critique of the Monthly Review School," *Review of Radical Political Economics*, vol. 11, no. 4, 1979, pp. 33–49.

25. Peter Evans, *Dependent Development: The Alliance of Multinational, State and Local Capital in Brazil* (Princeton, N.J.: Princeton University Press, 1979).

26. Folker Frobel, Jurgen Heinrichs, and Otto Kreye, *The New International Division of Labor: Structural Unemployment in Industrialised Countries and Industrialisation in Developing Countries* (Cambridge: Cambridge University Press, 1980). For an early and succinct version of their argument, see Frobel et al., "The Tendency Towards a New International Division of Labor," *Review*, vol. 1, no. 1, Summer 1977, pp. 73–88.

27. Frobel et al., op. cit., 1980, pp. 13–14.

28. Alain Lipietz, "Toward Global Fordism?" *New Left Review*, vol. 132, 1982, pp. 33–47.

29. One clear exception to this would be Warren who carries his analysis of the "progressive" nature of imperialism to the point of insisting that all forms of underdevelopment are being overcome.

30. James Caporaso, "Industrialization in the Periphery: The Evolving Global Division of Labor," *International Studies Quarterly*, vol. 25, no. 3, September 1981, pp. 347–84.

31. Joseph Grunwald and Kenneth Flamm, *The Global Factory: Foreign Assembly in International Trade* (Washington, D.C.: The Brookings Institution, 1985).

32. Peter Dicken, *Global Shift: Industrial Change in a Turbulent World* (London: Harper and Row, 1986).

33. See, for example, James Petras with A. E. Haven, M. H. Morley and P. DeWitt, *Class, State and Power in the Third World* (Montclair, N.J.: Allanheld, 1981).

34. Syzmanski, op. cit., falls into this category as does Thomas Weisskopf, "Imperialism and the Economic Development of the Third World," in Richard C. Edwards, Michael Reich, and Thomas Weisskopf, eds., *The Capitalist System*, 2nd ed. (Englewood Cliffs, N.J.: Prentice-Hall, 1978).

35. See chapter 4 for an explanation of Wallerstein's argument.

36. See Christopher Chase-Dunn, "The World System Since 1950: What Has Really Changed?," in C. Berquist, ed., *Labor in the Capitalist World Economy* (Beverly Hills: Sage, 1984).Another essay that links Third World industrialization to the crisis of U. S. hegemony is Philip McMichael, "Social Structure of the New International Division of Labor," in Edward Friedman, ed., *Ascent and Decline in the World-System* (Beverly Hills: Sage, 1982).

CHAPTER 6

1. Ernest Mandel, *The Second Slump: A Marxist Analysis of Recession in the Seventies*, Jon Rothschild, trans., (London: New Left Books, 1978); Manual Castells, *The Economic Crisis and American Society* (Princeton, N.J.: Princeton University Press, 1980); Samuel Bowles, David M. Gordon, and Thomas Weisskopf, *Beyond the Wasteland* (Garden City, N.Y.: Anchor Press–Doubleday, 1983); Thomas E. Weisskopf, "Marxian Crisis Theory and the Rate of Profit in the Postwar U. S. Economy," *Cambridge Journal of Economics*, vol. 3, 1979, pp. 341–78;Philip Armstrong, Andrew Glyn, and John Harrison, *Capitalism since World War II: The Making and Breakup of the Great Boom* (London: Fontana, 1984).

2. Albert Szymanski, *The Logic of Imperialism* (New York: Praeger, 1981), pp. 112–13; for his detailed argument, see ch. 10.

3. All of the data in this paragraph are from Szymanski, op. cit., p. 114.

4. U. S. Department of Commerce, Bureau of Economic Analysis, *Selected Data on U.S. Direct Investment Abroad, 1966–78*, Table 1, p. 3.

5. Supplement to above data received from the U. S. Department of Commerce, Bureau of Economic Analysis, September 24, 1982.

6. United Nations Centre on Transnational Corporations, *Transnational Corporations in World Development: Third Survey* (New York: United Nations, 1983), Annex Table II.8, p. 293.

7. Ibid., Annex Table II.9, p. 294.

8. Ibid., Annex Table II.10, p. 295.

9. Ibid., pp. 23, 193–254.

10. Ibid., p. 23.

11. See John Holmes, "The Organization and locational structure of production subcontracting," in Allen J. Scott and Michael Storper, eds.,

Production, Work, Territory: The Geographical Anatomy of Industrial Capitalism (Boston: George Allen and Unwin, 1986), pp. 80–124.

12. See Jeff Frieden, "Third World Indebted Industrialization: International Finance and State Capitalism in Mexico, Brazil, Algeria, and South Korea," *International Organization*, vol. 35, no. 1, 1981.

13. World systems theorist, Chase-Dunn, accuses some supporters of the new international division of labor thesis as maintaining the view that restructuring implies convergence or complete transference; we intend neither. See Chase-Dunn "Cycles, Trends or Transformation?: The World System Since 1945" in Terry Boswell and Albert Bergesen, eds., *America's Changing Role in the World-System* (Beverly Hills: Sage, 1985).

14. These two factors are also emphasized by Frobel, Heinrichs and Kreye, op. cit., pp. 13–15; and Grunwald and Flamm, op. cit., p. 7.

15. U. N. Centre on Transnational Corporations, op. cit., p. 142.

16. Frobel et al., op. cit., make the point for the German clothing and garment industry. See, also, North American Congress for Latin America, "Capital's Flight: The Apparel Industry Moves South," *Latin America and Empire Report*, vol. XI, no. 3, March 1977.

17. Grunwald and Flamm, op. cit., p. 7, draw similar conclusions for a number of items reported in U. S. Tariff Code data.

18. See, in particular, Frobel, Heinrichs, and Kreye, op. cit., ch. 6. As an example, on pp. 123, the authors quote the management of a major German textile firm that, "After years of stagnation...Triumph International AG, Munich has been able to increase its world turnover by a healthy 10% to DM 750 million. Profits may have risen more than 10%. Rationalisation and the *relocation of production abroad, with its lower wage costs, are paying off.*" (Emphasis added.)

19. See Kenneth Flamm, "Internationalization in the Semiconductor Industry," ch. 3, in Grunwald and Flamm, op. cit.

20. Julie Graham, *Economic Restructuring in the United States, 1958–1980: Theory, Method and Identification* (unpublished Ph.D. diss., Clark University, Worchester, Mass. 1983, Table 10, pp. 115–16.

21. U. N. Centre on Transnational Corporations, op. cit., p. 135.

22. Calculated from 1983 ILO *Yearbook*, op. cit. in Table 1, p. 580; and World Bank, *World Tables*, 3rd ed., vol. 1 (Baltimore, Md.: Johns Hopkins University Press, 1983), p. 159.

23. Singapore Chamber of Commerce, *Facts for Business*, (Singapore, 1981).

24. Ibid.

25. Calculated from data received from the U. S. Department of Commerce, September 24, 1982, op. cit.

26. The sources for these data are U. S. Department of Commerce, op. cit. and data received from U. S. Department of Commerce, September 24, 1982.

27. See Paul Bairoch, *The Economic Development of the Third World Since 1900,* Cynthia Postan, trans. (Berkeley: University of California Press, 1975),Table 18, p. 67.

28. Recent work by economic geographers has come to similar conclusions. See, for example, I. M. Clarke, "The Changing International Division of Labor Within ICI," in Michael Taylor and Nigel Thrift, eds., *The Geography of Multinationals* (New York: St. Martin's Press, 1982); and Richard Peet, "International Capital, International Culture," in Taylor and Thrift, op. cit.

29. United Nations Centre on Transnational Corporations, *Transnational Corporations in World Development: Third Survey* (New York: United Nations, 1983), p. 133.

30. Samir Amin, *Unequal Development: An Essay on the Social Formations of Peripheral Capitalism* (New York: Monthly Review, 1976), pp. 240–41.(Parentheses added.)

31. These data are taken from Simon Kuznets, *Economic Growth of Nations: Total Output and Production Structure* (Cambridge, Mass.: Belknap Press of Howard University Press, 1971) Table 21, pp. 146–51.

32. Ibid., Table 23, pp. 164–69.

33. Ibid., Table 39, pp. 259–60.

34. Warren, op. cit. uses this data to support his argument that capitalism and imperialism have always been a progressive force in the Third World. He rejects the view that the theory of monopoly capitalism and dependency theory have ever offered an accurate view of the impact of capitalism in the periphery.

35. Kuznets, op. cit., Table 38, pp. 250–54.

36. L. S. Stavrianos, *Global Rift: The Third World Comes of Age* (New

York: William Morrow, 1981), pp. 275–76, makes precisely this interpretation of the Kuznets data.

37. Amin, op. cit., p. 240.

38. Chile's pattern of growth was effected significantly by the election, overthrow, and aftermath of the Allende regime. On the response of international capital and the U. S. government to Allende's election, see James Petras and Morris Morley, *The United States and Chile: Imperialism and the Overthrow of the Allende Government* (New York: Monthly Review, 1975). For a somewhat different view that places more blame on mistakes of the Allende regime, but still recognizes that the investment strategies of multinationals effected the Chilean economy during the 1970s, see Paul Sigmund, *Multinationals in Latin America: The Politics of Nationalization* (Madison: University of Wisconsin Press, 1980), ch. 5. The Mexican case is highly complex. In part the relative decline of manufacturing in the late 1970s can be explained by the rapid expansion of the oil economy; however, most of the 1970s was a period of economic crisis for Mexico characterized by rising levels of class conflict which eventually diminished its attractiveness to global capital. For a detailed analysis, see James D. Cockcroft, *Mexico: Class Formation, Capital Accumulation and the State* (New York: Monthly Review, 1983), chs. 7 and 8.

39. International Labour Organization, *Employment Effects of Multinational Enterprises in Developing Countries* (Geneva: ILO,1981), p. 26.

40. See, for example, U. S. Congress, House of Representatives, Subcommittee on Labor-Management of the Committee on Education and Labor, *Oversight Hearings on the Nations Labor Relations Act*, Hearings, 94th Congress, 2nd Session, 1976, pp. 594–95. There has been considerable dispute over these claims; other studies find little or negligible impact, see, for example, International Labor Organization, *Employment Effects of Multinational Enterprises in Industrialised Countries* (Geneva: ILO, 1981).

41. United Nations Centre for Transnational Corporations, op. cit., p. 134, draws the same conclusion.

42. Taiwan and South Africa are also among the leading industrial producers in the Third World. They are not included because comparable data for those countries is not reported by the World Bank.

43. U.N. Centre for Transnational Corporations, op. cit., p. 133.

44. U.N. Centre on Transnational Corporations, op. cit., pp. 136–37.

45. Evans, op. cit., makes this clear in the Brazilian case, although he

also argues that foreign capital is the dominant partner of the triple alliance. For evidence that indigenous capital has played a substantial role in Hong Kong, South Korea, Taiwan, and to a lesser extent, Singapore, see Clive Hamilton, "Capitalist Industrialization in East Asia's Four Little Tigers," *Journal of Contemporary Asia*, vol. 13, no. 1, 1983, pp. 35–73.

46. Andre Gunder Frank, "Global Crisis and Transformation," in Richard Peet, ed., *International Capitalism and Industrial Restructuring* (Boston: George Allen and Unwin, 1987), pp. 293–312.

47. We calculated the value of exports divided by the population of each of the countries in Table 6.1. The relative growth in rates of the value of exported manufactured goods is similarly dramatic for the comparison of peripheral, semiperipheral, and "core" countries as those reported in Table 6.1. We calculated these data from the World Bank, *World Development Report, World Development Report 1982* (New York: Oxford University Press, 1982), and the United Nations, *Monthly Bulletin of Statistics*, vols. 20, 34, 38.

48. Although it is a primary commodity, petroleum exports are excluded from the table because of the exceptional price behavior of this primary good during the 1970s.

49. The case of the African periphery is an exception to this trend, which is discussed below.

50. The data in this paragraph were calculated from United Nations, *Monthly Bulletin of Statistics*, vols. 20, 24, 34, 39; and United Nations, *Year-book of International Trade Statistics 1977, Volume 1* (New York: United Nations, 1978).

51. The World Bank, op. cit.

52. Grunwald and Flamm, op. cit., p. 12. These authors indicate that U. S. tariff law encourages foreign assembly and outsourcing of parts to low-wage locations. The relevant tariff items are 806.30 and 807, "which permit the duty-free entry of U. S. components sent abroad for processing or assembly." For further explanation of the operation of these tariff items, see Grunwald and Flamm, pp. 34–37.

53. Ibid., pp. 24–34. Apparently reimport to Europe and Japan by their home firms is not as common as in the United States. Among other factors Grunwald and Flamm attribute this to the more restrictive application of provisions in European and Japanese trade law of legislation similar to the 806 and 807 sections of the U. S. tariff code.

54. Szymanski, op. cit., p. 324.

55. United Nations, *Yearbook of International Trade Statistics, 1979*, vol. 2. (New York: United Nations, 1980).

56. Grunwald and Flamm, op. cit., Table 2-3, p. 17.

57. For example, the percentage of African exports that were manufactured good actually declined from 1960 to 1980.African countries, with the exception of Nigeria, are also notable by their absence from the lists of both leading industrial powers and principal peripheral exporters of manufacturers. For a more detailed analysis of Africa's exclusion from the changes at work, see, Richard Higgott, "Africa, the New International Division of Labor and the Corporate State," paper presented at the 24th Annual Conference of the International Studies Association, Mexico City, Mexico, April 6, 1983.

58. Szymanski, op. cit., pp. 355-63.

59. See Irma and Cynthia Morris, *Economic Growth and Social Equity in Developing Countries* (Stanford: Stanford University Press, 1973); Christopher Chase-Dunn, "The Effects of International Economic Dependence on Development and Inequality," *American Sociological Review*, vol. 40, no. 6, 1975, pp. 720-39; Volker Bornschier, "World Economic Integration and Policy Responses: Some Developmental Impacts," in Harry Makler, Alberto Martinelli and Neil Smelser, eds., *The New International Economy* (Beverly Hills: Sage, 1982); Volker Bornschier, Christopher Chase-Dunn and Richard Rubinson, "Cross-National Evidence of the Effects of Foreign Investment and Aid on Economic Growth and Inequality: a Survey of Findings and a Reanalysis," *American Journal of Sociology*, vol. 84, 1978, pp. 651-83.

60. Frobel et al., op. cit., ch. 16.

61. See, for example, Wendy Chapkis and Cynthia Enloe, eds., *Of Common Cloth: Women in the Global Textile Industry* (Amsterdam: The Transnational Institute, 1983); Barbara Ehrenreich and Annette Fuentes, "Life on the Global Assembly Line," *MS*, January 1981, pp. 53-71; and Helen I. Safa, "Runaway Shops and Female Employment: The Search for Cheap Labor," *Signs*, vol. 7, Winter 1981, pp. 418-33.

62. Jeffrey Kentor, "Structural Determinants of Peripheral Urbanization: The Effects of International Dependence," *American Sociological Review*, vol. 46, April 198, pp. 201-211.

63. Among the first to elaborate the connections between peripheral industrialization and political authoritarianism was, Guillermo O'Donnell, *Modernization and Bureaucratic Authoritarianism* (Berkeley: University of California Press, 1973).

64. "Asia's New Bidders for Western Plants," *Business Week*, March 17,

1980, Special Report, pp. 48D–48P.

CHAPTER 7

Authors' Note: An earlier draft of the material presented in this chapter was originally published in the *International Journal of Urban and Regional Research*, 9, 2 (June 1985): 186–217.

1. Paul Lawrence and Davis Dyer, *Renewing American Industry* (New York: The Free Press, 1983), p. 31.

2. Richard Child Hill, "Transnational Capitalism and Urban Crisis: The Case of the Auto Industry and Detroit," paper presented at annual meetings of The Society of the Study of Social Problems, Toronto, Canada, August 23, 1982, p. 1.

3. The figures referred to can be found in Table 7.3.

4. Ibid., p. 2.

5. The phrase is one we were introduced to by Folker Frobel, Jurgen Heinrichs, and Otto Kreye, *The New International Division of Labor: Structural Unemployment in Industrialized Countries and Industrialization in Developing Countries* (Cambridge: Cambridge University Press, 1980). This idea of the depression as the executor of structural change will be developed in some detail toward the end of this chapter.

6. In our view, the slowdown of the world economy during the 1970s represents a restructuring crisis of capitalism. We also conceive of the cycle as the executor of structural change. Further developments of this point can be found later in this chapter.

7. For analyses of these processes in the Detroit metropolitan region, see Robert Conot, *American Odyssey* (New York: William Morrow, 1974); Stephen Friedman and Leon Potok, "Detroit and the Auto Industry: An Historical Overview," paper presented at "Economic Crisis and Political Response in the Auto City: Detroit and Turin," a Conference, organized by Harvard University's Center for European Studies, Detroit, Michigan, December 10–13, 1981; and Alex Schwartz, "The Auto-Industrial City: Detroit and the Auto Industry 1900–1982" (unpublished paper, Clark University, Worchester, Mass., February 20, 1983).

8. Lawrence and Dyer, op. cit., p. 29.

9. Ibid. Only Chrysler suffered during the period as it lost portions of its market share to both G. M. and Ford.

10. Note that this judgement about the disappearance of price competition is shared even by such conventional economists as Lawrence and Dyer. See Lawrence and Dyer, op. cit., p. 31.

11. Lawrence White, *The Automobile Industry Since 1945* (Cambridge, Mass.: Harvard University Press, 1970), p. 251.

12. See U. S. Department of Commerce, Bureau of the Census, *Statistical Abstract of the United States 1979* (Washington, D.C.: n.p., 1979), p. 427.

13. In 1961, wages of unskilled plant workers in Detroit were 117 percent of the national average while those of clerks were 114 percent of the national average. By 1978,the corresponding figures were 131 percent for unskilled plant and 121 percent for clerks. See U. S. Department of Labor, *Handbook of Labor Statistics* (Washington, D.C.: Bureau of Labor Statistics, 1983) Bulletin 2175.

14. For a discussion of hegemonic decline that agrees in general terms with our conclusions, but uses a different analytic framework, see Peter F. Cowhey and Edward Long, "Testing Theories of Regime Change: Hegemonic Decline or Surplus Capacity?" *International Organization*, vol. 37, no. 2, Spring 1983, pp. 157–188.

15. Motor Vehicle Manufacturers Association of the United States, *World Motor Vehicle Data*, 1986 ed., Detroit, 1986,pp. 11–13. The 1980 and 1982 percentages are calculated from U. S. Department of Commerce, *U.S. Automobile Industry, 1982: Report to the Congress from the Secretary of Commerce* (Washington, D.C.: n.p., June 1983), p. 4.

16. Ibid. At almost 6 percent of the world export market in cars, the countries of India, Mexico, Argentina, Brazil, Korea, Yugoslavia, S. Africa, exceeded Japan's 1960 2.9 percent share.

17. Motor Vehicle Manufacturers Association of the United States, *World Motor Vehicle Data*, 1986 ed., (Detroit, 1986),p. 36. The reader should be aware that even relatively small changes in world market shares produce dramatic revenue redistributions among automobile firms. We estimate that, as of 1979, each one percent of the world market produced a revenue flow in excess of $1.5 billion. This was calculated from data contained in U. S. Department of Transportation, *The U.S. Automobile Industry, 1980:Report to the President from the Secretary of Transportation* (Washington, D.C.: U.S. Government Printing Office, 1981), pp. 36, 47;as well as data in Table 1 of this chapter.

18. Calculated from U. S. Department of Transportation, Office of the Assistant Secretary for Policy and International Affairs, *The U.S. Automobile*

Industry, 1980 (Washington, D.C.: n.p., January 1981), p. 54; Motor Vehicle Manufacturers Association of the United States, *Motor Vehicle Facts and Figures, 1980* (Detroit: n.p., 1980). And Peter Dicken, *Global Shift: Industrial Change in a Turbulent World*, (London: Harper and Row, 1986), p. 296.

19. Motor Vehicle Manufacturers Association of the United States, *World Motor Vehicle Data*, 1986 ed., (Detroit: n.p., 1986), p. 36.

20. William J. Abernathy, Kim Clark, and Alan Kantrow, *Industrial Renaissance* (New York: Basic Books, 1983), p. 63.

21. U.S. Department of Transportation, *The U.S. Automobile Industry, 1980: Report to the President from the Secretary of Transportation* (Washington, D.C.: U.S. Government Printing Office, 1981), p. vii.

22. See *The New York Times* January 1, 1987, p. D1; George Russell, "The Big Three Get in Gear," *Time*, November 24, 1986, pp. 64.

23. Lawrence White, op. cit., p. 205.

24. See Lynn E. Browne, "Autos—Another Steel?" *New England Economic Review*, November/December 1985, pp. 14–29; Lawrence and Dyer, 1983, op. cit., ch. 2;Motor Vehicle Manufacturers Association of the United States, *Economic Indicators: The Motor Vehicle's Role in the U.S. Economy*, 2nd quarter, 1984 (Detroit: Motor Vehicle Manufacturers Association, 1984) p. 17.

A less conventional approach to the measurement of profits is taken by Julie Graham, *Economic Restructuring in the United States, 1958–1980: Theory, Method and Identification* (unpublished Ph.D. diss. Clark University, Worchester, Mass., 1983. Graham transformed conventional National Income Accounts data into data appropriate to Marxian value categories using input-output tables. The results showed that the post-World War II automobile industry suffered a decline in the rate of profit measured in value terms. Graham and her colleagues insist that Marxian value categories cannot be directly measured in price terms (i.e., profit or loss on a corporate balance sheet embodies a different calculus than that implied by the theory of declining rate of profit in value terms). Despite this qualification, we find it worthy of note that the empirical results of conventional profit measurements match the value results. This is even more interesting when we examine, below, the *timing* of the profit declines in relation to foreign investment.

In Chapter 5, we sketched the contradictions attendant upon rationalization as a strategy for increasing capital's share of value created in production. To recall the point briefly, as machines are substituted for workers, the rate of surplus extraction will increase but the rate of profit in value terms will decrease.

In the U. S. automobile industry this tendency became evident in the late 1960s. After a short recovery, it accelerated in the late 1970s.

25. The brief but intense upturn in the world economy from 1976 to early 1979 offered some respite from this tendency as a surge in worldwide and domestic purchases of automobiles led U. S. firms to add substantially and rapidly to the size of their work forces. Developments since then indicate clearly, however, that this boom only temporarily masked the underlying crisis facing the U. S. auto industry.

26. Data on investment in new plant and facilities in overseas subsidiaries are not available. The Department of Commerce suppresses them in order to avoid disclosure of the investments of individual firms. A crude estimate of the portion of this investment accounted for by motor vehicles can be arrived at by noting that from 1974 to 1981 domestic expenditures for new plant and equipment in motor vehicles and equipment average, annually, 57percent of domestic expenditures in the larger transportation equipment sector. Impressionistically, we have reason to think that in the foreign overseas investment, the share accruing to the motor vehicle sector may be even higher. See U. S. Department of Commerce, op. cit., 1981, p. 547, for the data upon which the motor vehicles as a percentage of transportation equipment calculation is based. For domestic data from 1966 to 1980, U. S. Department of Commerce, Bureau of the Census, *Statistical Abstract of the U.S., 1981* (Washington, D.C.: n.p., 1981), p. 547; for domestic data, 1981 to 1984, *Survey of Current Business*, vol. 64, no. 6,June 1984, p. 27; for data for foreign affiliates, U. S. Department of Commerce, Bureau of Economic Analysis, *Capital Expenditures of Majority-Owned Foreign Affiliates, 1966–76* (Washington, D.C.: n.p., 1978); after that date, *Survey of Current Business*, vol. 64, no. 3, March 1984, pp. 33–34.

27. The data on imports and profits for these years are drawn from Lawrence and Dyer, op. cit., ch. 2.

28. Motor Vehicle Manufacturers Association of the United States, op. cit., 1984.

29. Calculated from United Nations Centre on Transnational Corporations, *Transnational Corporations in the International Auto Industry* (New York: United Nations, 1983), p. 51.

30. Hill, op. cit., p. 8.

31. Calculated from tables, United Nations Centre of Transnational Corporations, op. cit., pp. 119–21.

32. Ibid.

33. Ibid., p. 118.

34. See Obie G. Whichard, "Employment and Employee Compensation of U. S. Multinational Companies in 1977," *Survey of Current Business*, vol. 62, no. 2, February 1982, pp. 37–49 or Ned G. Howenstine, "Gross Product of U. S. Multinational Companies, 1977," *Survey of Current Business*, vol. 63, no. 2, February 1983, pp. 24–29

35. For a fuller discussion, see Ruth Milkman, "The Anti-Concessions Movement in the UAW: Interview with Douglas Stevens," *Socialist Review*, vol. 65, 1982 p. 26.

36. Ann Job Woolley, "By a 3–1 margin, Ford Workers OK concessions to Get Job Security," *Boston Globe*, March 1, 1982, pp. 1, 6.

37. David Nyhan, "UAW votes to Resume Bargaining with GM," *Boston Globe*, March 12, 1982, p. 13.

38. On this phase of the negotiations, see Nyhan, op. cit.; and Milkman, op. cit.

39. John Holusha, "Snags Develop in Talks on General Motors Talks," *The New York Times*, March 21, 1982, p. 26.

40. For a cogent assessment of the contract and its implications, see Milkman, op. cit., pp. 26–27.

41. Milkman, op. cit., p. 33.

42. Motor Vehicle Manufacturer's Association of the United States, Policy Analysis Department, *Economic Indicators: The Motor Vehicle's Role in the U.S. Economy*, 2nd Quarter, 1984 (Detroit: Motor Vehicle Manufacturers Association, August 3, 1984), Table 14, p. 23.

43. Even the 1957–59 recession in the auto industry, during which the number of jobs lost were equal to the 1979–82 depression, did not bring about a decline in the real wages of auto workers.

44. In addition to the analysis presented above, see also United Nations Center for Transnational Corporations, op. cit.; Richard Child Hill, "The Auto Industry in Global Transition," paper presented at annual meeting, American Sociological Association, Detroit, Michigan, September 3, 1983; Bryan Berry, "For Auto Industry Road to Growth Leads Overseas," *Iron Age*, October 13, 1982, p. 47; and Shozo Hochi, "Auto Industry Charts Course for Internationalization," *Business Japan*, February 1981, p. 32.

45. Batelle Columbus Laboratories, "Identification of Location Criteria Related to the Development of Robotics and Biotechnology in the State of

Michigan," report to the High Technology Task Force and Michigan Department of Commerce, September 24, 1982.

46. This reconstruction of the Poletown incident is drawn from Barry Bluestone and Bennett Harrison, *The Deindustrialization of America* (New York: Basic Books, 1982), pp. 183–84.

47. Quoted in Eileen Ogintz, "Detroit's Renaissance Center in Trouble," *Chicago Tribune*, January 10, 1983.

48. *New York Times*, March 7, 1983.

49. P. Becker, "Historic Labor Force Levels and Unemployment Rates: Detroit SMSA Annual Averages," (Detroit: City of Detroit Planning Department, Data Coordination Division, December 1982).

50. Ibid.

51. Ibid.

52. Michigan Employment Security Commission, Bureau of Research and Statistics, Labor Market Analysis Section, "Civilian Labor Force and Employment Estimates," MESC 3221, March 1984.

53. Louis Fermin, "The Impact of the Current Recession of Human Services in Detroit," paper presented at "Economic Crisis and Political Response in the Auto City: Detroit and Turin" Conference, of the Harvard University Center for European Studies, Detroit, Michigan, December 10–13, 1981.

54. These data are unpublished data received during the fall of 1982 from P. Becker, Head, Data Coordination Division, City of Detroit Planning Department.

55. Fermin, op. cit., p. 31.

56. Ogintz, op. cit.

57. Fermin, op. cit., p. 4.

58. Thomas M. Stanback and Thierry Noyelle, *Cities in Transition* (Englewood Cliffs, N.J.: Allanheld, Osmun, 1982).

59. Barry Bluestone and Bennett Harrison, *The Economic State of the Union, 1984: Uneven Recovery—Uncertain Future* (San Francisco: Economic Education Project, January 1984).

60. Robert L. Simpson and John Koten, "Auto Makers Profits are Increasing Sharply Despite Mediocre Sales," *Wall Street Journal*, December 19, 1983, p. 1.

61. "The Amalgamated," as it was called in New York, is now The Amalgamated Clothing and Textile Workers Union (ACTWU).

62. Detroit, of course, was the recipient of a large number of black American migrants from the southern states during the period of agricultural mechanization in the south after World War II. On this, see, among others, Frances Fox Piven and Richard A. Cloward, *Regulating the Poor: The Functions of Public Welfare* (New York: Random House, 1971) chs. 7, 8.

CHAPTER 8

Authors' Note: Portions of this chapter, and earlier data, were originally published in *Review*, Vi, 3 (Winter 1983): 393–431.

1. Stephen Hymer, "The Multinational Corporation and the Law of Uneven Development," in George Modelski, ed., *Transnational Corporations and World Order* (San Francisco: W. H. Freeman, 1979) pp. 386–403.

2. Ibid., pp. 394–95.

3. Robert B. Cohen, "The New International Division of Labor: Multinational Corporations and Urban Hierarchy," in Michael Dear and A. J. Scott, eds., *Urbanization and Urban Planning in Capitalist Society* (New York: Methuen, 1981) p. 288.

4. Ibid., pp. 302, 305.

5. Saskia Sassen-Koob, "Recomposition and Peripheralization at the Core," *Contemporary Marxism*, vol. 5, Summer 1982, pp. 88–100; and E. Soja, R. Morales, and G. Wolff, "Urban Restructuring: An Analysis of Social and Spatial Change in Los Angeles," *Economic Geography*, vol. 59, no. 2, April 1983, pp. 195–230.

6. Soja, Morales, and Wolff, op. cit.

7. Ibid., pp. 195–96.

8. See, in particular, Samir Amin, *Unequal Development: An Essay on the Social Formations of Peripheral Capitalism*, Brian Pearce, trans. (New York: Monthly Review, 1976); Arghiri Emmanuel, *Unequal Exchange: A Study of the Imperialism of Free Trade*, Brian Pearce, trans. (New York: Monthly Review, 1972); and Immanuel Wallerstein, *The Capitalist World-Economy* (London: Cambridge University Press, 1979).

9. Wallerstein, op. cit., pp. 187–88, does speak of this possibility; however the manner of its incorporation into his larger theoretical perspective is not addressed.

10. Gerald Epstein, "Domestic Stagflation and Monetary Policy: The Federal Reserve and the Hidden Election," in T. Ferguson and J. Rogers, eds., *The Hidden Election: Politics and Economics in the 1980 Presidential Campaign* (New York: Pantheon, 1981) pp. 154–55.

11. Cohen, op. cit., pp. 302, 305.

12. Ira Katznelson, "A Radical Departure?: Social Welfare and the Election," in Ferguson and Rogers, op. cit., pp. 310–40.

13. U. S. Department of Labor, *Employment and Earnings, States and Areas, 1939–1978* (Washington, D.C.: Bureau of Labor Statistics, 1979), Bulletin 1370–13; U.S. Department of Labor, *Supplement to Employment and Earnings, States and Areas, Data for 1977–80*, (Washington, D.C.: Bureau of Labor Statistics, 1981) Bulletin 1370–15; and *Employment and Earnings*, vol. 33, no. 5, May 1987.

14. U. S. Department of Labor, op. cit., 1979,Bulletin 1370–13; U. S. Department of Labor, op. cit., 1981, Bulletin 1370–15; and for 1983,prepublication data received from U. S. Bureau of Labor Statistics.

15. U. S. Department of Labor, *Employment and Earnings, States and Areas, 1939–78* (Washington, D.C.: Bureau of Labor Statistics, 1979), Bulletin 1370–13; U.S. Department of Labor, *Supplement to Employment and Earnings, States and Areas, Data for 1977–80* (Washington, D.C.: Bureau of Labor Statistics, 1981), Bulletin 1370–15; and *Employment and Earnings*, vol. 33, no. 5, May 1987.

16. *Employment and Earnings*, op. cit., various issues.

17. Saskia Sassen-Koob, "Exporting Capital and Importing Labor: The Role of Caribbean Migration to New York City," paper presented at the Conference on Hispanic Migration to New York City, New York, December 4, 1981, pp. 7–10.

18. Rinker Buck, "The New Sweatshops: A Penny for Your Collar," *New York*, vol. XII, no. 9, January 29, 1979, p. 44.

19. Senator Franz Leichter, Glenn von Nostitz, and Maria Gonzalez, "The Return of the Sweatshop," Office of State Senator Leichter, New York, February 26, 1981, p. 40.

20. North American Congress for Latin America, "Capital's Flight: The Apparel Industry Moves South," *Latin America and Empire Report*, vol. XI, no. 3, March 1977.

21. Michael Flannery, "America's Sweatshops in the Sun," *AFL-CIO American Federationist*, vol. LXXXV, no. 5, May 1978, p. 16.

22. Ibid., p. 18.

23. Buck, op. cit., p. 46.

24. Personal communication, Research Department, International Ladies Garment Workers Union, April 1984.

25. Leichter et al., op. cit., p. 3; and Senator Franz S. Leichter, "Statement," *The Reemergence of Sweatshops and the Enforcement of Wage and Hour Standards*, Hearings before the Subcommittee on Labor Standards of the Committee on Education and Labor, United States House of Representatives, Ninety-Seventh Congress (Washington, D.C: U.S. Government Printing Office, 1982), p. 262.

26. Leichter et al., op. cit., p. 31.

27. See Table 1, above, for sources.

28. In New York City, as in other central cities in metropolitan areas, large fractions of the high wage "downtown" jobs are occupied by suburban residents. The city's retail sector (e.g., restaurants in Manhattan) are pegged to the managerial/professional clientele (both city-based and suburban) *and* cosmopolitan visitors. Housing costs reflect the pressure of demand on aging stock, and the premium which landlords can extract from the densest, most renter-based market in the U.S.

29. Peter Marcuse, *Rental Housing in the City of New York: Supply and Condition, 1975–78* (New York: Housing and Development Administration, 1979). These and the data in this paragraph compare changes in real purchasing power of median income in U. S. families with those of New York renter households. While these are not precisely comparable, it should be noted that about two-thirds of New York City's populace are renters. Thus, these data capture both large-scale realities of the income situation, and they also focus on those apt to be working class.

30. Peter Marcuse, *Rental Housing in the City of New York: Supply and Condition, 1975–78* (New York: Housing and Development Administration, 1979), p. 177.

31. Marcuse, op. cit., p. 208.

32. Ibid., p. 211.

33. Marcuse, op. cit., p. 179.

34. Friedrich Engels, *The Housing Question* (Moscow: Foreign Language Press, 1970); Michael Stone, "The Housing Crisis, Mortgage Lending and Class Struggle," *Antipode*, vol. VII, no. 2, September 1975, pp.

22–37; and Michael Stone, "Housing, Mortgage Lending and the Contradictions of Capitalism," in W. K. Tabb and L. Sawyers, eds., *Marxism and the Metropolis* (New York: Oxford University Press, 1978), pp. 179–207.

35. These observations are in addition to well-known facts, not reiterated here, concerning the grim conditions of life among New York City's sizable indigenous black, Hispanic, and Oriental populations.

36. As reported in Josh Barbanel, "Trickle Down: Economic Boom Helps Some of New York's Poor," *New York Times*, May 16, 1988,pp. B1, B2.

CHAPTER 9

1. See, for example, "Massachusetts Sets Post-War Record for Job Growth; Dukakis Hails Expanding Opportunities for All." News Release from the Office of Governor Michael S. Dukakis, January 9, 1985.

2. See, for example, Lynne Browne, "Can High Tech Save the Great Lakes States," *New England Economic Review*, November/December 1983, pp. 19–33. Also, Patricia M. Flynn, "Lowell: A High Technology Success Story," *New England Economic Review*, September/October 1984, pp. 39–47; and Peter David, "States Compete with Novel Bait," *Nature*, vol. 305, no. 1, September 1983, p. 7.

3. "High Tech: Blessing or Curse?" *U.S. News & World Report*, January 16, 1984, p. 16, as cited in The High Tech Research Group, *Massachusetts High Tech: The Promise and the Reality* (West Somerville, Mass., 1984), p. 13.

4. For the United States, 1950–1986: *Employment and Earnings*, vol. 34, no. 1, January 1987, Bureau of Labor Statistics, U.S. Department of Labor; for Massachusetts, *Employment and Earnings*, no. 5, May various years.

5. See, for example, Barry Bluestone and Bennett Harrison, *The Deindustrialization of America: Plant Closings, Community Abandonment, and the Dismantling of Basic Industry* (New York: Basic Books, 1982), pp. 92–96; and Bennett Harrison, *Rationalization, Restructuring, and Industrial Reorganization in the Older Regions: The Economic Transformation of New England Since World War II*, Joint Center for Urban Studies of the Massachusetts Institute of Technology and Harvard University, Cambridge, Mass., March 1981, pp. 31, 35–42, 90.

6. Examples are too numerous to list even a representative sample. James M. Howell, senior vice-president of the Bank of Boston and a major

business activist in regional affairs makes a more thorough than usual case for this view in "The New England Economic Revitalization and Future Research Priorities," *New England Journal of Public Policy*, Winter/Spring 1985, pp. 5–21. So does Lynne Browne, vice-president and Economist at the Federal Reserve Bank of Boston, in "Can High Tech Save ...," op. cit.

7. This lag is despite the fact that Massachusetts women—the fastest-growing group of labor force participants—have higher labor-force participation rates than the national average.

8. This figure is only illustrative, arguably dramatized; it overstates the effect. If labor force and population had grown as fast the nation's, even with subpar job formation in sectors that export goods or services out of state, more jobs would be created if only for the service needs of that population.

9. George Masnick, "The Demography of New England: Policy Issues for the Balance of This Century," *New England Journal of Public Policy*, vol. 1, no. 1, Spring 1985, pp. 22–43.

10. *Report of the Governor's Commission on the Future of Mature Industries: Appendix A: The Massachusetts Economy and Mature Industries*, Boston, June 1984, p. A–8, and Exhibit 9, p. A–20.

11. See *Report of the Governor's Commission on Mature Industries*, op. cit., Appendix B, "Industry Studies." Also, chapter 5, above, for data on the apparel industry and low-wage imports. Froebel, Heinrich, and Kreye, op. cit., have data on the global apparel industry in the 1970s.

12. For internal variation among the state's Labor Market Areas see *There is More Than One Massachusetts Economy*, Massachusetts Senate, Committee on Ways and Means, 1984. As of March 1985, average wages in manufacturing in Massachusetts were $8.88 per hour, 94 percent of the national average. The metropolitan area variation ranged from the Fall River, Mass., low of $6.81 per hour, 72 percent of the national average to the Boston high of $9.57 per hour, 101 percent of the national average. See Bureau of Labor Statistics (Boston regional office), "New England Unemployment Remains at 5.1 percent in March; Employment Totals 5,987,000," USDL–093, Release for May 28, 1985.

13. Federal Reserve Bank of Boston, *New England Economic Indicators: Monthly Update*, September 1987.

14. *Statistical Abstract of The United States*, 1985. U. S. Department of the Commerce, Bureau of the Census, Washington, DC., pp. 454, 457; Ellen McNamara, "While Massachusetts Economy Booms, Childhood Poverty Increases," *Boston Globe*, September 8, 1985, pp. 1, 16. Andrew Sum et al.,

Family Poverty in the New Boston Economy, Center for Labor Market Studies, Northeastern University, and Community Jobs Collaborative, Boston, Mass., October 1987.

15. Ellen McNamara, "While Massachusetts Economy Booms, Childhood Poverty Increases," *Boston Globe*, September 16, 1985, pp. 1, 16.

16. Division of Employment Security and the Center for Labor Market Studies [Northeastern University], Commonwealth of Massachusetts, *The Shrinking of Family Poverty: New Challenges for Opportunity*, May 1986.

17. Bluestone and Harrison, op. cit., p. 266. Compare this figure with the smaller 200,000 job loss previously cited for the traditional industries. These figures are not restricted to traditional industry or manufacturing; and they are gross numbers of losses, not the net of losses and gains.

18. Ibid., pp. 273–77.

19. See New York State Industrial Cooperation Council, *Research Report*, "New York Is Working This Labor Day: New Data on Business and Labor Growth In New York" (New York: n.p., August 1987), Appendix 2; methodology explained in Appendix 1. State level unionization data should be interpreted cautiously. Based on the Current Population Survey, the margin of error is relatively high, 3 to 5 percent. In Massachusetts, this results in a potential error of 130,000 union members.

20. *Report of the Governor's Commission on the Future of Mature Industries*, op. cit., p. 67; and Federal Reserve Bank of Boston, op. cit.

21. Division of Employment Security, Field Service Research Department, Commonwealth of Massachusetts, *High Technology Employment Developments: An Employer Perspective*, November 1986; and High Technology Research Group, op. cit., 1984, pp. 2–5; and Lynne Browne, "High Technology and Regional Economic Development," *New England Economic Indicators*, April 1984, pp. A3–A9.

22. High Tech Research Group, op. cit., p. 28.

23. Ibid.

24. See Division of Employment Security, op. cit., 1986; and Patricia M. Flynn, op. cit., 1984.

25. High Technology Report, op. cit., pp. 27–29.

26. Flynn, op. cit., pp. 43, 44.

27. Raytheon, the largest private employer, and a major defense contractor, is a unionized firm, as is Western Electric, accounting for this finding.

See, for example, High Technology Research Group, op. cit., pp. 29, 52.

28. High Technology Report, op. cit., pp. 55–56.

29. See, for example, Howell, op. cit.; Flynn, op. cit.; Browne, "High Tech and the Great Lakes States," op. cit.

30. High Technology Research Group, op. cit., pp. 61–63.

31. See, for example, Fred Brodie, "VDTs and Job Safety—Battle Shapes Up," *Boston Globe*, August 15, 1983, pp. 1, 16; and Bruce Mohl, "Business and Labor Debate VDT Legislation," *Boston Globe*, March 15, 1984, p. 37.

32. Harrison, op. cit., 1981, pp. 92–99.

33. John S. Hekman, "The Future of High Technology Industry in New England: A Case Study of Computers," *New England Economic Review*, January/February 1980, p. 11.

34. High Tech Report, op. cit., pp. 45–48; and High Technology Research Group, *Whatever Happened to Job Security: The 1985 Slow Down in the Massachusetts High Tech Industry* (Boston: High Tech Research Group, 1986), pp. 19–21; Division of Employment Security and Northeastern University, op. cit., pp. 21–24.

35. Charles Stein, "Uncertainty Shadows Future of High Tech," *Boston Globe*, June 9, 1985, pp. 1, 30, and numerous stories on June 18 and 19.

36. Bennett Harrison and Jean Kluver, "Reassessing the 'Massachusetts Miracle,'" December 20, 1988 (forthcoming in *Environment and Planning*).

37. Ronald Rosenberg, "Shift to Cheaper Asian Labor Cuts U. S. High-Tech Jobs," *Boston Globe*, June 9, 1985, p. 30.

38. High Tech Research Group, op. cit., p. 47.

39. *Business Week*, "Even the IBM PC Isn't All-American," March 11, 1985, Box, p. 60.

40. Robert Rosenberg, *Boston Globe*, op. cit.

41. Cf. Harrison and Kluver, op. cit.

42. *Report of the Governor's Commission on Mature Industries*, Boston, 1984, Appendix A, Exhibit 14.

43. The calculation is as follows: in 1950 41percent of all Massachusetts nonagricultural jobs were in manufacturing, while 34 percent of the nation's were. The Massachusetts ratio was thus 121 percent of the nation's. In 1982, 21 percent of U. S. nonagricultural employment was in manufacturing. 121

percent of 21 percent is equal to 25.4 percent. 25.4 percent of the Massachusetts employment base in 1982 equals 670,315. Actual Massachusetts manufacturing employment in that year was 640,000. Thus, if Massachusetts had maintained its relative concentration in manufacturing, despite national manufacturing losses, there would have been 30,000 more manufacturing jobs than there were in 1982.

By 1987, both the United States and Massachusetts experienced further deconcentration from manufacturing: to 18.7 percent and 20 percent, respectively. If Massachusetts had maintained its 1950 (121 percent) relative concentration in manufacturing it would have had 22.5 percent of all of its April 1987 jobs (3,041,200) in manufacturing (i.e., 685,290) instead of its 608,200. See *Governor's Commission*, op. cit., and Sources for Table 3, above, and Federal Reserve Bank of Boston, *New England Economic Indicators: Monthly Update*, September 1987.

44. Harrison and Kluver, op. cit.

45. See Harrison, op. cit., pp. 74–80.

46. Harrison and Kluver, op. cit.

47. The most detailed analysis of the Boston Coordinating Committee, the Vault, is in Boston Urban Study Group, *Who Rules Boston: A Citizen's Guide to Reclaiming the City* (Boston: Institute for Democratic Socialism, 1984), pp. 36–45. This source gives the history of the Vault in the making of the New Boston, and profiles members and their web of associations.

48. About Boston, see Boston Urban Study Group, op. cit., p. 37.

49. Boston Urban Study Group, op. cit., p. 60.

50. See Massachusetts Business Roundtable, *The Massachusetts Agenda 1983: A Competitive Assessment of Our Economy*, 1983.

51. March 19, 1984; reprinted in The New England Council, Report, April 1984.

52. In 1979, the state and local tax burden in Massachusetts was 11.4 percent higher than the national average, and ranked eleventh among the states. *State Budget Trends 1976–1985* (Boston: Massachusetts Taxpayers Foundation, May 1984).

53. Massachusetts Taxpayers Foundations, op. cit., p. 5.

54. High Tech Research Group, op. cit., pp. 70–71.

55. See Sarah Kuhn, "Computer Manufacturing in New England: Structure, Location, and Labor in a Growing Industry," Report to the Office of

Economic Analysis and Research, Economic Development Agency, U. S. Department of Commerce, grant no. OER-620-G78-14 (99-7-13440), March 31, 1981, Harvard–MIT Joint Center for Urban Studies, Cambridge, Mass. Also, Kenneth Geiser and Bennett Harrison, "The High Tech Industry Comes Down to Earth," *Boston Globe*, June 23, 1985, pp. 22–24.

56. Deborah Ecker and Richard Syron, "Personal Taxes and Interstate Competition for High Technology Industries," *New England Economic Review*, September/October 1979, pp. 25–32.

57. See Geiser and Harrison, op. cit., and Massachusetts High Technology Council, "The High Tech Agenda: 1985–1990," December 1984.

58. See *New York Times*, "Bankers Advance Deadline on Massachusetts Budget," November 4, 1975, p. 22; and John Kifner "Massachusetts Raises Taxes Sharply Under Pressure of Banks," *New York Times*, November 10, 1975, p. 55. Also, Stephen Curwood, "Bankers Say Bond Default Averted by Mass. Tax Vote," *Boston Globe*, November 10, 1975, pp. 3.

59. Commenting on an early draft of this material, a knowledgeable legislative staff person put the situation differently: " . . . the governor had an enormous stake in resolving the issue without taking sides. To achieve this result, the governor's negotiators found the price necessary to get labor to back down from insistence on a mandatory notice bill." The price was the benefits discussed below.

60. Howard P. Foley, "Two Issues Will Help Determine State Business Climate," *Boston Globe*, January 17, 1984, p. 78.

61. Andrew Blake, "Teradyne May Call Off Expansion if Closing Bill Passes," *Boston Globe*, February 24, 1984, p. 1.

62. Eileen McNamara, "Murphy Jeered at Closing-Bill Airing," *Boston Globe*, April 21, 1983, p. 45.

63. The Legislature also added a technical assistance—"Industrial Service Program"—to the package. Drafted by then Representative and Chair of the Commerce and Labor Committee Timothy Bassett and his aide Karl Seidman, these changes were supported by the original advocates of the mandatory plant closing bill—Gallagher and D'Amico. Together with the monitoring functions written into the bill, they seemed to represent, in embryo, a start at industrial policy at the state government level.

64. Division of Employment Security, Commonwealth of Massachusetts, *The Final Report of the Mature Industries Research Project on Partial Plant Closings*, Boston 1986, ch. 2.

65. Tom Gallagher, with editorial assistance from Bob Ross, *The Massachusetts Mature Industries Law: Promise and Reality*, (Boston: New England Equity Institute, 1987), p. 3.

66. Ironically, Dukakis supported a mandatory notice law as a presidential candidate. Republicans paniced at being on the wrong side of a popular issue. After vetoing the bill once, Reagan allowed it to become law during the summer of 1988. A long campaign had ended in a major advance in industrial relations.

CHAPTER 10

Authors' Note: This chapter is based on an earlier essay, "Global Capitalism and Regional Decline: Implications for the Strategy of Classes in the Older Regions," by Robert Ross, with K. Gibson, J. Graham, P. Susman, and P. O'Keefe in P. O'Keefe, ed., *Restructuring Regions in Advanced Capitalism* (London: Croom Helm, 1984). When not otherwise referenced, the observations on the strategic situation of local community organization and the populiist component of it stem from Ross's work as advisor and consultant to such groups from 1975 to 1981 and his work on the staff of a Massachusetts state Senator from 1983 to 1986.

1. Harvey Molotch, "The City as A Growth Machine," *American Journal of Sociology*, vol. 82, no. 2, 1976, pp. 309–332.

2. See R. Ross with D. Shakow and P. Susman, "Local Planners—Global Constraints," in *Policy Sciences*, vol. 12, 1980, pp. 1–25.

3. Unibook (editorial staff), *Houston: City of Destiny* (New York: MacMillan, 1980), p. 60, 82, as cited by Joe R. Feagin, "The Social Costs of Houston's Growth: A Sunbelt Boomtown Reexamined," *International Journal of Urban and Regional Research*, vol. 9, no. 2, June 1985, p. 167.

4. Massachusetts Business Roundtable, *The Massachusetts Agenda 1983: A Comparative Assessment of Our Economy* (n.p.: n.p., 1983).

5. See New York State Industrial Cooperation Council, *Research Report*, "New York Is Working This Labor Day: New Data on Business and Labor Growth In New York" (New York: n.p., August 1987), Appendix 2.

6. William Serrin, "U. S. Cities Continued Drop in Union Membership," *New York Times*, February 8, 1985.

7. International Union, United Automobile, Aerospace, and Agricultural Implement Workers of America, "A UAW Program to Get America Back to Work," *Solidarity*, vol. 23, no. 5, May 1–15, 1980, pp. 12–13.

8. German Marshall Fund, Joint Report of the Labor Union Study Tour Participants, *Economic Dislocation: Plant Closings, Plant Relocations, and Plant Conversion* (Washington, D.C.: German Marshall Fund, May 1, 1978).

9. See John Cavanagh, et al., *Trade's Hidden Costs: Worker Rights In A Changing World Economy* Washington, D.C.: International Labor Rights Education and Research Fund, 1988,and *Worker Rights News: A Newsletter of the International Labor Rights Education and Research Fund*, vol. 5, no. 2, February, 1989, pp. 1, 2, 12. See also Stephen Coats "When International Labor Solidarity isn't International Labor Solidarity," *In These Times*, February 22, 1989, p. 6. According to Bill Goold, a staff aide to Congressman Don Pease (D-Ohio), the various amendments which embody this approach are of too recent vintage to test their efficacy yet (Interview, March 9, 1989).

10. For example, Steven Greenhouse, "Business and The Law: Wide Debate Over N.L.R.B.," *New York Times*, February 19, 1985, p. D2.

11. Manuel Castells, *The Urban Question* (Cambridge, Mass.: MIT Press, 1977).

12. Cf. William Kornblum, *Blue Collar Community* (Chicago: University of Chicago Press, 1974).

CHAPTER 11

Authors' Note: An early version of this chapter was prepared for the Conference on State Change of the Program on Political and Economic Change at the University of Colorado, Boulder, May 25–27, 1988.

1. Hal Draper has convincingly demonstrated that the notion of state autonomy was central to Marx's and Engel's views in *Karl Marx's Theory of Revolution, Vol. 1: State and Bureaucracy* (New York: Monthly Review Press, 1977), e.g., p. 319. See David A. Gold, Clarence Y. Lo, and Erik Olin Wright, "Recent Developments in the Marxist Theories of the Capitalist State," *Monthly Review*, vol. 27, no. 5, 1975,pp. 29–43; Bob Jessop, *The Capitalist State: Marxist Theories and Methods* (New York: New York University Press, 1982); Martin Carnoy, *The State and Political Theory* (Princeton, N.J.: Princeton University Press, 1984); and Robert R. Alford and Roger Friedland, *The Powers of Theory: Capitalism, The State and Democracy* (Cambridge: Cambridge University Press, 1985).

2. Marx actually put it this way in the *Communist Manifesto:* "The executive of the modern State is but a committee for managing the common affairs of the whole bourgeoisie."

3. "Marx and I are ourselves partly to blame," Engels continues, "for the fact that young people sometimes lay more stress on the economic side than is due to it. We had to emphasize the main principle vis-a-vis our adversaries who denied it, and we had not always the time, the place or the opportunity to give their due to the other elements involved in the interaction." Engels to J. Bloch (September 21–22, 1890),*Selected Correspondence of Karl Marx and Friedrich Engles* (Moscow: Foreign Language Publishing House, n.d.), pp. 498–500. These excerpts are taken from Robert Freedman, ed., *Marxist Social Thought* (New York: Harcourt, Brace and World, 1968) pp. 129, 131.

4. See Bertell Ollman, *Alienation: Marx's Conception of Man in Capitalist Society*, 2nded. (Cambridge: Cambridge University Press, 1976 [1971]), pp. 7–8.

5. See Louis Althusser and Etienne Balibar, *Reading Capital* (London: New Left Books, 1970), especially the translator's Glossary, p. 319.

6. A major exception is to be found in Edward Greer's study of Gary, Indiana—the home of the monopolist U. S. Steel Corporation, now USX. Greer found that the corporation and the local petite bourgeoisie were in a long-term alliance and that interests of the junior partners in that alliance were, from the founding of the city, a matter of both planning and compromise by the corporation. Particularly telling was his analysis of landlords and police. See Greer, *Big Steel: Black Politics and Corporate Power in Gary, Indiana* (New York: Monthly Review Press, 1979).

7. Gabriel Kolko, *The Triumph of Conservatism: A Reinterpretation of American History, 1900–1916* (New York: Free Press, 1963).

8. Even apparent exceptions prove this proposition. Conservative German Bismark's famous founding of social insurance took place in a context where the *illegal* Social Democratic Party was the largest political party in Germany.

9. See David Gordon, Richard Edwards, and Michael Reich, *Segmented Work, Divided Workers* (New York: Cambridge University Press, 1982).

10. Cf. James O'Connor, *The Fiscal Crisis of the State* (New York, St. Martin's Press, 1973). Also, Barry Bluestone and Bennett Harrison, *The Deindustrialization of America: Plant Closings, Community Abandonment, and the Dismantling of Basic Industry* (New York: Basic Books, 1982). Once again we note that an *accord* is a pact, an agreement; its antonym is conflict: one does not require a pact with a party with which one has no potential conflict of interest.

11. See the Poulantzas-Miliband debate, in part: R. Miliband, "Poulantzas and the Capitalist State," *New Left Review*, no. 82, November/December 1973, on Nicos Poulantzas, *Political Power and Social Classes* (London: New Left Books, 1973);Miliband, *The State in Capitalist Society* (New York: Basic Books, 1969); Poulantzas, "The Capitalist State: A Reply to Miliband and Laclau, *New Left Review*, no. 95, January/February 1976, pp. 65–83. Also Philip Kasinitz, "Neo-Marxist Views of the State," *Dissent*, vol. 30, Summer 1983, pp. 337–46.

12. Ralph Miliband, *Marxism and Politics* (Oxford: Oxford University Press, 1977), p. 74.

13. See Richard Peet, ed., *International Capitalism and Industrial Restructuring: A critical analysis* (Boston: George Allen and Unwin, 1987), esp. "Global Crisis and Transformation," Andre Gunder Frank, pp. 293–312.

14. This approach differs from Fred Block and others—cf., Block, "The Ruling Class Does Not Rule: Notes on The Marxist Theory of the State," *Socialist Review*, no. 33 May/June 1977; "Beyond Relative Autonomy: State Managers as Historical Subjects," *New Political Science*, vol. 2, 1981, pp. 33–49; and Nicos Poulantzas, *Political Power and Social Classes* (London: New Left Books, 1973)—in its *disaggregation* of interests within "monopoly capital" and its assertion that the monopoly capitalism framework does define a limit of autonomy. It also differs from the "orthodox" critics who assert that under monopoly capitalism autonomy *declines*. See, for example, Berch Berberoglu, *New Political Science*, op. cit., pp. 135–40.

15. C. Wright Mills, *The Sociological Imagination* (New York: Oxford University Press, 1959), p. 149.

16. See the essays in Peter Evans, Dietrich Rueschemeyer, and Theda Skocpol, eds., *Bringing the State Back In* (Cambridge: Cambridge University Press, 1985), esp. Theda Skocpol, "Bringing the State Back In: Strategies of Analysis in Current Research," pp. 3–37; also Stephen D. Krasner, "Approaches to the State," *Comparative Politics*, January 1984, pp. 223–46, and Fred Block, "Beyond Relative Autonomy: State Managers as Historical Subjects," *Socialist Register*, 1980, pp. 227–242.

17. The determinants of the *length* of such lags, as a general question, will not be addressed here.

18. James O'Connor's usages are adopted here. See *The Fiscal Crisis of the State* (New York: St. Martin's Press, 1973), "Introduction," pp. 1–12.

19. This point has also been noted by Francis Fox Piven and Richard Cloward, in *The New Class War* (New York: Pantheon, 1982).

20. See Michael Useem, *The Inner Circle: Large Corporations and The Rise of Business Political Activity in the U. S. and U. K.* (Oxford: Oxford University Press, 1984).

21. Joel Krieger, *Reagan, Thatcher and the Politics of Decline* (Oxford: Oxford University Press, 1986), ch. 7.

22. Krieger, op. cit., p. 33, pp. 162–67.

23. It should be noted that in the course of his discussion of the Reagan deficit, Krieger's analysis of the institutional fragmentation of American fiscal and monetary policy and the ways the early Reaganites worked this system is incisive and valuable.

24. Krieger, op. cit., pp. 161–162.

25. See Bluestone and Harrison, op. cit.; and Piven and Cloward, op. cit.

26. In 1964, Henry Ford III led a corporate fundraising effort for Lyndon Johnson in the campaign against Barry Goldwater.

Bibliography

Abernathy, William J., Kim Clark, and Alan Kantrow. *Industrial Renaissance.* New York: Basic Books, 1983.

Aglietta, Michel. *A Theory of Capitalist Regulation: The U. S. Experience.* London: New Left Books, 1979.

Alford, Robert R. and Roger Friedland. *The Powers of Theory: Capitalism, The State and Democracy.* Cambridge: Cambridge University Press, 1985.

Althusser, Louis and Etienne Balibar. *Reading Capital.* London: New Left Books, 1970.

Amin, Samir. *Unequal Development: An Essay on the Social Formations of Peripheral Capitalism.* New York: Monthly Review, 1974.

Armstrong, Philip, Andrew Glyn, and John Harrison. *Capitalism since World War II: The Making and Breakup of the Great Boom.* London: Fontana, 1984.

Arrighi, Giovanni. "Towards a Theory of Capitalist Crisis." *New Left Review* 111 (September/October 1978):3–24.

Bachrach, Peter and Morton Baratz. "The Two Faces of Power." *American Political Science Review* 56 (1962): 947–52.

Bairoch, Paul. *The Economic Development of the Third World Since 1900.* Cynthia Postan, trans. Berkeley: University of California Press, 1975.

Baran, Paul. *The Political Economy of Growth.* New York: Monthly Review, 1957.

Baran, Paul and Paul Sweezy. *Monopoly Capital.* New York: Monthly Review, 1966.

Barbanel, Josh. "Trickle Down: Economic Boom Helps Some of New York's Poor." *New York Times* (May 16, 1988): B1, B2.

Batelle Columbus Laboratories. "Identification of Location Criteria Related to the Development of Robotics and Biotechnology in the State of Michigan." Report to the High Technology Task Force and Michigan Department of Commerce, September 24, 1982.

Becker, P. "Historic Labor Force Levels and Unemployment Rates: Detroit SMSA Annual Averages." Detroit: City of Detroit Planning Department, Data Coordination Division, December 1982.

Bergesen, Albert. "Long Economic Cycles and the Size of Industrial Enterprise." In Richard Rubinson, ed. *Dynamics of World Development.* Beverly Hills: Sage, 1981, pp. 179–91.

Berry, Bryan. "For Auto Industry Road to Growth Leads Overseas," *Iron Age*, October 13, 1982.

Blake, Andrew. "Teradyne May Call Off Expansion if Closing Bill Passes." *Boston Globe* (February 24, 1984): 1.

Blake, David and Robert S. Walters. *The Politics of Global Economic Relations*. Englewood Cliffs, N.J.: Prentice-Hall, 1976.

Block, Fred. "The Ruling Class Does Not Rule: Notes on The Marxist Theory of the State." *Socialist Review* 33 (May–June 1977): 6–28.

_____. "Beyond Relative Autonomy: State Managers as Historical Subjects." *New Political Science* (1981): 33–49.

Bluestone, Barry and Bennet Harrison, *The Deindustrialization of America*. New York: Basic Books, 1982.

_____. *The Economic State of the Union, 1984: Uneven Recovery— Uncertain Future*. San Francisco: Economic Education Project, January 1984.

Boddy, Raford and James Crotty. "Class Conflict and Macro Policy: The Political Business Cycle." *Review of Radical Political Economics* 7, 1 (1975): 1–19.

Bornschier, Volker. "World Economic Integration and Policy Responses: Some Developmental Impacts." In Harry Makler, Alberto Martinelli and Neil Smelser, eds. *The New International Economy*. Beverly Hills: Sage, 1982.

Bornschier, Volker and Christopher Chase-Dunn, *Transnational Corporations and Underdevelopment*. New York: Praeger, 1985.

Bornschier, Volker, Christopher Chase-Dunn, and Richard Rubinson, "Cross-National Evidence of the Effects of Foreign Investment and Aid on Economic Growth and Inequality: A Survey of Findings and a Reanalysis." *American Journal of Sociology* 84 (1978): 651–83.

Boston Urban Study Group. *Who Rules Boston: A Citizen's Guide to Reclaiming the City*. Boston: Institute for Democratic Socialism, 1984.

Bottomore, Tom. *Theories of Modern Capitalism*. London: George Allen and Unwin, 1985.

Bowles, Samuel, David M. Gordon, and Thomas Weisskopf. *Beyond the Wasteland*. Garden City, N.Y.: Anchor Press–Doubleday, 1983.

Braverman, Harry. *Labor and Monopoly Capital*. New York: Monthly Review Press, 1974.

Brenner, Robert. "The Origins of Capitalist Development: A Critique of Neo-Smithian Marxism." *New Left Review* 109 (July/August 1977): 25–92.

Brewer, Anthony. *Marxist Theories of Imperialism: A Critical Survey*. London: Routledge and Kegan Paul, 1980.

Brodie, Fred. "VDTs and Job Safety—Battle Shapes Up." *Boston Globe*, August 15, 1983: 1, 16.

Browne, Lynn E. "Autos—Another Steel?" *New England Economic Review* (November/December 1985): 14–29.

_____. "Can High Tech Save the Great Lakes States." *New England Economic Review* (November/December 1983): 19–33.

_____. "High Technology and Regional Economic Development." *New England Economic Indicators* (April 1984): A3–A9.

Buck, Rinker. "The New Sweatshops: A Penny for Your Collar." *New York*, XII, 9 (January 29, 1979): 40–46.

Business Week. "Even the IBM PC Isn't All-American," box, (March 11, 1985): 60.

_____. "Asia's New Bidders for Western Plants." Special Report (March 17, 1980): 48D–48P.

Caporaso, James. "Industrialization in the Periphery: The Evolving Global Division of Labor," *International Studies Quarterly*, 25, 3(September 1981): 347–84.

Cardoso, Fernando Henrique. "Dependency and Development in Latin America." *New Left Review*, 74 (July/August 1972): 83–95.

Cardoso, Fernando Henrique and Enzo Faletto. *Dependency and Development in Latin America*. Marjory Mattingly Urquidi, trans. Berkeley: University of California Press, 1979.

Carney, J., R. Hudson, and J. Lewis, eds. *Regions in Crisis: New Perspectives in European Theory.* London: Croom Helm, 1980.

Carnoy, Martin. *The State and Political Theory*. Princeton, N.J.: Princeton University Press, 1984.

Castells, Manuel. *The Urban Question*. Cambridge: MIT Press, 1977.

_____. *The Economic Crisis and American Society*. Princeton, N.J.: Princeton University Press, 1980.

_____. "High Technology, Economic Restructuring and The Urban-Regional Process in the United States." In Manuel Castells, ed. *High Technology, Space, and Society*, vol. 28, Urban Affairs Annual Reviews. Beverly Hills: Sage, 1985.

Chapkis, Wendy and Cynthia Enloe, eds. *Of Common Cloth: Women in the Global Textile Industry.* Amsterdam: The Transnational Institute, 1983.

Chase-Dunn, Christopher. "Stages of Dependency or Cycles of World System Development?" *Humboldt Journal of Social Relations*, 8, 1 (Fall/Winter 1980–81): 1–24.

_____. *Global Formation: Structures of the World-Economy.* New York: Basil Blackwell, 1989.

_____. "Cycles, Trends, or Transformation?: The World System Since 1945." In Terry Boswell and Albert Bergesen, eds. *America's Changing Role in the World System.* Beverly Hills: Sage, 1985.

_____. "The World System Since 1950: What Has Really Changed?" In
C. Berquist, ed. *Labor in the Capitalist World Economy*. Beverly Hills:
Sage, 1984.

_____. *Socialist States in the World-System*. Beverly Hills: Sage, 1982.

_____. "International Economic Policy in a Declining Core State." In
William P. Avery and David P. Rapkin, eds. *America in a Changing World
Political Economy*. New York: Longman, 1982.

_____. "The Effects of International Economic Dependence on Develop-
ment and Inequality." *American Sociological Review*, 40, 6 (1975):
720–39.

Clarke, I. M. "The Changing International Division of Labor Within ICI."
In Michael Taylor and Nigel Thrift, eds. *The Geography of Multinationals*. New York: St. Martin's Press, 1982.

Cockcroft, James D. *Mexico: Class Formation, Capital Accumulation and the
State*. New York: Monthly Review, 1983.

Cohen, Robert B. "The New International Division of Labor: Multinational
Corporations and Urban Hierarchy." In Michael Dear and A. J. Scott,
eds. *Urbanization and Urban Planning in Capitalist Society*. New York:
Methuen, 1981.

Committee on Ways and Means. *There is More Than One Massachusetts
Economy*. Boston: Massachusetts Senate, 1984.

Conot, Robert. *American Odyssey*. New York: William Morton, 1974.

Cowhey, Peter F. and Edward Long. "Testing Theories of Regime Change:
Hegemonic Decline or Surplus Capacity?" *International Organization*
37, 2 (Spring 1983): 157–88.

Crenson, Matthew A. *The Un-Politics of Air Pollution*. Baltimore, MD: Johns
Hopkins University Press, 1971.

Curwood, Stephen. "Bankers Say Bond Default Averted by Mass. Tax Vote."
Boston Globe (November 10, 1975): 3.

Cypher, James M. "The Internationalization of Capital and the Transformation of Social Formations: A Critique of the Monthly Review School."
Review of Radical Political Economics 11, 4 (1979): 33–49.

Damette, Felix. "The Regional Framework of Monopoly Exploitation: New
Problems and Trends." In John Carney and Ray Hudson, eds., *Regions
in Crisis*. London: Croom Helm, 1980.

David, Peter. "States Compete with Novel Bait." *Nature*, 305, 1(September
1983): 7.

Dicken, Peter. *Global Shift: Industrial Change in a Turbulent World*. London:
Harper and Row, 1986.

Division of Employment Security and the Center for Labor Market Studies
of Northeastern University. *The Shrinking of Family Poverty: New*

Challenges for Opportunity. Boston: Commonwealth of Massachusetts, May 1986.

_____. Field Service Research Department. Commonwealth of Massachusetts. *High Technology Employment Developments: An Employer Perspective.* Boston: n.p., November 1986.

_____. Commonwealth of Massachusetts. *The Final Report of the Mature Industries Research Project on Partial Plant Closing.* Boston: n.p., 1986.

Domhoff, G. William. *The Bohemian Grove and Other Retreats.* New York: Harper and Row, 1974.

_____. *The Higher Circles.* New York: Random House, 1970.

_____. *Who Rules America?* Englewood Cliffs, N.J.: Prentice-Hall, 1967.

Draper, Hal. *Karl Marx's Theory of Revolution, Vol. 1: State and Bureaucracy.* New York: Monthly Review Press, 1977.

Ecker, Deborah and Richard Syron. "Personal Taxes and Interstate Competition for High Technology Industries." *New England Economic Review* (September/October 1979): 25–32.

Ehrenreich, Barbara and Annette Fuentes. "Life on the Global Assembly Line." *MS* (January 1981): 53–71.

Eitzen, S. Stanley with Maxine Baca Zinn, *In Conflict and Order: Understanding Society.* 4th ed. Boston: Allyn and Bacon, 1988.

Emmanuel, Arghiri. *Unequal Exchange: A Study of the Imperialism of Trade.* New York: Monthly Review, 1972.

Engels, Friedrich. *The Housing Question.* Moscow: Foreign Language Press, 1970.

_____. "Letter to J. Bloch September 21–22, 1890." *Selected Correspondence of Karl Marx and Friedrich Engels.* Moscow: Foreign Language Publishing House, n.d.

Epstein, Gerald. "Domestic Stagflation and Monetary Policy: The Federal Reserve and the Hidden Election." In T. Ferguson and J. Rogers, eds. *The Hidden Election: Politics and Economics in the 1980 Presidential Campaign.* New York: Pantheon, 1981.

Evans, Peter. *Dependent Development: The Alliance of Multinational, State and Local Capital.* Princeton, N.J.: Princeton University Press, 1979.

Evans, Peter, Dietrich Rueschemeyer, and Theda Skocpol, eds. *Bringing the State Back In.* Cambridge: Cambridge University Press, 1985.

Federal Reserve Bank of Boston. *New England Economic Indicators*, various issues.

Feagin, Joe R. "The Social Costs of Houston's Growth: A Sunbelt Boomtown Reexamined." *International Journal of Urban and Regional Research* 9, 2 (June 1985): 186–217.

Fermin, Louis. "The Impact of the Current Recession on Human Services in Detroit." Paper presented at the Economic Crisis and Political Response in the Auto City: Detroit and Turin Conference, Harvard University Center for European Studies, Detroit, Mich., December 10–13, 1981.

Flamm, Kenneth. "Internationalization in the Semiconductor Industry." In Joseph Grunwald and Kenneth Flamm, eds. *The Global Factory: Foreign Assembly in International Trade.* Washington, D.C.: The Brookings Institution, 1985.

Flannery, Michael. "America's Sweatshops in the Sun." *AFL-CIO American Federationist.* LXXXV, 5 (May 1978): 15–16.

Flynn, Patricia M. "Lowell: A High Technology Success Story." *New England Economic Review.* (September/October 1984): 39–47.

Foley, Howard P. "Two Issues will Help Determine State Business Climate." *The Boston Globe* (January 17, 1984): 78.

Foster, John Bellamy. "Marxian Economics and the State." *Science and Society* XLVI, 3 (1982): 257–83.

Foster-Carter, Aiden. "The Modes of Production Controversy." *New Left Review* 107 (January/February 1978): 47–77.

Gallagher, Tom, with editorial assistance from Bob Ross. *The Massachusetts Mature Industries Law: Promise and Reality.* Boston: New England Equity Institute, 1987.

Frank, Andre Gunder. *Capitalism and Underdevelopment in Latin America.* New York: Monthly Review, 1967.

———. "Global Crisis and Transformation." In Richard Peet, ed. *International Capitalism and Industrial Restructuring.* Boston: George Allen and Unwin, 1987.

Frieden, Jeff. "Third World Indebted Industrialization: International Finance and State Capitalism in Mexico, Brazil, Algeria, and South Korea." In Jeffrey A. Frieden and David A. Lake, eds. *International Political Economy: Perspectives on Global Power and Wealth.* New York: St. Martin's Press, 1987.

Friedman, Stephen and Leon Potok. "Detroit and the Auto Industry: An Historical Overview." Paper presented at the Economic Crisis and Political Response in the Auto City: Detroit and Turin Conference, Harvard University Center for European Studies, Detroit, Mich., December 10–13, 1981.

Frobel, Folker, Jurgen Heinrichs, and Otto Kreye. *The New International Division of Labor: Structural Unemployment in Industrialized Countries and Industrialization in Developing Countries.* Cambridge: Cambridge University Press, 1980.

———. "The Tendency Towards a New International Division of Labor." *Review: A Journal of the Fernand Braudel Center for the Study of Economics, Historical Systems, and Civilizations.* 1, 1 (Summer 1977): 73–88.

Galbraith, John Kenneth. *The New Industrial State*. Boston: Houghton Mifflin, 1967.

Geiser, Kenneth and Bennett Harrison. "The High Tech Industry Comes Down to Earth." *Boston Globe* (June 23, 1985): 22–24.

German Marshall Fund, Joint Report of the Labor Union Study Tour Participants. *Economic Dislocation: Plant Closings, Plant Relocations, and Plant Conversion*. Washington, D.C.: German Marshall Fund, May 1, 1978.

Gibson, Katherine. *Structural Change Within the Capitalist Mode of Production: The Case of The Australian Economy*. Unpublished Ph.D. diss., School of Geography, Clark University, Worcester, Mass., 1982.

Gibson, Katherine D. and Ronald J. Horvath. "Global Capital and The Restructuring Crisis in Australian Manufacturing." *Economic Geography* 59, 2 (April 1983): 178–96.

Gibson, Katherine D., et al. *Toward a Marxist Empirics*. Unpublished ms., 1986, Clark University, Worcester, Mass.

Gibson, Katherine, et al. "A Theoretical Approach to Capital and Labor Restructuring." In Phil O'Keefe, ed. *Regional Restructuring Under Advanced Capitalism*. London: Croom Helm, 1984.

Glyn, Andrew and Bob Sutcliffe. *British Capitalism, Workers and the Profit Squeeze*. London: Penguin, 1972.

Gold, David, Clarence, Lo, and Erik Olin Wright. "Some Recent Developments in Marxist Theories of the State." *Monthly Review*, 27, 5 (October 1975):29–43; 6 (November 1975):36–51.

Goodman, Robert. *The Last Entrepreneurs*. New York: Simon and Schuster, 1979.

Gordon, David. "Capitalist Development and the History of American Cities." In William K. Tabb and Larry Sawers, eds. *Marxism and the Metropolis: New Perspectives in Urban Political Economy*. 2nd ed. New York: Oxford University Press, 1984.

———. "The Global Economy: New Edifice or Crumbling Foundations?" *New Left Review* 168 (March/April 1988): 24–64.

Gordon, David, Richard Edwards, and Michael Reich. *Segmented Work, Divided Workers: The Historical Transformation of Labor in the United States*. Cambridge: Cambridge University Press, 1982.

Gordon, David M., Thomas E. Weisskopf, and Samuel Bowles. "Power, Accumulation, and Crisis: The Rise and Demise of the Postwar Social Structure of Accumulation." In vol. I, R. Cherry et al., eds., *The Imperiled Economy*. New York: n.p., 1988.

Graham, Julie. *Economic Restructuring in the United States, 1958–1980: Theory, Method and Identification*. Unpublished Ph.D. diss., School of Geography, Clark University, Worcester, Mass., 1983.

Gramsci, Antonio. *Selections from the Prison Notebooks*. Quintin Hoare and Geoffrey Nowell Smith, eds. and trans. New York: International Publishers, 1971.

Greenhouse, Steven. "Business and The Law: Wide Debate Over N.L.R.B." *New York Times* (February 19, 1985): D2.

Greer, Edward. *Big Steel: Black Politics and Corporate Power in Gary, Indiana*. New York: Monthly Review, 1979.

Grunwald, Joseph and Kenneth Flamm. *The Global Factory: Foreign Assembly in International Trade*. Washington, D.C.: The Brookings Institution, 1985.

Hamilton, Clive. "Capitalist Industrialization in East Asia's Four Little Tigers." *Journal of Contemporary Asia* 13, 1 (1983): 35–73.

Harrison, Bennett. "Institutions in the Periphery." In David M. Gordon, ed. *Problems in Political Economy: An Urban Approach*. 2nd ed. Lexington, Mass.: D.C. Heath, 1977.

_____. *Rationalization, Restructuring, and Industrial Reorganization in the Older Regions: The Economic Transformation of New England Since World War II*. Cambridge, Mass.: Joint Center for Urban Studies of the Massachusetts Institute of Technology and Harvard University, March 1981.

_____. and Barry Bluestone. *The Great U-Turn*. New York: Basic Books, 1988.

_____. and Sandra Kantor. "The Political Economy of States' Job-Creation Business Incentives." *Journal of the American Institute of Planners* 44 (October 1978): 424–35.

_____. and Jean Kluver. "Reassessing the 'Massachusetts Miracle'". (December 20, 1988) Forthcoming in *Environment and Planning*.

Harvey, David. *The Limits to Capital*. Chicago: University of Chicago Press, 1982.

Hekman, John S. "The Future of High Technology Industry in New England: A Case Study of Computers." *New England Economic Review* (January/February 1980): 5–17.

Higgott, Richard. "Africa, the New International Division of Labor and the Corporate State." Paper presented at the 24th Annual Conference of the International Studies Association, Mexico City, Mexico, April 6, 1983.

High Tech Research Group. *Massachusetts High Tech: The Promise and the Reality*. West Somerville, Mass.: High Tech Group, 1984.

_____. *Whatever Happened to Job Security: The 1985 Slow Down in the Massachusetts High Tech Industry*. Boston: High Tech Research Group, 1986.

Hill, Richard Child. "Transnational Capitalism and Urban Crisis: The Case of the Auto Industry and Detroit." Paper presented at the Annual Meeting of the Society for the Study of Social Problems, Toronto, Canada, August 23, 1981.

_____. "The Auto Industry in Global Transition." Paper presented at the Annual Meeting, American Sociological Association, Detroit, Mich., September 3, 1983.

Hirschberg, Lynn. "The Unbearable Rightness of Michael Kinsley: The *New Republic* Editor Mouths Off." *Rolling Stone* 526 (May 18, 1988): 105–8.

Hochi, Shozo. "Auto Industry Charts Course for Internationalization." *Business Japan* (February 1981): 32.

Holloway, John and Sol Picciotto. *State and Capital: A Marxist Debate*. London: Edward Arnold, 1978.

Holmes, John. "The Organization and Locational Structure of Production Subcontracting." In Allen J. Scott and Michael Storper, eds. *Production, Work, Territory: The Geographical Anatomy of Industrial Capitalism*. Boston: George Allen and Unwin, 1986.

Holusha, John. "Snags Develop in Talks on General Motors Talks." *New York Times* (March 21, 1982): 26.

Hopkins, Terence and Immanuel Wallerstein, eds. *World-Systems Analysis: Theory and Methodology*. Beverly Hills: Sage, 1982.

_____. "Patterns of Development of the Modern World-System." In Terence Hopkins and Immanuel Wallerstein, eds. *World-Systems Analysis: Theory and Methodology*. Beverly Hills: Sage, 1982.

_____. "Cyclical Rhythms and Secular Trends of the Capitalist World-Economy: Some Premises, Hypotheses and Questions." In Hopkins and Wallerstein, eds. *World-Systems Analysis: Theory and Methodology*. Beverly Hills: Sage, 1982.

Howell, James M. "The New England Economic Revitalization and Future Research Priorities." *New England Journal of Public Policy* 1, 1 (Winter/Spring 1985): 5–21.

Howenstine, Ned G. "Gross Product of U.S. Multinational Companies, 1977." *Survey of Current Business* 63, 2 (February 1983): 24–29.

Hudson, R. and D. Sadler, "Contesting Works Closures in Western Europe's Old Industrial Regions: Defending Place or Betraying Class?" In Allen J. Scott and Michael Storper, eds. *Production, Work and Territory: The Geographical Anatomy of Industrial Capitalism*. Boston: George Allen and Unwin, 1986.

Hymer, Stephen. "The Multinational Corporation and the Law of Uneven Development." In George Modelski, ed. *Transnational Corporations and World Order*. San Francisco: W. H. Freeman, 1979.

International Labour Organization. *Employment Effects of Multinational Enterprises in Developing Countries*. Geneva: ILO, 1981.

International Union, United Automobile, Aerospace, and Agricultural Implement Workers in America. "A UAW Program to Get America Back to Work." *Solidarity* 23, 5 (May 1–15, 1980): 12, 13.

Jessop, Bob. "Recent Theories of the Capitalist State." *Cambridge Journal of Economics* 1, 4 (1977): 353–73.

_____. "Accumulation Strategies, State Forms and Hegemonic Projects," *Kapitalistate*, Double Issues 10/11 (1983): 89–112.

_____. *The Capitalist State: Marxist Theories and Methods.* New York: New York University Press, 1982.

Kasinitz, Philip. "Neo-Marxist Views of the State." *Dissent* 30 (Summer 1983): 337–46.

Katznelson, Ira. "A Radical Departure?: Social Welfare and the Election." In T. Ferguson and J. Rogers, eds. *The Hidden Election: Politics and Economics in the 1980 Presidential Campaign.* New York: Pantheon, 1981.

Kentor, Jeffrey. "Structural Determinants of Peripheral Urbanization: The Effects of International Dependence." *American Sociological Review* 46 (April 1981): 201–11.

Kifner, John. "Massachusetts Raises Taxes Sharply under Pressure of Banks." *New York Times* (November 10, 1975): 55.

Kolko, Gabriel. *The Triumph of Conservatism: A Reinterpretation of American History, 1900–1916.* New York: Free Press, 1963.

Kornblum, William. *Blue Collar Community.* Chicago: University of Chicago Press, 1974.

Krasner, Stephen D. "Approaches to the State." *Comparative Politics* (January 1984): 223–46.

Krieger, Joel. *Reagan, Thatcher and the Politics of Decline.* New York: Oxford University Press, 1986.

Kuhn, Sarah. "Computer Manufacturing in New England: Structure, Location, and Labor in a Growing Industry." Report to the Office of Economic Analysis and Research, Economic Development Agency, U. S. Department of Commerce, grant no. OER-620-G78-14 (99-7-13440)(March 31, 1981), Harvard-MIT Joint Center for Urban Studies, Cambridge, Mass.

Kuznets, Simon. *Economic Growth of Nations: Total Output and Production Structure.* Cambridge, Mass.: Belknap Press of Harvard University Press, 1971.

Landsberg, Martin. "Export-Led Industrialization in the Third World: Manufacturing Imperialism." *Review of Radical Political Economics* 2, 4 (1979): 50–63.

Lawrence, Paul and Davis Dyer. *Renewing American Industry.* New York: The Free Press, 1983.

Leichter, Senator Franz S. "Statement." In *The Reemergence of Sweatshops and the Enforcement of Wage and Hour Standards.* Hearings before the Subcommittee on Labor Standards of the Committee on Education and Labor, United States House of Representatives, Ninety-Seventh Congress. Washington, D.C.: U.S. Government Printing Office, 1982.

_____, Glenn von Nostitz, and Maria Gonzalez, "The Return of the Sweatshop." Office of State Senator Leichter, New York, February 26, 1981.

Lenzner, Robert. "Revolution on Wall Street: New Mobility of Capital is Altering Market." *Boston Globe* (July 5, 1986): 1, 20.

Lipietz, Alain. "Towards Global Fordism." *New Left Review* 132 (March/April 1982): 33–47.

Magdoff, Harry. *The Age of Imperialism*. New York: Monthly Review, 1969.

Mandel, Ernest. *The Second Slump: A Marxist Analysis of Recession in the Seventies*. Jon Rothschild, trans. London: New Left Books, 1978.

_____. *Long Waves of Capitalist Development*. Cambridge: Cambridge University Press, 1980.

Marcuse, Peter. *Rental Housing in the City of New York: Supply and Condition, 1975–78*. New York: Housing and Development Administration, 1979.

Masnick, George. "The Demography of New England: Policy Issues for the Balance of This Century." *New England Journal of Public Policy* 1, 1 (Spring 1985): 22–43.

Massachusetts Business Roundtable. *The Massachusetts Agenda 1983: A Competitive Assessment of Our Economy*. 1983.

Massachusetts High Technology Council. "The High Tech Agenda: 1985–1990." December 1984.

Massachusetts Taxpayers Foundation, Inc.. *State Budget Trends* 1976–1985. Boston, Mass.: n.p., May 1984.

McMichael, Philip. "Social Structure of the New International Division of Labor." In Edward Friedman, ed. *Ascent and Decline in the World-System*. Beverly Hills: Sage, 1982.

McMichael, Philip, James Petras, and Robert Rhodes, "Imperialism and the Contradictions of Development." *New Left Review* 85(May/June 1974): 83–104.

McNamara, Ellen. "While Massachusetts Economy Booms, Childhood Poverty Increases." *Boston Globe* (September 8, 1985): 1, 16.

_____. "Murphy Jeered at Closing-Bill Airing," *Boston Globe* (April 21, 1983): 45.

Michigan Employment Security Commission, Bureau of Research and Statistics, Labor Market Analysis Section. "Civilian Labor Force and Employment Estimates." MESC 3221, March 1984.

Miliband, Ralph. *The State in Capitalist Society*. New York: Basic Books, 1969.

_____. "Poulantzas and the Capitalist State." *New Left Review* 82 (November/December 1973): 83–92.

_____. *Marxism and Politics*. Oxford: Oxford University Press, 1977.

Milkman, Ruth. "The Anti-Concessions Movement in the UAW: Interview with Douglas Stevens." *Socialist Review*, 65 (1982): 18–42.

Mills, C. Wright. *The Power Elite*. New York: Oxford University Press, 1956.

_____. *The Sociological Imagination*. New York: Oxford University Press, 1959.

Mohl, Bruce. "Business and Labor Debate VDT Legislation." *Boston Globe* (March 15, 1984): 37.

Molotch, Harvey. "The City as A Growth Machine." *American Journal of Sociology* 82, 2 (1976): 309–32.

Morris, Irma and Cynthia. *Economic Growth and Social Equity in Developing Countries*. Stanford: Stanford University Press, 1973.

Motor Vehicle Manufacturers Association of the United States, Inc. *Economic Indicators: The Motor Vehicle's Role in the U.S. Economy: 2nd Quarter*. Detroit: Motor Vehicle Manufacturers Association, 1984.

_____. *Motor Vehicle Facts and Figures, 1980* Detroit: Motor Vehicle Manufacturers Association, 1980.

_____. *World Motor Vehicle Data 1986 Edition*, Detroit: Motor Vehicle Manufacturers Association, 1986.

Munck, Ronald. "Imperialism and Dependency: Recent Debates and Old Dead-Ends." In Ronald C. Chicote, ed. *Dependence and Marxism: Toward a Resolution of the Debate*. Boulder, Co.: Westview, 1982.

New York State Industrial Cooperation Council. *Research Report*. "New York Is Working This Labor Day: New Data on Business and Labor Growth In New York." New York: n.p., August 1987.

New York Times. "Bankers Advance Deadline on Massachusetts Budget." November 4, 1975: p. 22.

North American Congress for Latin America. "Capital's Flight: The Apparel Industry Moves South." *Latin America and Empire Report*, XI, 3 (March 1977), entire issue.

Nyhan, David. "UAW Votes to Resume Bargaining with GM," *Boston Globe* (March 12, 1982): 13.

O'Connor, James. *The Fiscal Crisis of the State*. New York: St. Martin's Press, 1973.

_____. *Accumulation Crisis*. Oxford: Basil Blackwell, 1984, 1986.

O'Donnell, Guillermo. *Modernization and Bureaucratic Authoritarianism*. Berkeley: University of California Press, 1973.

Office of Governor Michael S. Dukakis. "Massachusetts Sets Post-War Record for Job Growth; Dukakis Hails Expanding Opportunities for All." News Release (January 9, 1985).

Ogintz, Eileen. "Detroit's Renaissance Center in Trouble," *Chicago Tribune* (January 10, 1983).

Ollman, Bertell. *Alienation: Marx's Conception of Man in Capitalist Society.* 2nd ed. Cambridge: Cambridge University Press, 1976.

Palloix, Christian. "The Self-Expansion of Capital on a World Scale." *Review of Radical Political Economics* 9, 2 (Summer 1977): 3–28.

_____. "The Meaning of Economic Imperialism." In K. T. Fann and Donald Hodges, eds. *Readings in U.S. Imperialism.* Boston: Porter Sargent, 1971.

Peet, Richard. "Introduction: The Global Geography of Contemporary Capitalism." *Economic Geography* 59, 2 (April 1983): 105–11.

_____. "The Relocation of Manufacturing Capital within the United States." *Economic Geography* 59, 2 (April 1983): 112–43.

_____, ed. *International Capitalism and Industrial Restructuring: A Critical Analysis.* Boston: George Allen and Unwin, 1987.

_____. "International Capital, International Culture." In Michael Taylor and Nigel Thrift, eds. *The Geography of Multinationals.* New York: St. Martin's Press, 1982.

Petras, James with A. E. Haven, M. H. Morley, and P. DeWitt. *Class, State and Power in the Third World.* Montclair, N.J.: Allanheld, 1981.

Petras, James and Morris Morley. *The United States and Chile: Imperialism and the Overthrow of the Allende Government.* New York: Monthly Review, 1975.

Piven, Frances Fox and Richard A. Cloward. *Regulating the Poor: The Functions of Public Welfare.* New York: Random House, 1971.

_____. *The New Class War.* New York: Pantheon, 1982.

Poulantzas, Nicos. *Political Power and Social Classes.* London: New Left Books, 1973.

_____. "The Capitalist State: A Reply to Miliband and Laclau." *New Left Review* 95 (January/February 1976): 65–83.

Report of the Governor's Commission on the Future of Mature Industries: Appendix A: The Massachusetts Economy and Mature Industries. Boston: n.p., June 1984.

Rosenber, Ronald. "Shift to Cheaper Asian Labor Cuts U. S. High-Tech Jobs." *Boston Globe* (June 9, 1985): 30.

Ross, Robert. "Facing Leviathan: Public Policy and Global Capitalism." *Economic Geography* 59, 2 (April 1983): 144–60.

_____. "Regional Illusion, Capitalist Reality." *Democracy* II, 2 (1982): 93–99.

Ross, Robert, et al. "Global Capitalism and Regional Decline: Implications for The Strategy of Classes in Older Regions." In Phil O'Keefe, ed. *Regional Restructuring under Advanced Capitalism.* London: Croom Helm, 1984.

Ross, Robert, Don Shakow, and Paul Susman. "Local Planners—Global Constraints." *Policy Sciences* 13 (1980): 1–25.

Ross, Robert and Graham Staines. "The Politics of Analyzing Social Problems." *Social Problems* 20, 1 (1972): 18–40.

Ross, Robert and Kent Trachte. "Global Cities and Global Classes: The Peripheralization of Labor in New York City." *Review* VI, 3 (Winter 1983): 393–431.

Rowthorn, Bob. "Imperialism in the Seventies—Unity or Rivalry?" *New Left Review* 69 (September/October 1971): 31–51.

Russell, George. "The Big Three Get in Gear." *Time* (November 24, 1986): 64.

Safa, Helen I. "Runaway Shops and Female Employment: The Search for Cheap Labor." *Signs* 7 (Winter 1981): 418–33.

Saskia Sassen-Koob, "Recomposition and Peripheralization at the Core," *Contemporary Marxism* 5 (Summer 1982): 88–100.

_____. "Exporting Capital and Importing Labor: The Role of Caribbean Migration to New York City." Paper presented at the Conference on Hispanic Migration to New York City, New York, December 4, 1981.

Schumpeter, Joseph. *Capitalism, Socialism, and Democracy.* 5th ed. London: George Allen and Unwin, 1976.

Schwartz, Alex. "The Auto-Industrial City: Detroit and the Auto Industry, 1900–1982." Unpublished paper, Clark University, Worcester, Mass., February 20, 1983.

Skocpol, Theda. "Bringing the State Back In: Current Research." In Peter Evans, Dietrich Rueschemeyer, and Theda Skocpol, eds. *Bringing the State Back In.* Cambridge: Cambridge University Press, 1985.

Seers, Dudley. "The Congruence of Marxism and Other Neoclassical Theories." In K.Q. Hill, ed. *Towards a New Strategy for Development.* New York: Pergamon, 1979.

Serrin, William. "U. S. Cities Continued Drop in Union Membership." *New York Times* (February 8, 1985): B5.

Shaikh, Anwar. "Political Economy and Capitalism: Notes on Dobb's Theory of Crisis." *Cambridge Journal of Economics* 2 (1978): 233–51.

Sigmund, Paul. *Multinationals in Latin America: The Politics of Nationalization.* Madison, Wisconsin: University of Wisconsin Press, 1980.

Simpson, Robert L. and John Koten. "Auto Makers Profits are Increasing Sharply Despite Mediocre Sales." *Wall Street Journal* (December 19, 1983): 1.

Singapore Chamber of Commerce. *Facts for Business.* Singapore: n.p., 1981.

Soja, E., R. Morales, and G. Wolff. "Urban Restructuring: An Analysis of Social and Spatial Change in Los Angeles." *Economic Geography* 59, 2 (April 1983): 195–230.

Stanback, Thomas M. and Thierry Noyelle. *Cities in Transition.* Englewood Cliffs, N.J.: Allanheld, Osmun, 1982.

Stavrianos, L. S. *Global Rift: The Third World Comes of Age.* New York: William Morrow, 1981.

Stein, Charles. "Uncertainty Shadows Future of High Tech." *Boston Globe* (June 9, 1985): 1, 30, and numerous stories on June 18–19, 1985.

Stone, Michael. "The Housing Crisis, Mortgage Lending and Class Struggle." *Antipode* VII, 2 (September 1975): 22–37.

_____. "Housing, Mortgage Lending and the Contradictions of Capitalism." In W.K. Tabb and L. Sawyers, eds. *Marxism and the Metropolis*. New York: Oxford University Press, 1978.

Storper, M. and R. Walker. "The Theory of Labor and the Theory of Location." *The International Journal of Urban and Regional Research* 7, 1 (1983): 1–41.

_____. "The Spatial Division of Labor: Labor and the Location of Industries." In Larry Sawers and William K. Tabb, eds. *Sunbelt/Snowbelt: Urban Development and Regional Restructuring*. New York: Oxford University Press, 1984.

Sum, Andrew, et al. *Family Poverty in the New Boston Economy*. Boston: Center for Labor Market Studies, Northeastern University, and Community Jobs Collaborative, October 1987.

Susman, Paul and Eric Schutz. "Monopoly and Competitive Firm Relations and Regional Development in Global Capitalism." *Economic Geography* 59, 2 (April 1983): 161–77.

Sweezy, Paul. *The Theory of Capitalist Development*. 2nd ed. New York: Monthly Review, 1970.

_____. "Some Problems in the Theory of Capitalist Accumulation." *Monthly Review* 26, 1 (May 1974): 38–55.

Szymanski, Albert. *The Logic of Imperialism*. New York: Praeger, 1981.

Tabb, William K. "Economic Democracy and Regional Restructuring: An Internationalization Perspective." In William K. Tabb and Larry Sawers, eds. *Sunbelt/Snowbelt: Urban Development and Regional Restructuring*. New York: Oxford University Press, 1984.

Taylor, John G. *From Modernization to Modes of Production: A Critique of the Sociologies of Development and Underdevelopment*. London: MacMillan, 1979.

Trachte, Kent and Robert Ross, "The Crisis of Detroit and The Emergence of Global Capitalism." *International Journal of Urban and Regional Research* 9, 2 (June 1985): 186–217.

United Nations Centre on Transnational Corporations. *Transnational Corporations in World Development: Third Survey*. New York: United Nations, 1983.

_____. *Transnational Corporations in the International Auto Industry*. New York: United Nations, 1983.

United Nations. *Monthly Bulletin of Statistics*, vol. 20 (1966), vol. 34 (1980), and vol. 38 (1984). New York: United Nations.

_____. *Yearbook of International Trade Statistics 1977, Volume 1*. New York: United Nations, 1978.

_____. *Yearbook of International Trade Statistics, 1979, Volume 2*. New York:

United Nations, 1980.

U. S. Congress, House of Representatives, Subcommittee on Labor-Management of the Committee on Education and Labor. *Oversight Hearings on the Nations Labor Relations Act*, 94thCongress, 2nd Session, 1976.

U. S. Department of Commerce, *U.S. Automobile Industry, 1982: Report to the Congress from the Secretary of Commerce.* Washington, D.C.: U.S. Government Printing Office, June 1983.

_____, Bureau of the Census. *Statistical Abstract of the United States.* Washington, D.C.: U.S. Government Printing Office, various years.

_____, Bureau of Economic Analysis. *Selected Data on U.S. Direct Investment Abroad, 1966–78.*Washington, D.C.: U.S. Government Printing Office, 1980.

_____. *Survey of Current Business.* Washington, D.C.: U.S. Government Printing Office, various years.

_____. *Capital Expenditures of Majority-Owned Foreign Affiliates, 1966–76* Washington, D.C.: U.S. Government Printing Office, 1978.

U. S. Department of Labor. *Handbook of Labor Statistics.* Washington, D.C.: Bureau of Labor Statistics, 1983. Bulletin 2175.

_____. *Employment and Earnings, States and Areas, 1939–1978*Washington, D.C.: Bureau of Labor Statistics, 1979. Bulletin 1370–13.

_____. *Supplement to Employment and Earnings, States and Areas, Data for 1977–80* Washington, D.C.: Bureau of Labor Statistics, 1981. Bulletin 1370–15.

_____. *Employment and Earnings.* Washington, D.C.: U.S. Government Printing Office, various issues.

U. S. Department of Transportation. *The U. S. Automobile Industry, 1980: Report to the President from the Secretary of Transportation.* Washington, D.C.: U.S. Government Printing Office, 1981.

Useem, Michael. *The Inner Circle: Large Corporations and The Rise of Business Political Activity in the U. S. and U. K.* Oxford: Oxford University Press, 1984.

Veblen, Thorstein. *The Theory of Business Enterprise.* New York: Charles Scribners' Sons, 1904, 1963.

Vernon, Raymond. *Sovereignty At Bay.* New York: Basic Books, 1971.

Wallerstein, Immanuel. "The Rise and Future Demise of the World Capitalist System: Concepts for Comparative Analysis." *Comparative Studies in Society and History* 4 (1974): 387–415.

_____. "The Present State of the Debate on World Inequality." In I. Wallerstein, ed. *World Inequality: Origins and Perspectives on the World System.* Montreal: Black Rose Books, 1975.

_____. *The Capitalist World Economy.* Cambridge: Cambridge University Press, 1979.

_____. *The Modern World System I: Capitalist Agriculture and the Origins of the European World-Economy in the Sixteenth Century.* New York: Academic Press, 1974.

_____. *The Modern World System II: Mercantilism and the Consolidation of the European World-Economy, 1600–1750.* New Yrok: Academic Press, 1980.

_____. "Semiperipheral Countries and the Contemporary World Crisis." *Theory and Society* 3 (Winter 1976): 461–83. Reprinted in Wallerstein (1979): 95–118.

_____. "World-Systems Analysis: Theoretical and Interpretive Issues." In T. Hopkins and I. Wallerstein, eds. *World-Systems Analysis: Theory and Methodology.* Beverly Hills: Sage, 1982.

_____. "Crisis As Transition." In Samir Amin et al. eds. *Dynamics of Global Crisis.* New York: Monthly Review, 1982.

Warren, Bill. "Imperialism and Capitalist Industrialization." *New Left Review* 81 (September/October 1973): 3–44.

_____. *Imperialism: Pioneer of Capitalism.* London: New Left Books, 1980.

Weeks, John. *Capital and Exploitation.* Princeton, N.J.: Princeton University Press, 1981.

Weeks, John and Elizabeth Dore. "International Exchange and the Causes of Backwardness." *Latin American Perspectives* VI (Spring 1979): 62–87.

Weisskopf, Thomas E. "Marxian Crisis Theory and the Rate of Profit in the Postwar Economy." *Cambridge Journal of Economics* 3 (1979): 341–78.

_____. "Imperialism and the Economic Development of the Third World." In Richard C. Edwards, Michael Reich, and Thomas Weisskopf, eds. *The Capitalist System.* 2nd ed. Englewood Cliffs, N.J.: Prentice-Hall, 1978.

Whichard, Obie G. "Employment and Employee Compensation of U. S. Multinational Companies in 1977." *Survey of Current Business* 62, 2 (February 1982): 37–49.

White, Lawrence. *The Automobile Industry Since 1945.* Cambridge, Mass.: Harvard University Press, 1970.

Woolley, Ann Job. "By a 3–1 Margin, Ford Workers OK Concessions to Get Job Security." *Boston Globe* (March 1, 1982): 1, 6.

World Bank. *World Development Report, 1982.* New York: Oxford University Press, 1982.

_____. *World Tables.* 3rd ed., vol. 1. Baltimore, Md.: Johns Hopkins University Press, 1983.

Wright, Erik Olin. *Class, Crisis and the State.* London: New Left Books, 1978.

Index